As Time Goes By
2008-2009

As Time Goes By
2008-2009

Edited by

Elaine Cousino

Pittsfield Seniors Creative Writing Group

ISBN: 978-0-557-09092-1

~Acknowledgments~

About five years ago, I suggested to our Senior Coordinator, Carol Presley, that perhaps a Creative Writing Group might be an activity that our Center would support. In her enthusiastic way she said, **"Go for it!"**

Now that wasn't exactly what I had in mind when I made that suggestion. However, it has proven to be one life's most gratifying experiences to be a part of and to facilitate this spectacularly talented group of authors.

Imaginations soar and mind-boggling adventures flow out of each session. At times we are triggered to write about a recent harrowing experience and at other times we suffer together with writer's block. Our lively discussions about the world about us, locally and nationally have led to many exciting ideas.

May I express my very deepest thanks and appreciation to each person who contributed in any way.

Special thanks to Carol Presley and Cindy Deery for their encouragement and understanding. To my dear friend and extremely kind Technical Advisor, Janis Shuon, and John Vidolich, The Grand Computer Wizard and Master of Patience. Thanks also to all the thoughtful volunteers that freed up my time to be able to part of this wonderful learning experience.

It was amazing just to be a small part of this big adventure!

Fondly,

'Elle' (Elaine Cousino)

10/20/09

Bless you Sue!
Happy Reading
'Elle'

~Dedication~

It is my very great pleasure to dedicate this book to Lucile Holtz. Lucile – quick to point out that her name was spelled with only one L. She was one of the charter members of Pittsfield Creative Writers Group. Lucile both charmed and delighted us with her wisdom and most gentle of all souls. We miss her.

~ TABLE OF CONTENTS~

Fiction and Factual

Slice of Life Opinions & Essays

Memories

Poetry

SEA DREAM *'ELLE' ELAINE COUSINO* 220
Book Excerpts

Meet The Authors

DAN KENT
BEVERLY LEE BIXLER
BONNIE BRANIUM
JOANNE SAVAS
JANIS SHUON 5
THOMAS (TOM) TORANGO 5
G. OTTO FANGER 5
MICHAEL ANDERONI
WALTER PALESCH
MARGE ANDERSON
CAROLE HENDRICKSON
EDNA MASSEY
SALLY WU
PAT SPRIGGEL
ELAINE 'ELLE' COUSINO

"THE BEAUTY OF THE WRITTEN WORD IS THAT IT CAN BE HELD CLOSE TO THE HEART AND BE READ OVER AND OVER AGAIN."
~FLORENCE LITTARIER

Fictional and Factual Short Stories

"There has never been a statue
erected in the memory of someone
who left well enough alone."
Jules Ellinger

Ghost River Landing

by Dan Kent

The story of Jordan Mackenzie has been around since just before World War I. Jordan was a rather tall, beautiful Irish r ed head from South Carolina that met and married Sawyer T. Mackenzie around 1912. Sawyer was the cherished son of Tobias Mackenzie, founder of Mackenzie Pacific Mills, a lumbering firm with extensive forestry reserves.

In the years that followed, Jordan and Sawyer raised two daughters and all went well until that fateful Fourth of July outing when disaster came to call.

As a treat for the children, their father put them aboard a borrowed canoe for a brief trip downstream to the next landing. An hour later, horrified people on the landing saw an overturned canoe drifting by. The bodies of Sawyer and his youngest were recovered shortly before nightfall. Down the river searching for the missing child continued for a week after the mishap, but the body of the second daughter was never recovered.

In a cleared forest area, Sawyer and his child were laid to rest in a special memorial plot with an angel as guardian surrounded with high iron fencing. A grief stricken grandfather never recovered from the accident or what followed in unbelievable succession.

Five months after the tragedy, Jordan and her companion, Emily Easton left for San Francisco to visit friends. The two women arrived, stayed four days and journeyed on to San Jose. From that point on, no one knows exactly what happened to Jordan and Emily. Tobias Mackenzie spent a small fortune on investigation to no avail. This included services of the famed

Pinkerton Detective Agency. Jordan's brother, John O'Donovan also came all the way from Charleston, South Carolina to assist in the search. Several months of effort yielded nothing of real worth. Foul play was all too clear, but who and why was never resolved.

Strange sightings began to occur around 1923, in each case a tall red haired woman was seen standing on the river bank near the scene of the Mackenzie boating accident. She was always seen wearing a pale blue dress and straw hat with a long blue ribbon trailing behind. Over the years, the appearance was reported at least six times, most recently, three years ago in July. In the latest instance, a person in a canoe passing near the river landing was hailed by a woman on the shore that beckoned him and quite clearly said: "Did you find her?"

Since he had no idea what was meant by the woman's question, he began working his way toward the riverbank for an explanation. He attempted to keep her in sight while avoiding boulders near the landing. In doing so, he briefly glanced away as he made his way to shore. He looked for her once more and he was astonished that she had vanished.

Pulling the canoe up on the bank, he saw other people in the vicinity, but no evidence of the woman that had hailed him. Baffled he looked about for footprints in the sand and found a long blue ribbon at the water's edge. ©

U S O Pen Pals

by Elaine 'Elle' Cousino

"Will I ever find the guy on my mind, the one who is my ideal?" the crooner inquired as Janie sank deeper into the bubble bath. Reading until a sleepy stupor came over her, a hot bath, all of mom's old remedies for sleeplessness seemed to be working. The hot milk was waiting on the nightstand.

Janie had been working ten and twelve hour days at the nearby defense plant, building B-24's. A tiny thing only 4'9", weighing 93 pounds she'd been assigned to the wing section, along with many other little people. Her size and theirs made it possible to fit in and rivet where others could not.

Bills last letter had upset Jamie, affecting her sleeping. God only knows where he was stationed, because of the censuring of his letters, and the meaning of his letters had become somewhat convoluted. She had written him asking for some space, some time to think. Janie felt that their pen pal relationship was moving too fast and the fact that she was alone and he was overseas had everything to do with what was happening

She had begun writing to Bill as part of an USO effort to keep up the morale of our service men and women. First the letters flew back and forth; both could not wait to learn more about the other. Then she eased off, his two letters to her occasional one.

Looking back, she mused from the warm tub, she thought, "What do I really know about him, except what he had written her about himself?' Stepping out she wrapped a bath towel around her slim body, then walked to the bedroom humming as she snuggled into flannel pajamas that smelled like fresh air. She sat on the edge of the bed drinking the hot milk; slowly she could almost feel herself slipping away into sleep.

From somewhere a muffled sound made her aware that she was not alone in the apartment. Her eyes opened wide, the sleepiness disappearing instantly. Janie saw a faint fluttering movement under the heavy drapes that she had pulled for the night. Her heart thudded loudly. It seemed to fill the room with the sound of beating. Her hand moved toward the phone next to the bed.

The drapes flew open and a uniformed figure leaped out, waving a pistol in front of him. "Don't go for the phone Sweetie. I've got you right where I want you." Janie felt as if the air had been suddenly sucked from the room. She sat very still on the edge of the bed. "Donald?" she questioned. "Yeah Baby, it's me, home from the war, to see my favorite Pen Pal!"

He answered sarcastically, still waving the gun.

"Please put the gun away, Donald." Janie managed to say in a calm voice, although she could feel the pulsation of her heart beating in her ears. "I suppose you're right, since you're such a tiny twerp. I doubt that you could do anyone much harm." He taunted as he laid the pistol on the marble-topped table. He gently touched Janie's clean dark hair that shone in the lamplight. "My sister used to have hair like yours," he muttered aloud. Janie's mind raced to think of something, anything to distract him. "Oh you have a sister? Is she younger or older than me." Abruptly he turned away, "Okay now, I'll ask the questions around here, not you little lady-love." Janie never once took her eyes off from him, never lowered them. She surmised he was suffering from battle fatigue or had serious mental problems, in either case, she decided not to be his victim.

Slowly she eased to a standing position beside the bed. "I have to go to the bathroom." She said quietly. After a moment's hesitation, he said, "Alright, but I'll go in first to make sure you don't try anything really cute." He sauntered to the bathroom door. Janie stood by the bed. "Come on now, you said you had to go." He said, raising his voice at her. She moved fast now, walking swiftly, she gave him a shove with all her might. Janie had thrown Donald off balance, towards the graceful claw-foot tub, still filled with water. He must have slipped on the wet tile floor and over he went. In one smooth motion, Janie swept the radio into the tub with him.

The lights dimmed momentarily and the water vibrated as Donald shook with the charge of electricity. The pistol glowed blue in the water. ©

A Sign of Spring in the Yukon

by G. Otto Fanger

It had been a long frigid winter in the Eskimo village of Alibaki. The village was built on a small peninsula jutting out between the outlets of the Kahlo, and the Sakami Rivers, where both emptied out into West Beacon Sound.

The winter wind howled outside and into their dwellings. Even the double walls of the log or driftwood cabins and huts could not stop the frigid blasts of air. It found small fissures in the mud packed between the walls, and flowed into the smoky interiors of what they called their 'igloos'. The gusts of sub zero wind was fierce here in the Arctic Circle, and winter was so...so long.

But finally, the winter was ending. There was a stretched seal hide on the back wall of the cabin in the village's most respected resident, referred to as The Respected One. It showed the charcoal X's marking off the cold winter days, one by one, and indicating the spring days rapidly approaching. The cracking ice was also a sure sign of the coming of spring. It would not be long before the tribe would be able to begin their seasonal sea hunt for seals. This, along with other ocean fishing would help to replenish the meager food supplies left after the severe winter. Early that morning the sun had begun its climb from near the horizon, to its apex almost directly overhead. The photographic team had known that there would be no darkness. This was the land of the midnight sun.

The Continental Explorer Magazine team of photographers and technicians had been aware of the hazardous conditions when they accepted the assignment. Still, they eagerly signed up knowing that the event they were traveling to cover was worth all of their hardships.

Laura Bradford, the chief photographer of the team, understood that the unique position of the sun, relative to the surface of the still frigid earth was something else that would make this traditional event even more meaningful! It was time for The Spring Tradition still practiced, and documented for hundreds of years in Eskimo folklore. Laura had long before learned that the Inuit social structure was centered on the survival of the group. These people believed that this yearly ritual would insure that the village would prosper, and that younger life would be given a better chance of survival.

The Respected One and his consul had worked diligently on the preparations for this ceremony. Their traditional dress was brought out from storage, repaired and cleaned. The consul had carefully explained to each family member who would be featured in the ceremony, exactly what his or her role would be.

Travel had always been exciting to these simple people living north of the Arctic Circle, and this spring travel was no exception. The Inuit's had always been a nomadic culture. In the winter quarters they lived near of source of their food and clothing, seals in the sea. In the summer they traveled into the interior, living in seal skin tents and hunting caribou, bears, and wolves.

Laura was busy taking film clips of the villagers. Almost everyone she saw was specially dressed for this occasion. The men were wearing their cleanest reindeer parkas, and insulated Kaniks. The women had on their brightly colored ceremonial parkas, signifying the beauty inherent in this event. She had already filmed some clips of The Respected One, and also of the village consul wearing their traditional clothes for this Inuit ceremonial (Inuit clothes). She also captured, on film, the Angakok, adorned in his carved wooden mask darkened with charcoal sticks, and displaying a full eagle headdress above the mask. A collection of 'lucky' Amulets hung down to his chest from the seal gut cord around his neck. He had been in the midst of preparatory spiritual concentration.

She made some final adjustments of the camera lens. The village people had all paused for a minute in front of the town's carved cedar totem. She started photographing; focusing her camera lens on the Angakok chanted an ancient prayer. Then he suddenly raised his feathered baton. This motion signaled the official start of the pageant. Other photographers of the team were recording the events at the front of the procession. The most elderly members of the village were first in line. The team already knew that they were an important component of this event. Dressed in their finest clothes, each carried a blanket. All wore their heaviest kamiks, to insulate their feet from the icy earth surface.

Meanwhile, Laura shifted the position of the variable 1000 MM to 350MM lens, and focused in on the consul members, next in line. They were waving long carved sticks. The Respected One, walking with his head high, followed close behind them in the procession. There was a break space. Then the Angakoh appeared in the camera lens. As he performed a ceremonial dance, she was barely able to hear the soft chant of his ancient prayer. Most likely, he was appealing to the sacred helping spirit, Toornaq. Now, directly behind him, her film was recording the band. It was led by seven Aqunnaaki, (meaning between two skins, their word for teenagers. Each young person was fingering wooden flute-like instruments producing owl-like sounds. Accompanying them were seven drum players, walking along beating their drumsticks on selected spots on the stretched drum skins stretched over large wooden hoops. The entourage was completed by seven youngsters shaking their traditional whalebone rattles.

It was a glorious sight, reminding Laura of the New Orleans Parade to the cemetery that she had photographed some weeks before. The big difference was that here there were no tarnished or bandaged brass instruments, nor any black ladies circling with colorful parasols. Laura focused her attention back onto the scene being filmed. The first row of the villagers seemed to be composed of the closest relatives of the elderly group in the front. Then a crowd of other villagers followed at a friendly distance behind them in this official Intuit ceremony. They were also chanting an ancient folklore story in guttural major clef utterances. A few of the young mother's in this group were carrying their papooses in Anarts on their backs. Slowly the long winding procession made its way out of Alabila and down a worn path leading to a wooden platform extending far out into the river.

Laura turned the filming over to Gloria Blakely, one of the junior assistant photographers. "Is this really going to come about?" She wondered. Looking over at the river, her eyes could see large cracks in the ice, and more and more icy water exposed between the ice floes slowly making their way to the Arctic Ocean. She scanned the area with the full power of her 1000 MM telephoto lens of her overview camera, swinging the lens over to view the long wooden pier. It stood firm, strongly resisted the pressure of the chunks of ice that crashed into its side, and thereby broke them into smaller chunks of frozen water. She panned down to the river's edge, past the piled up kayaks, and back up to the larger Umiaq leaning against the pier on the snow-covered shoreline.

Laura resumed the responsibility for the filming in this position, locking in the camera lens on the front of the procession, which had now reached the far end of the pier. Listening, she heard what started out as a soft drum roll that built to a crescendo…then the drum beat slowly decreasing in volume until it stopped. Other than the ceaseless barking of the malamutes from the village, only a few sobbing cries broke the silence of the moment.

Through the viewer, she saw the 'Respected One' raise his hand and motioned to the consul members standing at the front. At his signal, each pair of them escorted one of the groups of eldest members of the village onto a specific spot at the edge of the pier. The two counselors at the end of the pier both lowered their long wooden poles over the side of the pier until, together, they secured a medium sized ice floe close to the pier. The elderly lady they had escorted, turned and waved to her family, then sat down on the edge of the pier, and cautiously stepped onto the ice floe. She carefully placed her folded blanket on top of the ice, and sat down on it, crossing her arms and legs, placing her traditional woven scarf around her head and shoulders. Another ice floe was secured, and another elderly lady went through the same procedure. This continued until there were nine chunks of frozen ice, each housing an elderly lady in a stoic sitting position. There were no elderly men in the village. They had died off long ago, either from excessive alcohol, or as polar bear food. The nine chunks of ice boats surrounding the pier were carefully held in place by the long poles of the council members.

Laura's ears were greeted by another long and bold drum roll, and when it suddenly stopped, all of the counselors simultaneously lifted up their poles. The village crowd, watching from the shore either yelled in excitement, or gasped in terror! Laura was too busy to be emotional. She was capturing the whole event on film from her position on the shore. The film recorded the ice boats bumped along the pier, jostling the seated travelers. Then, one by one, each jagged chunk of ice entered the river water. The travelers on their 'ice boats' had begun their journey! The Spring Tradition had been completed, just as it had been every spring for thousands of years.

From her extended visit to this same village last summer, Laura understood. These grandmothers feeling that they were seqijuk (worthless individuals) in the village and just a burden to their family had elected to take this traditional trip to sea. Their final trip would complete the natural cycle of life. Their bodies would become food for the animals that the villagers would later kill and eat. It was their Life to Death to Life cycle.

The cameras recorded the travelers embarking on their trip to the open sea, shimmering beneath the morning sun. The villagers on the pier and on the shore also watched the figures on their rafts of ice boats move faster and faster up to the mouth of the river. The stillness of the crowd was dramatic. This was their Sign of Spring!

Suddenly, one of the ice boats shattered, spilling its occupant into the icy river. In a moment she popped up waist high in water and retrieved her wet blanket, began walking to the shore not far away. Then another boat broke up, and then another.

The crowd on the pier and shore gave a tumultuous chorus of cheers. Soon all of the traveling elderly ladies were plodding their way to the shore. Meanwhile, their relatives were running to meet them. The first there were the grandchildren, who lovingly hugged their grandmas oblivious of their cold, wet bodies. Other relatives soon arrived, holding thick wrapping blankets.

Laura was about to conclude what she felt had been a successful filming session. She separated the camera from its tripod. As she did so she reasoned, "This would have never played out this way before global warming. In the past the ice had been thick enough and the water cold enough to support the weight of a frail human body, but not now!" She folded up her tripod, shook her head, and wondered, "Perhaps the Bush agenda ignoring global warning turned out to do some good after all…or had it?" Now the village had nine more adults to feed in the next year. New babies would be born. Meanwhile global warming was contributing to a significant reduction in the size of the winter ice. The ice the Ignites depended on, to catch the winter seals. Meanwhile, she noticed that the procession back from the shore was even more joyful than the return march from a New Orleans funeral. ©

ESKIMO GLOSSARY

1) AMAUT- a hooded pouch to carry a baby
2) ANGAKOK- a shaman, or type of witch doctor
3) AQUNNAAKI – (BETWEEN TWO SKINS) teenagers
4) IGLOO- a generic term used for any Eskimo dwelling
5) INUET- A culture of peoples descended from those crossing a land bridge from Russia to The north American continent, now living within the Arctic circle

6) KAYAK- A small hand-built boat made from sealskin stretched over a whalebone or wood frame
7) KAMIK- sealskin or bearskin boot
8) SEQIJUK- a worthless individual
9) TINNEH-Indians of the Yukon, speaking the Athabasca language
10) TOORNAQ- a helping spirit
11) UMIAQ- a large boat, usually rowed by women

George and the Angel

by 'Elle' Elaine Cousino

He slashed and slashed again and again, hacking at the wild vines that covered the old outside basement door. Then George crept into the hidey-hole basement as he had done as a child. He was a small man, seemingly made smaller by the large hump on his back. Inside, the earthly smell of the basement reminded George of the falls long ago when Mama had him carry bushel after bushel of apples and potatoes down to the fruit cellar. This musty green scent of dark places shut up too long proceeded to lead George down the rickety stairs where he slowly made his decent checking for rotten wood as he went.

His high working shoes were worn, heavy and wet from the long trek through the woods. George sighed loudly, thinking to himself, "No one would look for me here." Reaching the bottom of the stairs, he leaned against the damp green wall, his eyes growing accustomed to the dimness. Yes, he could see the shelves where Mama's pickles, canned peaches, and preserves were stored. One empty jar that escaped lay on its side, making a home for spiders. George found an old stool and sat down slowly, recollecting the strange twists and turns that life had dealt him. That was the way it is, he thought, life was in control, not him. He was not responsible for the things that happened, they just happened and they happened to him.

But the escape had been easier than he'd imagined. George just followed two inmates as if he had been part of their plan. Of course, he was not. They were in for bank robbery and had a long number of years left on their sentence, whereas, George was in for life. What did he have to lose anyway? Burt and Lee were surprised and unhappy about him cutting into their break but since he didn't hold them up on the escape route, they ignored him. Once out of the fenced area, they went one way, George another. He was sure where he was going and remembered the old house in the Tennessee woods where Mama had hidden him away for years until Angel came.

George remembered her clearly. All dressed in snow white, those golden curls, shining in the sunlight. Her voice tinkled like little bells when she spoke, tiny pink hands, exquisitely dainty gestured with her speech. Until she appeared, he did not know such beauty existed. A

11

few others whom George had encountered earlier in his life had been cruel and somewhat afraid of his appearance, but Angel, oh no.

Remembering her first visit, when George had hidden behind the door where she could not see him, while Angel convinced Mama to let her home school on a weekly time-table. George saw Angel through the crack. "Please Mama, Mama," he begged in his sleepy mind.

Finally Angel won and every Thursday she would appear with books, markers and games in the large tote bag. Mama hated Angel from the beginning. She only went along with the schooling to keep the sheriff out of the picture.

There was no trouble until that day when Angel's hair shone so brightly in the shaft of light coming through the kitchen window. George felt compelled to touch that hair. Angel ignored his light touch at first, then he began to caress a little more, a little harder, then suddenly he found her whole head in his large knotty hands. He was not aware of her screaming, only when Mama burst into the room, he could hear her.

Mama's eyes burned with anger. "Oh you little hussy! You jest wanted to get yer hands on my sweet Georgie boy and get him all riled up!" She yelled. Her remarks were punctuated with the loud banging of the shovel that she had carried in from the garden. She swung it into the table, then in a fit of anger she swung it wildly, hitting Angel squarely in the face. Crimson fountains of blood spurted from her mouth and her bright blue eyes still had the surprised look of an animal caught in the headlights as her body fell to the floor in a heap.

George was weeping now, deep in sorrow, remembering the terrible incident. He had cried then too. Mama put him to sleep in her big bed while she cleaned up. Mama gave him the medicine that made him sleep really deep. As he drowsed off he heard her going in and out the back door and the sound of something heavy being dragged across the kitchen floor.

When he awoke, Mama was rocking on the back porch, gently humming to herself. "Have some milk and there are cookies on the counter," she had called out. George was not hungry.

"What happened Mama?" He asked sleepily.

"You must have had a bad dream." She replied, still rocking.

"Where is the Angel?" He asked, more concerned.

"Everything is peaceful now Georgie. You just come and sit out here with Mama."

All of this before the sheriff came looking for Angel. This was before they looked in the freezer and found all that meat wrapped up in pink butcher paper, tied up with string. This was before Mama just up and died right there before them all, falling down dead on the shiny kitchen floor.

They took George in back seat of the sheriff car. He stayed in the jail. When he found out that I had to go to jail and to court because Angel was gone, George cried. "Where is she?" he loudly demanded over and over again. But no-one answered him or even looked like they heard.

"Yes, life does take its twists and turns." George reminisced out loud and shifted back on the stool, causing the quart jar that was laying on its side to fall and break at his feet.

He bent over to pick up the shards of glass when he fell. Laying there on the packed dirt floor, he heard the whispery rattling sounds. Turning his head slowly, he saw that rattlesnakes had made their home in the old basement. Slowly they came, in their slithery dance toward him, seeming to float just above the dirt floor, wicked red tongues flickering. He kept watching, mesmerized by the snake's approaching rhythmical fatal dance. Just before they began striking George heard magnificent music, somewhat like tinkling bells playing far away in the distance.©

The Mystery of the Small White Seashell

by Marge Anderson

She found herself lying on the sore of an island somewhere in the Caribbean. She didn't know how she got there or why. She tried to think but her mind was completely muddled and she had a terrific headache. As she lay there drifting in and out of consciousness, she had flashes of memory, "Who am I?" she cried. Her mind cleared slightly and she blurted out, "Nina, my name is Nina, and I am a first year graduate student at the University of Michigan, studying marine biology." She recalled being aboard a sailboat with friends, lazily sailing around the islands of the Bahamas. The group was supposed to be searching for rare marine specimens – for college credit, no less – but in truth, they were really out for a good time.

It was December 31, 2000 and they were celebrating. Nina remembered the night air turning chilly. She was wearing shorts and a t -shirt over her swimsuit and decided to go below to put on a warm-up suit and jogging shoes. Coming back on deck she realized a storm was brewing. The wind had picked up and there was an ominous looking glow in the tropical sky. "Hurry up Nina," called her friends, "we're about to toast the New Year and the new century." As they raised their glasses, a gigantic wave engulfed the boat, capsizing it, throwing everyone into the choppy sea. Again she was overcome by weakness. When she awoke she looked around. "Where is everyone?" She cried when she realized she was completely alone. Tired, wet, and though the sun was hot on her skin, she felt very cold. As she lay there she felt something or someone tugging at the sleeve of her shirt. Struggling to open her eyes, she found a monkey chattering wildly in what seemed to be Spanish. "Si, Si! Si, Si!" she called. Finally, Nina realized that this animal was trying to get her to move up the beach, away from the water's edge. The tide was coming in and she surely would be swept out to sea. With great effort she pulled herself out of danger and collapsed, exhausted in a shady spot on the sand. She must have lay there for many hours, for as she became conscious the sun was beginning to descend in the western horizon. She struggled to her feet and with her new friend Nina had named Marcheta went looking for shelter. After a short walk down a path that led through the thick jungle growth, she came upon what looked to be an abandoned village. The few buildings, weather worn from tropical storms seemed to be empty. There was a small hotel still in fair condition. Over the door was a sign that read, "Casa Blanca." The door was unlocked. Nina entered, half expecting to find Humphrey Bogart and Igrid Bergman smooching at a corner table. She was just happy to have a roof over her head. She took off her wet clothes and wrapped herself in a blanket. She found a small cot and with Marcheta snuggling next to her, cried herself to sleep.

Nina woke in the morning, lonely, scared, sad and very hungry. However, she smiled in spite of herself, for there was little Marcheta offering her bananas, papaya and even a coconut. Her clothes were dry so she put on her swimsuit, pulled on the T-shirt and set about investigating her situation. She found candles, and oil lamp, a fireplace and thank goodness, matches! Also, and old gramophone and a stack of '78's – all in Spanish.

In the hotel kitchen she found a tin of crackers, jars of peanut butter and jelly and a sack of ground corn. There was plenty of fresh water in the rain barrel. Finding food and water lifted Nina's spirit somewhat but she longed for an ice cold Coke or a Sprite. She vowed if I ever get home, I'll never again bitch if mom or grams bring home the wrong brand of soft drink!

Not having a calendar, she needed a way to keep track of her time on the island, no that she expected to be stranded here very long. Surely someone would come to rescue her. At any rate, she decided to put a seashell in a safe place every morning. In that way, she could count the days. Besides, she and her little companion would while away time looking for shells. Nina would call, "Come on Marcheta. It's time to go on our treasure hunt." One day during one of these island excursions, Nina came across a fresh water spring. "Wonderful!" She cried. "I have my own private pool! It's a good thing I have my bathing suit, not that it would matter if I went skinny dipping, there's no one around to hide in the bushes to sneak a peek."

Even though the cool water was comforting, despair engulfed her as she realized again, how alone she was and how hopeless her situation had become. She kept scanning the skies for a rescue plane and the endless blue ocean for the Coast Guard. They always searched for people that were missing in movies or television shows, but no one came looking for her. So Nina and Marcheta kept gathering seashells, keeping track of the days, then weeks and finally months she had been stranded.

One morning, Nina saw someone walking toward her down the road. As the figure came closer, she could see that it was a woman. She wore a long black dress and her jet-black hair shone in the sunlight. Nina could not believe her eyes, it was her grandmother! "Ah Buella, she called in Spanish, "Ah Buella Rosa, what are you doing here? How did you get here? You live in Spain!"

Grandmother Rosa just smiled and kissed Nina on both cheeks, murmuring, "My dear little one." Then faded from sight as quickly as she had arrived.

Each morning Grandmother Rosa would appear, bearing fresh eggs. Together she and Nina would make tortillas and feast on wild berries and papaya. Then as day faded into evening, she would vanish as mysteriously as she had appeared in the morning. Nina tried to follow her, but to no avail. She simply disappeared into the dusk. Sometimes she would stay a little longer and Nina would wind up the gramophone then she and Marcheta would dance around the room. Rosa joyously tapped her feet and clapped her hands in time with the lively music calling out, "Ole, Nina! Ole, Marcheta, Ole!"

Then one day as Nina was about to place a seashell in a new pile, she realized it was December 31. She was not only starting to count the days of a new month, but a New Year. At that moment, Grandmother Rosa approached. As usual, she kissed Nina on both cheeks. Then she whispered "Adios, my little one, I must leave you. Vaya con Dios, Vaya con Dios – go with God." Like a vision the older woman faded from sight. Nina cried, "Ah Buella! Come back. Don't leave me!" But she was gone.

Nina was filled with remorse. Her sadness was more than she could bear. She gave up hope of ever returning home. With tears streaming down her cheeks, still clutching the seashell in her hand, she lay down on the water's edge, hoping the tied would carry her out to sea. Bidding adios to Marcheta, she tired to shoo her away but her faithful friend snuggled by her side. Suddenly, as she looked out over the water, everything became white. It was as if a curtain had fallen from the sky. A bright light began to slowly penetrate the thick whiteness. Confused and scared, Nina tightly clamped her eyes shut. As she lay there, she heard a voice – her mother's voice. Cautiously, she opened her eyes and heard her mother say, "Oh Nina, you've come back to us. My prayers have been answered!"

Gradually, Nina became aware of her surroundings. She couldn't believe it! She was in her own room with her little cat, Polka Dot snuggled up next to her and her loving family standing around her bed.

"But Mom, Nina cried with the little strength she could muster, " the deserted island, my little friend Marcheta, the seashells…"

"No my dear, said her mother, "you have been here in your own room. When the sailboat you were on capsized, you hit your head and you got a concussion. Your friends are all safe, but you've been in a coma for a whole year."

"But Mom, what about Grandma Rosa?" Nina asked.

"Yes your grandmother was here. When she heard about your accident she came right away. She flew back home to Spain just this morning. Before she left, she kissed you on both cheeks and whispered, Vaya con Dios, my little one, Vaya con Dios."

A faint smile crossed Nina's face and as she drifted off into a peaceful slumber, her left hand slowly opened. A gasp went around the room. For there in the palm of her hand lay a small, white seashell. ©

A Sneak Attack

by G. Otto Fanger

As they gazed toward the enemy shore, the troops in the trailing vessels of the fleet were inspired by the emblem of their country fluttering above the front of the lead attack ship. The weather was typical for an early December morning. However, that was inconsequential. They would bear any and every possible hardship to complete this mission. This was a battle for their homeland. This was the big one. Every man knew that if they won the war, they would be celebrated as heroes. If they lost the war they would be executed as war criminals.

Thoughts went back to the pre-boarding activities. Their leader had given them an inspiring message, about doing their duty for Deity and Country. At the end they had all given three cheers to the general. Then their officers separated them into companies. They all gathered, and carried their equipment onto the boats, preparing for the long water crossing.

Now, all of their attention was focused back to their water passage. The ships crept closer and closer to their target. If they could gain total surprise, their success was almost assured, but that was far from certain. Everyone was quiet, not making a sound that the enemy might hear.

Finding the boats had been a real problem. Their country did not have the type of transports the high command wanted. Scouts had to locate others, and laboriously ship in these substitutes. They were much slower, heavier, and offered less protection to the personnel, if attacked on the water.

Now the enemy shore was becoming clearer. They could just make out details through the fog. These last few minutes would be crucial to the success or failure of this operation.

They approached the shore line; then scrambled over the sides of the ships, and into the cold water. After wading ashore the soldiers split into two groups. As planned, one group, lead by the general headed for the north side of the enemy base. The Lt. Colonel led the other group south along the coastline in an attempt to skirt the enemy camp, and attack from the far side.

In a few minutes the lead company of the northern attack force reached their objective, methodically leveling devastating fire on the surprised enemy. Enemy soldiers ran in every direction in utter confusion. The attacking force pressed forward, toward the enemy troop garrisons.

Meanwhile, the southern attack group, following along the coast, was encountering more foggy weather. However, it seemed to work to their advantage, because they skirted by several ground defensive positions without being recognized. The sleepy guards in their stations believing that these they were their own men coming back from patrol.

Finally past the shore sentries, the southern force swung inland. When they came to the main road turned to the north driving toward the enemy in a pincher movement. It was classic Napoleonic strategy with southern group completing the pincher begun by their comrades on the north. The battle was over, almost before it began. It was a stunning victory.

Their commanding general had successfully led their sneak attack across the icy river into Trenton New Jersey. General George Washington and his second in command Lt. Colonel Benedict Arnold had secured total victory. From this day on mercenary Hessian soldiers would never again touch this continent. British soldiers would have to do their own fighting.

The attack was something that no one had thought possible. It turned the ragged revolutionary troops into instant heroes, and the victory came just when almost all the citizens of the fledgling county had given up hope for their revolt against England.

This historic victory would turn the whole war around, and arouse other countrymen to join their cause, to drive the British from this country once and for all. It laid the groundwork for the eventual defeat of the British at Yorktown two years later, and the eventual birth of a new free country! It had been a very successful sneak attack!

Some 68 years later an Imperial armed force from the far east would make another sneak attack on an American island shore. The date of this attack, December 7, 1941 would in the words of President Roosevelt, "go down in infamy."

The winning side always writes the history! ©

CRANBERRY LAKE

by Walter Palesch

As I step into my leaky old rowboat, a small turtle scurries around my feet. He's got a worried, panicky look about him, and hurriedly dives off the dock. Considering he carries his suit of armor with him at all times, it's hard to fathom why he should be worried. Maybe he is unhappy that I'm trespassing here at four thirty in the morning. It's still almost dark. A slight chill clings to the late August air as I gently lower the paddles and drift into the fog that hangs like a shroud over the black waters.

I'll stop by old man Jeb McCorkle's place today. He's the oldest resident on the lake, at 93, and by far the most interesting. His cabin is on the other side of the lake. Always has a story, given a near century of experience to talk about. Now some think he's a crotchety old geezer, but if you're a real person, as he sees you, he will do just about anything for you. Jeb gave me this leaky boat. Said:"My Pappy brung it with him from Kaintucky in 1901." Explains the leaks, I guess. Says my little boat saved their lives. Stopping by his place is always pleasant,'cause he will entertain you with coffee and homemade sausage. Don't know what he makes it from, but it's good.

As I glide through the reeds, the visible world drops off into dark oblivion just ten feet away. A barking dog on the far shore registers his complaint about the almost imperceptible sounds coming from my boat. He is the only sensory connection to the outside world now. It is truly as still as a medieval cathedral at midnight.

I can make out lily pads as they glide into view. I try not to make waves. A big frog with swiveling eyeballs proudly surveys his eminent domain from a large lily pad. His glassy eyes look me over with a frog's concern. He decides that I might be trouble. He bellows out an ungodly note like playing a bass fiddle with a hacksaw. Then he dives into the murky waters. Hard to believe he can actually attract a mate with those lyrics.

In the distance I hear tree frogs, crickets, birds and bullfrogs. Given the cadence they maintain, they must be communicating. A loud splash startles me. It's a big fish jumping out of the water, followed by two more. They're toying with me. They know I haven't caught a fish in eight years of trying. I did catch a sneaker once, and a bicycle wheel, next a toilet seat, and a bra! Hmm! Well, the lake is after all advertised as an "All Sport Recreational" Lake. With that kind of luck, I gave up fishing. But to add insult to injury, the neighbor's nine-year-old daughter, Corbin, purposely tiptoes across my yard with a big fish in hand, sporting an exaggerated smile, about once a week.

I notice the fog is lifting from the lake, slowly rising like a delicate curtain. Its color changes from a milky gray to an eerie, shimmering, phosphorescing hue. I can see fish of all sizes, beetles, and myriads of bugs. Dragonflies, with their iridescent wings are all around me. Insects whose names I don't know are busily going about their daily chores. Following genetic orders programmed long before any human or even human like creature ever walked this earth.

I'm too busy to notice the sun pierced the horizon. A spray of golden laser beams radiate from the sun and race across the lake. Simultaneously, the piercing shriek of a hawk wakes up the rest of this microcosm with its millions of miniature inhabitants. Suddenly, a chevron shaped shadow glides across the waters. Canadian geese demonstrate their precision aerial skills. At the last moment, they see me. Instantly, the formation pulls out of the landing pattern to pick a new place to touch down. How do they do that? They never collide! Maybe Jeb knows. Course he hates the geese. They like to camp out on his lawn, have late night parties, and plain mess his yard. Anyway the flock furiously complains about my being here, with their honking. They keep up their tirade for some time. I don't think I'm welcome here. They probably guessed that I contacted the DNR this year to evict them and move them to some other deserving lake. I mean a few geese are O.K., but not an armada of 400 illegal, alien birds. Soon they'll be taking food and jobs away from our birds. Jeb will have a lot to say about these geese.

By now the entire lake is bathed in brilliant light. A heron, like a statue, stands on his stilts near the shore. Two swans swim by majestically. These are huge birds, and not afraid of much. They are so white, only fresh snow can match them. Swans are beautiful, but their voices are awful. This is no lie. They sound like a tuba filled with mud, mixed in with the sound of a cement mixer full of rocks.

Jeb McCorkle's cottage is about 400 feet up ahead. He's sitting on his porch, smoking his pipe. He just doesn't know smoking is bad for you; and he's had 93 years to figure that out.

"Hey Jeb" I holler out as I coast in. "It's Walt."

"You think my eyes ain't good enuff to figure out who you is? He hollers back.

"Naw, just bein friendly, Jeb"

"Well come on up an get you some coffee and vittles."

"Thanks, Jeb."

I haul the leaky boat up on the lawn, and he starts to laugh and laugh some more, slapping his lap.

"I gave you that boat for kindling wood. Don't wanna be responsible for you to go out and drown in it, you fool. Your wife Nancy would give me hell and then some."

"got a gallon jug in it for bailin out water. Hey, you know anybody else who's got a 90 year old rowboat."

"Can't say I do. Nobody with a half a brain would".

That's what made this dude Jeb so cool. He had what I call headroom. Always had room to laugh, joke and have some fun. And live a productive life.

"You look prosperous, he opines." This is an expression, from another century, when only wealthy people were portly. They had enough money and food to overeat. Their waistline proved they were prosperous.

"Hey, go easy, Jeb. Maybe I put on five or ten pounds."

"Yeah, you're half again the man you used to be, Walt. Beetles wrote a song on that." Then he mouths the song. He's got a tongue!

"How is your Dad and Mom? Gotta get over there an taste some of your mother's Strudel and your dad's smoked ham."

"You're overdue on that," I offer.

"Did 'ja see the geese land out there?" I ask, knowing that will light a fire under him.

"Sho 'nuff. Damn birds. Noisy, dirty, crap all over lawns, docks, everythin. Dem Kanucks, oughta stay in their own country. It's big enuff, that Canada, ain't it? Gotta mind to pull out the shotgun."

"Whoa, Jeb, you remember where that got you last time?"

"Yup, that was a ordeal alright. Guess that's not the answer."

Jeb had fired at the illegal, immigrant, alien birds with his shotgun two years ago. Didn't hit none, just scared them away. Neighbor turned him in to Johnny Law. Got arrested, spent the night in jail. Deputy played cards with him all night. Jeb won 15 bucks off of him. Thirty-five of his neighbors showed up for the arraignment. Jeb told the judge that soon it'll be illegal to stomp on a damn bug on a damn sidewalk. That was not good etiquette in a really, really green county courtroom like ours. Considering Jeb's age, the Judge let him off with a stern warning. I couldn't help noticing that the judge had a hard time keeping a straight face. Imagine reprimanding a centurion, a man in whose lifetime shooting geese was considered sport for food. Centurion is not really the right word here, but I like it.

"Hey Jeb, you was married once, right?" (Christ, I'm starting to talk like him now!)

"Married the woman of my life when I was 20 and Irene was 17. She was a looker, a good wife, an the best thing ever happened to me, ever. Had a child hood sickness. Couldn't bear children. She died when she was 30. Been alone ever since. Never could find nobody like her, so I quit lookin."

" Hold it right there, Jeb. Who was the woman we saw you with a few years back?"

"A woman friend, nice lady. She died because of some complicated woman thing."

"So she was with you until you were about 82?"

"Sounds about right."

"Have you got a lady friend now?"

"Naw, I can't remember anymore what I would even do with one. No use wrackin your brain over stuff you can't remember. Let's get some food."

"How'd you know I was coming?"

"I got ESD."

"You mean ESP?"

"What I said. ESD! Naw, just joshen you, Walt. My dawg Elvis been pointy eared and prancin around ever since you stepped into your sieve, I mean boat. Dogs can hear stuff four miles out and smell about 1000 times better'n you. Elvis knew you was commin."

"I smelled your bacon half a mile out."

"You're good at sniffin out food. Explains why you're half again the manyou...." He trails off.

He had lean bacon slab turning over a wood flame, hearth baked bread that he made, eggs and a cheap cigar. You would hold your chunk of bread under the pork to catch a few of the bacon drippins. Delicious! At the end he served a shot of decent whisky.

I thought the time was right to ask: "How did that leaky boat save your life?"

"Well, my Pappy an Ma an me came up from Kaintucky right about the year 1901, to find work in Michigan. Bought a wagon an a team of horses in Detroit. Left for Oscoda and Harrisville, up yonder, north of the Michigan thumb. Settled into a small logging town with a big sawmill operation. Pappy was good at runnin and repairin machines, so they made him chief mechanic, nothing to sneeze at in those days. Some 'o them ridgerunner hillbillies come up from the South were pretty dense. These dumb clodhoppers were hired by the sawmill, and kept busting machines like clockwork. Pappy said that Michigan was covered with huge Oaks, Beech an Pine trees the likes he ain't ever seen. Kinda like those jungles down in Mexico."

"You mean Brazil, don't you?" I interrupt.

"There you go again, you horse's arse. Always acting smarter than thou. I say it's Mexico."

"Of course, Jeb. You're right. My geology really stinks."

"The word's geography, you know, Mister smarter than thou." I gave him that one, so he'd cool down.

He starts back up. "Remember, Michigan wasn't a State until 1837 or so. Not much goin on then to wreck the trees until we started loggin them. Course by the time it was all over, we had clear-cut the whole damn State. Shame that people never know when to quit, whether its, whales, buffalo, seals, or you name it. Anyway, the sawdust, shavings, barks an bad quality boards were all put on the muddy dirt roads, until it was a bout 3 feet thick for miles. Before that, the roads were mud 2 feet deep in the spring. Couldn't get around for weeks."

"Three feet of sawdust?"

"Yup, seemed like a great idea for paving roads. The heavy lumber wagons and horses compacted the stuff. Water sank into that thick sawdust sandwich an made it hard, an we were pretty smug about all that."

"And then it hit. Some dang fools, probably the McGaffee twins, those daffy idiots, careless and all were clearing land up by Cottrell Creek and started a forest fire. Ma saw it out the window, screamed out "Oh my Lord, my savior God," dropping the dishes in her hand. The pieces skidded across the floor. In less than half hour, the inferno was rolling towards town, driven by a hellacious west wind. Cinders were already raining down on everything. Old man Mercer's barn an livery stables were up in flames. People was runnin around like ants on a ant hill that's just been stomped on, with about the same touch of organization. They were throwen their belongings onto wagons. More worried about things than themselves. Cost Jarred Smythe his life. "Dang idiot." Pappy ran down the street to get Jim Borst, our fastest rider. Jim was already on the case. He raced up the North road, and then galloped back, screaming at Pappy: "On fire!" Marco Ciuffetelli, we called him Cuffy, was our Italian neighbor. He was galloping south, disappeared into the smoke, and then came flying back two minutes later "On fire! Both roads!" he bellowed out as he reappeared out of the dense smoke, jumping off the horse on the run. "The roads are on fire, Zeke!" He screamed at my Dad. "All the roads are burning, every which way! No way out."

"What the hell is all burning?" somebody yells out through the commotion an smoke. "The damn roads are on fire now, the forest's on fire, the whole valley is burning, full circle," yelled Jim.

"Those thousands of tons of sawdust were now burning with a vengeance. Fire all around! The wall of flames circled our little town, our settlement of fifty four souls. It was the driest fall in a while, a tinderbox. The houses were built of, you guessed it, wood. They had a flame retardin rating of about four seconds. Now the tall pines on the Huron ridge exploded into flame, and roared like thunder. The thick smoke was choking people now. Dad yelled, "Put kerchiefs over your mouth and nose." Only way out is the lake. Pappy barked orders at the small group of men, and took over.

"Untie all the animals! Let the chickens and pigs loose! Get the rowboats out. Take only blankets and food, you hear! Jeb, get all the matches, lanterns and candles you can find and carry. You fellas, get ropes, some metal tubs and kindling wood, more blankets an straw. Let's go; let's go. Move it! Move it or fry!"

Pappy was the boss now. That fool Joe Kennedy took what he could, loaded his wife Emma and lil Clifford on his wagon and tore out down the south fork. There were only eleven boats with room for forty-four total. Adding more would capsize the boat. There was fifty of us left now. Women and children were loaded first, then the men. Six had no seats. They waded into the Lake, staying as close to the shore as was possible. Used wet blankets to shield agin the heat. Four of those six perished due to the cold waters and breathing in burning hot smoke. They could only wade out about 50 feet in the shallow or drown, surrounded by that inferno. The horses mostly perished, a horrible sight.

Some ran into the lake, were caught between burning and drowning. The next morning we saw three of them floatin by, one with stiff legs up in the air. Caleb McClintock died weeks later from exposure. Imagine the upper body fried by the heat an lower body frozen by the lake. Two lived outta dem six. My Pappy an that Pollack, what's his name. Got 40 letters in his name, mostly z's, y's,w's and a bunch if skis. The Italian, Marco, and Jim kept the boats together and took care of the people. Some were at the edge of losing it, for fear. The Pollack got himself a job with Henry Ford at the new factory and became quite prosperous. He was a enforcer in Henry's private Police Force. The 11 rowboats floated about a half mile out, all tied together in a group, safe in that place. Funny thing was the Steamship Shenandoah left the night before with a load of lumber. Headed for Canada. Woulda had room for all of us, easy. Stayed offshore in the little boats for about 18 hours, watching everything we owed turn to ashes. Praying to God that no storm would come up. If it had we would have all drowned. Hadn't been for Pappy, Marco the Italian, an Jim, we would never have made it. Those men were heroes. There was a storm on the Great Lakes maybe six years before and two hundred eight ships was sunk, about everything that was floating at the time. Killed hundreds. These lakes are small oceans, you know. Some of the storms kick up 30 foot waves, but not that night. Our boat did have a leak though, something that don't surprise you much, does it? But that little rowboat saved our lives. Can you beat that?"

"This here 'lil boat?"

"Yup."

"By the way Joe, that fool, tried to gallop his horses through that wall of flames. Horses wouldn't have it. Reared up, capsized the wagon. No way to go now, forward or back. Found their bones weeks later, the dead horses too. Eighteen woodsmen died in their cabins, near Harrison's landing. Had no chance to go in any direction. Streets were still burning 2 months later. So they built a new sawmill 15 miles up the lake. A place we could now call home again. Weren't nothing left of the old, including the McGuffee twins."

Takes me a while to come back to the here an now after listening to that. We needed one more shot of whiskey.

I thank him for the hospitality. Ask him if he would mind if write his story down.

"Now who in tarnation would wanna read about a old fool like me, he grumbles?"

"You'd be surprised, Jeb."

"Really?

"Yup".

"Don't forget, full name's, " Jebediah Timothy McCorkle, II. You'll get it right, won't you?"

"Yes sir!" as I salute him.

Although we have other old timers on the lake, Jeb is the most colorful. He is another reason life is good here. I pull my boat back into the water and head back home. I'm thinking I'll take a day off and write, and stain the deck. My office is forty miles away, and won't be located any closer for another three years. Does it make sense to drive that distance, or should we move? Jeb says I must be teched to drive that ever day. Guess I'll go out on the lake in the morning and find out if it's worthwhile. No use bein in a huff to make a decision. It might take several trips to get the answer. A body cain't hardly make up a mind, less'n it has all the facts. Reckon I told you I'm startin to talk like ol Jeb.

Postscript:

Jebediah Timothy McCorkle II had no children. His wife died young. Both younger brothers died in their 70's. One nephew was killed in "Nam, another in a car accident. The only niece simply vanished. All his contemporaries, every one, now belong to the ages. Seven years ago, I recall him saying mournfully,

"Today my very last friend died."

This is a drawback of a long, long life. His genetic train is heading for that last stop on that long journey. Most precious, he has been a participant and observer in a century of unparalleled change, the likes which humanity has never witnessed or even dreamed of. A century filled with miracles, wonders, achievements, and hope; and horrors, and man's inhumanity to man. All of that will be lost with his passing unless...

Unless, if you're in the neighborhood, or even if not, you stop by and say hello to Jeb. He is really a friendly cuss. And you will learn more things than you ever imagined. You will take home some of his priceless wit and wisdom; all that from a man who in a handful of years will leave his footprint in three different centuries.©

Liberty Point Station

by Dan Kent

Her incessant complaining about everything he did was making her a prime case for spousal abuse. His only relief from Midge's mouth invariably came on Saturday morning when he liberated himself by leaving the house with the newest of metal detectors.

Sometimes he had the whole Saturday, when Kansas football season was in full swing and several cronies of his would come over to enjoy a game. Midge usually left the house for a full day of shopping somewhere. She said she could not stand to hear grown men whooping and hollering over some silly game.

Last Saturday was especially bad for their teetering relationship when she started riding him at the breakfast table. "Why can't you find a decent, respectable hobby that both of us can enjoy instead of gallivanting all over creation waving that dumb detector around. Let me refresh your memory, in the past two years, all of the treasures you have brought home. Let's see, as I recall: you have found sleigh bells, buttons, belt buckles, dime store diamond rings, another diamond ring that wasn't, ear rings, one of each, a wrist watch that will never find noon again, all this with an assortment of coins so badly worn they are virtually worthless. You are really something. Why don't you act your age and forget about finding other people's lost baubles. Oh yeah, on the way out, take the trash."

Midge really had a mouth on her, he thought of Jackie Gleason when she was on one of her tirades. As Ralph said: "One of these days, Alice, its pow…to the moon!" But today, James Templeton Starling, (J.T.) was looking forward to another taste of freedom.

He had a new target in mind this morning. A friend told him about the old railroad station at Liberty Point that was nearly demolished by a tornado last month. The Home Owners Association had been harping about the site for years as it was reflecting on their properties up the hill. There was a time, long ago, that the station brought the well-to-do home or sent them on a journey only they could afford. A number of them came home in a fancy box, for them it was literally the end of the line.

Old Liberty Point suburb was still an exclusive residential neighborhood with all types of restrictions with which the home owners needed to comply. You could not paint your house anyway you chose. First you needed to get committee approval. Improvements such as planting a tree, well actually anything had to be approved after seeking permission. When the old railroad station was nearly blown away, the committee members finding that it was railroad property became upset because they wanted the debris removed immediately. The railroad people said demolition would start the first of July however; the tornado came five days earlier.

What was left of the old station was a real mess. Two walls had collapsed, bringing the roof down on the ground floor. The tornado skirted the western edge of the community sparing many magnificent homes but the historic railroad station suffered extensive damage. According to the legend attached to the gable of the station, it was built in 1882 and operated by the Atchison, Topeka and Santa Fe Railroad until recent years and railroad decline.

It took J.T. almost twenty minutes to locate a pathway beneath the wreckage. He wanted to find an area underneath the ticket counter and waiting room if at all possible. From his calculations, he had found the correct position. It may be the right place, but entering it was somewhat of a risk. For one thing, at the first sign of a rat, he would depart in maximum haste. Surprisingly, he could breathe fairly well with the paper mask. He was grateful as considerable dust arose at his every movement. Crawling on his knees, he reached the area he had been seeking. Comforting beeps from the detector were heard in short order to the left of where he was positioned. He sifted through the sand and to his delight; a number of coins came to light. Three silver dollars, four nickels, with two quarters were soon in his hand, together with a number of pennies. Then his flashlight picked up a yellow gleam in the dark, dirty sand. It turned out to be an odd brass colored coin or perhaps a token of some kind. The dust was becoming bothersome, getting in his ears, eyes and nose with a maddening itching. Well, he thought, enough for now. As he wiggled out of the threatening confinement, he could hear ominous creaking and sighing from above.

Given the light of day and fresh air, he paused near his car with its open trunk. Finding a rag, and with water from his thermos, he washed his face, neck and hands of the black soot-like residue that covered him. Lordy, he must look like a coal miner. Before leaving for home he studied his findings, in particular, the strange gold token marked Cincinnati Mining and Trading Company, with an Indian head on one side, and on the reverse, California Ten Dollars, dated 1849. It must be gold! How did it get there? How did this lowly token have a value of ten dollars? If it was made in 1849, it had to arrive after 1882 when the depot was built. Could a mining company make its own coins? As he drove away, he pondered these questions and wondered how the items had found their way into the crawl space.

Since the flooring was wooden, he suspected cracks appeared in the boards after thousands of feet that brought in snow, mud, rainwater and sand into the structure. Eventually failures in the flooring had to make an appearance. He mused on. Having so many wealthy patrons using the building, he doubted they would make an issue of a coin that had been lost. Now, a gold piece that vanishes surely must have got someone's dander up! Who had owned it? Where did it come from? Why was it here in Kansas?

Other coins might be found, but J.T. found himself saying that he was not going back into that hellish place again. It was like working under a mountain of splintered wood and rusty nails. By the time he neared his home he noticed that the wind had picked up and he was grateful that he was not under that pile of rubble now. He reasoned that the blackness on his clothing and person must be coal dust that had filtered down through the wooden flooring. Oh great! Midge was going to have a fit when he got back into the house.

Sure enough, as he opened the back door, Midge was there to greet him. "Well, for God's sake, look at you! You're absolutely filthy. Now don't you set a foot inside this house looking that way. You stand right where you are until I think of something. Listen to me. Here is what I want you to do. Go down to the basement, take all your clothes off where I can get them in the washing machine, then go upstairs for a bath, leave your shoes off down there too. I'll get to those later. What in heavens name is all that black stuff anyway?"

"Coal dust."

"I won't even ask where you got it. I just hope you had sense enough to cover the car seat, as I intend to go to church tomorrow in that car."

After a bath and a change of clothing, he explained to Midge the importance of getting to the library before they closed. With a wave of the hand he was dismissed.

At the library he could find nothing about the unique token. If the item was indeed gold, he did learn a few things. Gold could not be held privately in the United States from about 1933 to 1961. At the turn of the century it was valued at $20.00 an ounce. In 1961 it rose to $38.00 an ounce and after 1975, all restrictions on possession were lifted.

J.T. walked to the public phone outside the library and called a coin shop known as "Empty Pockets" run by the Morgan Brothers. He described the find the best he could to the shop owner.

"Could you hold on for a minute? Who did you say you were?"

"I did not say." After a short delay another voice came on the line. "We were about to close, however, if you would like to bring it over for us to examine, we will stay open until you arrive."

One half - hour later he unwrapped the item from its tissue blanket as the brothers looked on. Larry Morgan's eyes widened and anything resembling a dead poker face or a cold eyed banker vanished.

"Where did you find this?"

"I would rather not say." J.T. replied

"Who are you? I don't recall…"

"What was the Cincinnati Mining Company?" J.T. queried.

The brothers were silent, taking turns studying the item with their jeweler's loupes. Finally, they laid it down carefully on the tissue. They appeared to be in awe.

"What in hell is that thing?" J.T. said impatiently.

One of the brothers offered to let the other speak. "It is a California Territorial gold coin. It was made during a period of severe coin shortage and an unusual glut of gold in circulation. So private companies or gold assayers made coins for public use when nothing was provided by the government. At that time there was a huge surplus of raw gold in California. Your specimen seems somewhat worn and we are puzzled at that." Both brothers nodded to one another and one spoke. "We will buy it from you, if you are willing to sell."

"You haven't told me about the Cincinnati Mining and Trading Company." J.T. entreated once again.

"Ah yes, that is a bit of a mystery. No one seems to know much of anything about the firm. I have heard that records of the company may have been lost in the San Francisco earthquake and fires of 1906. Of course no actual proof of that exists, it is just speculation."

J.T. was lost in thought for a spell. Then he inquired, "I see, what would you offer me if I decided to sell?"

The brothers turned their back and conferred, and then they turned in unison to face him. "Would you take $2,500.00? Wouldn't that be a nice surprise for the missus?"

"Really, that much?" J.T.'s eyebrows lifted at that. The brothers smiled broadly. "Well, perhaps I should inquire a little further, perhaps another appraisal to assess its worth…a verification of sorts."

"Alright, we can go $5,000.00, cash on the barrelhead right now. You can walk out that door with cash in your pocket. This is our final offer; as far as we dare go. Where are you from? Do you live around here? Have you a phone number where you can be reached?"

J.T. offered no further information. By the look on the brother's faces it was obvious that the situation reached a standoff. J.T. began wrapping up his prize, the thin balding brother said, "Here, let me put it in a capsule to protect it from further harm."

He waited as they fitted the coin in a clear plastic container, then thanked them and turned to leave. "Call us if you change your mind." They said in harmony.

J.T. found himself sweating again after only walking half a block. His mind was reeling as he supported himself, leaning on the fender of his car. It took a while for him to calm down to think straight. One thing for sure, now was the time to keep his mouth shut until he had a better picture of the matter as a whole. As he sat in his car watching traffic, he made a few decisions. At no time would he reveal his name, address, or telephone number. Nor would he say where the coin had been found as he had heard stories of people finding objects of value that had been lost, with all manner of claimants coming forth for their "rightful" share. He soon realized if a dealer would offer him $5,000.00 today, what might the coin generate at an auction?

After that he began to call himself, "Mr. Jones" as he sought further information by phone from all dealers within a hundred miles and one as far away as Wichita. The phone numbers were all gained from the phone books in the collection of the Topeka Public Library. He thought eventually he might face the wrath of Midge over the unusual number of long distance calls, then maybe not, when he explained himself. He always thought that Midge had a beautiful smile and this would surely provoke the desired reaction.

He wished he knew how to take photographs for the look on Midge's face was one to remember. That was when he told her one dealer had offered him $5,000.00 and others when contacted offered twice as much and more, pending examination and proof of authenticity. She had paled at this, plumped down on the recliner holding her hands to her face. Plainly the news had left Midge shaken. It gave J.T. a great measure of pleasure so long denied to see her thus and hear her say repeatedly, "Oh my God, Oh my God! Is it real? Let me see it!"

The following Saturday morning brought a totally new atmosphere to the household. Midge Starling was up early preparing a vegetable omelet for her husband. She had also prepared him a lunch, including a salad, now in an iced cooler ready for his weekly foray.

She was all smiles as he was leaving with a kiss on the cheek. "Now, do you have everything you need? Don't forget to buy gas. Take your time, and enjoy yourself. Try to be home by six, I'll have dinner ready about then. Good bye, dear."

He smiled to himself when the screen door closed behind him. She knows the auction in Dallas is still a long way off. J.T. remained closed mouth as to where he had found the coin. Even Midge had asked repeatedly about it but he refused to disclose its origin, fearing that she might say something leading to a knock on his door.

One thing for sure, that at an auction it would bring a tidy sum into his pocket. Many times he wondered how the coin had found its way into that grimy crawl space. His most recent theory was that it was someone's "Lucky Pocket Coin" that slipped from his grasp and disappeared from view. To think that it had once belonged to a wealthy traveler was a fair assumption. ©

Night Adventure

(On the Shelf Marked N)
by G. Otto Fanger

He woke abruptly, immediately jolted with a splitting headache. At first he supposed it was night, but then he reasoned, that there is always some light at night. This was total darkness as if he were inside a closed cave. Then he knew the truth…he was blind.

Where was he? And, more importantly who was he? There was no memory to draw on, just an empty space in his mind needing to be filled in. It felt just a bit cool. The grass beneath him was slightly damp. He wet his finger, and held it up. There was a mild wind from his left.

Interesting, doing that just now. He thought I must have some knowledge of the outdoors. There was something else…a certain odor. He thought it smelled familiar, but he could not identify it. Trying to rise, the pain exploded in his left temple. He felt it with his left hand, and discovered a bump above and in front of his ear. His fingers explored the hair around the wound. They located a few pieces of fiber in his hair. It could be tree bark. Had he fallen into a tree and been knocked unconscious? Perhaps that had caused his temporary loss of memory, and his blindness. If so, he thought, it would come back in a few days. He tried again to rise, this time making it to his feet. He was unsteady. As he stumbled on the grassy ground, his hand brushed against what felt like a small evergreen bush or tree.

Then it began…a deep pressure in his chest – like someone pushing down hard. A pressure he instantly remembered…angina; a heart crying for more blood, struggling to supply the body with its rhythmic pulsing. Instinctively, he felt for the nitro pills. He found the small vial, over his heart, in his left front pocket. He opened the cap, shook out 1 of the tiny pills, and placed it under his tongue. The tingling burning sensation started almost immediately. Soon, he felt the relief.

He sat down on the grass to gather his thoughts. In his search for the nitro pills, he had discovered a wallet in his left front pocket. He examined it. There were a few bills, three credit cards, some paper cards, probably identification cards. The cards would tell him who he was, but that must wait until his sight returned.

He had only the personal items that were on his body. The rest must have been lost in the plane crash. That's what he told himself had happened. He was on the top of a hill, thrown from the plane, and very lucky to have survived. Were there any other survivors? He heard no one. No cries for help, no human voices of any kind. There was only the occasional hoot of an owl nearby...that was all. He touched his chin. He had a beard. The hair was coarse and kinky. He was older, maybe 50, maybe more. He now also felt some arthritis pain in his knees and ankles. Definitely more, he thought ...more like late 60's or mid 70's. That made him feel better. He had a good long life. Faced lots of other adversity; and must have had many experiences to upon. Overall, he knew that he had an excellent chance of surviving.

His technical training began to kick in. Systematically, he began to mentally review his needs and options in this situation. He remembered the "Survivor TV Shows." Their first needs on arriving at a location: water, shelter, warm clothing, and food. The basics that man had needed through his short existence on this planet. It was then that he heard the sound of a liquid gurgling and splashing on rocks, as if it was from a small waterfall. It was to his right. He moved, carefully, steadily in that direction, catching the ends of brush, or holding onto small trees as he went. He could sense that s he was descending, and then the ground was soft and wet under his feet. The sound of the falling water was close. In a moment, he felt a rock edge. Reaching down his hand was caressed by the touch of cool water; He brought the hand to his lips. It tasted refreshing. His primary need had been found. He had not realized just how thirsty he had become.

Without a carrier or holding container, he would need to build his camp nearby the water supply. Perhaps under the extended branches of an evergreen tree, using some other soft evergreen branches for his bed on the ground under the tree branches...just like in the Survivor TV show!

He sat on a nearby rock and pondered his plans. Shivering a bit from his wet feet, his thoughts turned to fire. That would be tougher. He had seen the survivors use a pointed stick, patiently, quickly rotated on a stone to produce enough heat to ignite dry moss. If they could do it, so could he. After all, he had years of experience. He knew he needed to keep track of this place. He once more wet his fingers, and raised it above his head. Standing with the water behind him the wind was now from his left side. He could feel no heat from rays from the sun. It was either a cloudy day, or night. Considering the owl's calls, it was probably night or early morning. He would use the wind direction as an indicator of space, keeping the wind to his left as he headed away from the water. On the return it would be on his right. Very soon, he ran into a larger tree. Its small needles told him it was either a spruce or fir, and not a longer leafed pine. How did he know that? He seemed to be familiar with the outdoors. Perhaps I am a hunter. This thought cheered him. It would be helpful in his quest for survival. I will not panic, he said.

His head throbbed again. "I need pain medicine," he thought. Then words from the chapter of an adventure book he had read as a teenager flipped up in his memory. He remembered," The Indians chewed birch bark to extract the salicylic acid, just as we had later done by taking an aspirin. He saw the molecular configuration in his head, The benzene ring with the salicylic acid side group, and the acetyl group attached to the oxygen atom of the acid. How did he know that? He must have had college chemistry; maybe he even had been a chemist! Interesting. He was reassured. Bits of memory were returning. "It would be just a matter of time before his sight returned," he mused.

Walking to the left a short distance he found a clump of birch trees, soon locating some loose bark. He ripped off pieces, and shoved it in his pockets until they were full. Then took a small piece, placed it in his mouth, and began chewing. It was bitter at first, but he thought, "That's good, it's the acid coming out of the bark." As he continued chewing the bitterness became less noticeable. He made his way back to the camping tree area. He began working on his shelter. He had labored a short time when he heard an eerie, terrifying sound. There, in the distance, a wolf howled, then another, then a third, then a fourth, then a fifth. After several minutes, their howling became louder. It sounded to him like the pack was coming closer.

His heart was pounding with fear. He grabbed for the vial in his pocket, flipped a nitro pill into his cupped hand, and then carefully positioned it under the front of his tongue. What had his cardiologist said? " Check your blood pressure to make sure it is over 120. If it is you can take one pill, three times, checking the pressure before each one. If the pain persists after three, then head for the emergency room, or call 911."

Some time elapsed while the canines were making their way up the various paths, exchanging information with their howls, and barks. He quickly ripped some more evergreen branches, and threw them onto the ground below the overhanging attached tree branches. The howling was becoming louder. It brought him back to his immediate situation.

Should he try to conceal himself under a tree branch, among the downed branches? Or, should he stand tall, and appear as large as possible?

"To hell with the "tall" idea," he thought. What chance would he have? A blind man fighting off a pack of hungry wild wolves? Quickly, he crouched under the evergreen tree branches, and attempted to cover himself with some of the other branches he had gathered for the bedding. He lay very still, and prayed that they would not find him. But, his breathing was heavy, and labored. He was wheezing now, desperately trying to catch his breath. He needed to elevate his head. It was time for another pill. He knew his pressure must still be over 120. (maybe 220!). He found, opened, and turned over the vial…but no pill came out. The vial was empty!

The animals came bounding up to the oasis, barking loudly as they came, a wild unearthly sound. They knew a man was near. Their keen sense of smell immediately picked up his odor. A few directional sniffs and they located the man under a small evergreen tree. He, of course, could not see how it was impossible to hide in this small outdoor landscape.

The leader stopped barking, and gave out a low whimper. He sensed that something was wrong with the man. The others also stopped barking, and watched the leader intently. The beautiful German Shepherd lowered his head until it was over the man's outstretched hand. Then he tenderly licked the hand. The hand remained limp and motionless. The dog leader whimpered again, and waited for the man to move. The other dogs relaxed, and watched the man and their leader.

But, the man did not move. His reaction to what he believed was the rush of a wolf pack had caused a major artery to burst in his wildly beating heart. The break quickly deprived the heart of its blood supply. It had palpitated wildly for a few seconds, quivered, and then completely stopped moving.

About an hour later, Ben, a security guard, pulled up in front of a large store. As he exited his Tahoe SUV. He saw the lighted sign high above the door proclaiming, "LaVana's Sports Palace". Below this, in smaller sized letters it read," We Sell Everything the Sportsman Needs." Ben unlocked one of front doors using a key on his ring of keys, and stepped inside. Something was different tonight. The watchdogs were not wagging their tails and waiting for his treats.

"Watchdogs, indeed," he scoffed, " any stranger could easily placate these dogs by offering them some scraps of meat." He had spoiled them into household pets. As he walked down the center aisle, past the gun dept. on the right, and the men's sports clothing on the left, he saw nothing unusual. Proceeding toward the back, he next passed the knife department and the woman's sport clothing (right and left sides, respectively). When he reached the camping supplies, and the tent area, he spotted one of the guard dogs further ahead in the recreational area by the Oasis.

He broke into a run. As he neared the dogs, and they spotted him, their tails began wagging. They looked back and forth between him, and the Oasis. At the same time they gave out intermittent soft whimpers. It was as if they were saying to him: "Come on Ben, look at what we found...what should we do now?"

"What is it boys?" He asked. He called to the leader, "King, what did you find?" The dogs were clustered around the back of the large oasis landscape that the store had recently installed. It was the high point of the store for visitors and customers. They marveled at the real trees and shrubs. They were excited to see the large pond of water in the central oasis, with a magnificent flowing four-foot waterfall! Everything was living, and real, even the grass.

A large fan was concealed behind bushes on one side. It constantly blew moist air through the Oasis display. And, to add to the realism, above the fan stretched a large live tree. A very special tree, with a hollowed –out burrow near one tree crotch. "Hooter," a half-grown screech owl sat on the branch next to the burrow. He turned his head from side to side and periodically hooted. Hooter and the tree were furnished by the local nature center. They had been loaned to the store for the opening of the display. Hooter was healing broken wing, so he could only sit in his tree home and make owl talk.

On another side, under a twelve-foot fir- tree, Ben saw a man's body. One hand was outstretched, clutching a small brown vial that appeared to be empty. Ben felt for a pulse, and found none. He reached for his cell phone, and called 911. Then he called the store manager and appraised him of the situation.

About 45 minutes later people started arriving. The attending coroner declared, after inspecting the body, that death was probably caused by a myocardial infart. He also recorded a large bump on the victim's left temple, most likely caused by striking a blunt force object. He noted that this injury could well have traumatized the victim, making him more vulnerable to a heart malfunction.

One of the police investigators found a stone out of place on the edge of the nature exhibit. About 5 feet away, they spotted blood on the top edge of a tree stump. They reasoned that the victim must have tripped on the rock, hit his head on the stump when he fell. They collected a sample of the blood from the stump, to check against the victim's. However, they were fairly certain that this was the blunt force object he had fallen against.

The head Inspector also made a note that the victim had an empty vial of nitroquick tablets clutched in his right hand. He wondered why the man had not walked over to the new pharmacy department 15 feet away, and either called someone, or found a bottle of nitroquick medication himself. It was sitting in plain view on the pharmacy shelf marked N.

With the family's input, he put together the rest of the puzzle. John Whittaker (the victim) had gone out late Friday night to pick up his nitro medication. He needed it replenished before the weekend. When questioned, the pharmacist at the drug store down the street explained that Mr. Whittaker had left after placing his order. He had told the pharmacist that he'd be back in 30 minutes to pick up the filled prescription. He never returned.

His wife reasoned that he had probably dropped by Lavana's to check on the display. It seems he had been commissioned, as a chemical consultant to develop a fragrance duplicating the fresh clean air of an evergreen forest. Evidently, he was checking on the test site at the Oasis, when he had tripped on the edge rock and hit his head in the fall. The clerks and manager on duty that night had not realized that he was still in the store at the time they closed Friday night. He had been locked inside, unconscious. The patrol dog gate automatically opened 1 hour later.

Normally his wife would have become concerned and called him on his cell phone. When he would not have responded, she would have notified the police of his disappearance. However, that night his wife had been out of town visiting her sister in Springfield. She had not known that he did not return home until she returned the morning after the ordeal.

On Saturday afternoon of the next day, the Chief Inspector was finishing writing up his report on the death incident. He reviewed what he had just written, and shook his head, "It sure was not Mr. Whittaker's lucky day," he thought. Then he filled out the last line of the report:

Inspector Jack Collins, Chicago PD Saturday, June 14th, 2008©

The Glitter Frock Lives

by Joanne Savas

I have a faint memory of my mother, Kalliope, in a dress bursting with faded orange and brown flowers. She was passionate about that dress, even having her portrait done, full length, wearing the creation. I am starting to understand how she felt.

The "glitter frock" I own has a history, too. She got her name not long ago from my grand kids. They love to add glitter to their pictures and wondered who put all that glitter on my dress. The frock takes on a persona immediately as it exits the closet. The light blue, sometimes purple frock first came to life at my son Zachary's wedding. That was a decade ago! Then it traveled here and there at various social gatherings receiving many accolades. It even took a trip to France and as far as New Zealand, proudly worn by me, the mother of the groom for my eldest son Jack. This frock withstands. Jack says to anyone within hearing distance, "I bought my mother this thing, its great isn't it!" Who would disagree?

Once again, glitter frock is out of the closet. I'm amazed at the number of times she has come to my rescue. I recall, the theatre performance in New York City of "Death of a Salesman," the Yasoo Dinner Dance; the night I sat with the famous pianist Gregory Hines at the Detroit Auto Show; the wedding of Peggy, the beautiful bride from Saginaw, Michigan; and on and on, too many to recount. Christmas festivities not withstanding, the frock's favorite, the glitter will continue a social circuit that puts Emelda Marco's traveling shoe collection to shame!

Glitter frock has been there for me in sickness and in health, standing sturdy; a frock I upon which I can rely. Today may be the exception. A crisis has ensued, or maybe just a glitch. My dear lifelong friend Mary arrives from Florida so we can attend our 50th. high school reunion in Dearborn, Michigan. She calmly assures me this temporary crisis can be overcome. I express my sentiments, "It is all up to you glitter frock." My expanding girth for the last decade complicates.

"If I can just get the zipper going," Mary muses out loud, "and how are your arms in the sleeves, can you move them freely?"

She is too polite to say this is not working. All this is said and done in a very serious demeanor. Then suddenly we both burst out laughing realizing how ridiculous it appears. Glitter frock is steadfast. It cooperates. But who knows, we are still a day away from the actual showing. Disaster could strike! That zipper could descend and never ascend again!

So, my plan at this moment is to hold my breath, refuse to select an alternate, and let glitter frock continue to do what she does best, to make me look good at the fancy Dearborn Country Club Gala.©

Boogies Last Ride

by Dan Kent

I was still shaking, thoroughly rattled as I glimpsed at all the flashing lights in the windows and the body being taken out the front door to the waiting EMS unit. That kid was only seventeen years old and would not get any older or smarter. All I can say he was old enough to scare the living daylights out of me barely an hour ago.

A young uniformed officer sat down next to me and put his arms around my shoulders. His badge read, James D. Rockwood, Jr. As you might have guessed everyone just had to call him "Rocky."

"How do you feel now Mr. Bennett, can I get you anything?"

"A cup of strong coffee might help. I'm also late in taking my insulin as a result of all the excitement. I'm getting the low sugar shakes on top of being scared silly. I think I have one more vial upstairs and I'll need it before much longer."

With an encouraging smile, Officer Rockwood said, "I know you have your statement to the detectives however, they tell me that you were some kind of a technical writer at one time. It might help you adjust to this incident if you tried to put it all down on paper while it is fresh on your mind. Somebody other than cops may be interested in what you have to say. Why don't you at least think about it while I try to find you some coffee. Mrs. Robinson from next door is concerned, so I'll ask her to make a pot. No cracks, please, about cops and doughnuts, I've heard them all." He finished with a chuckle. At the moment, all I could manage was another involuntary shiver and a weak smile. The ringing in my ears from the gunfire still filled me.

When the last of the police cars left, my friends and neighbors crowded into the living room. It was a comfort to realize their concern. I excused myself and headed for the upstairs bathroom to administer my needed insulin from what remained.

Mrs. McTavish, the widow from across the street met me coming back down the stairs. "You know Stan, I have a friend that works for that disaster company in Monroe. I bet they could clean that mess up in the basement for you. Do you think your home owner's insurance would cover something like that?"

"Don't know, but come to think of it, I've seen their trucks off and on around town. I understand the crime lab people are coming back later this morning. They had to leave for a more pressing matter on the other side of town. No one is permitted to enter the basement while the investigation is still underway. Did you see the yellow tape across the doorway? They are also trying to determine the identity of the other man. I told them the other guy called him Leon. Then I asked them if they knew the dead kid's name."

"Oh yes, young Mr. Ainsworth has been known to us since he was thirteen. A constant pain to just about everyone. I'm told the street name 'Boogie' stems from a little brother who was teased early on by Jason, which is Boogie's given name. Most likely it was taken from "Boogeyman." Some say he has boasted of several car thefts, and if given more time perhaps a carjacking at gun point would be in order. A smart kid in school, (when he went.) Too bad he couldn't grasp that someone could be smarter."

By the next morning, I had calmed down enough to make coffee and think over what had happened to me earlier. In the study, I found a yellow pad and began to write down what I remembered. Little Marcie from across the street offered to stay the night on my sofa if I needed someone to talk to or just to keep me company, but I declined – nice of her anyway.

Words came surprisingly easy. I'm calling my story, "Boogies Last B. & E. or "His Last Ride." As that is exactly what it turned out to be for him.

I'm Stanford Bennett and last month I had my 70 birthday. I am alone now, lost my wife six years ago, but I still have Bubba, my old tom cat. I am a retired draftsman of a welding equipment maker. We have had this house for more than forty years. The place is two stories with a bedroom study and bath upstairs, on the first floor, the usual array for rooms to make things work for a family.

In the basement, I have a small metalworking shop and a security room that once housed my large gun collection of military rifles and pistols. A couple of years ago, I gave up on guns, sold them and with the money I thought I would see the world; taking trips to Australia, Alaska, Hawaii and New Zealand. I had my reasons for unloading the guns. All I have left in my world is a distant brother and two nieces. Why burden them with the disposal of the weapons? I might as well do it right. As a rule gun collectors are not as nuts as coin collectors, but they come awfully close.

Oddly enough, of all the guns I had, I kept just one and that one turned out to be my life saver. It was my old Colt automatic. The police took it for some reason not fully explained to me. I've had the fool thing thirty years or more, and now I'm some kind of threat to the community. Maybe it was to make sure it was not involved in another crime. I didn't bother to ask questions.

I was restless last night when I heard a little creak outside on the wood fire escape. Somebody must be out there. I was out of bed in an instant looking out the tiny window in the door. Sure enough two figures dressed in dark clothing were mounting the stairs.

"Go away or I'm calling the police," I yelled. To my surprise, a voice answered, "Don't think so old man, we cut the wires. Give us the keys to both your cars and some money and maybe we won't break down your door."

"Bull to that!" I replied. I had my doubts if they could get past the dead bolt. In the meantime, I wasn't going to wait to see if they could. I grabbed my keys from the dresser and headed downstairs, turning on lights as I went. I was clad only in my boxer shorts and a black t-shirt from Alaska. If I had been fully awake, I might have gone immediately to the strong room. The door was fireproof, covered in steel, opened outward and you could not kick it in. It would take a lot of work with a sledge hammer or an explosive charge to get in as even the walls were reinforced concrete block. Trouble was, the door lock was somewhat screwed up and I had been slow in repairing it because nothing was stored there. Guess it doesn't make much difference, but I didn't give the strong room a thought.

I made a bee line for the gray metal locker standing in one corner of the basement. I was in such a panic, I had a hard time finding the right key for the locker. In short order the doors popped open to reveal what lay on the middle shelf. It was my Colt .45 Government Model automatic pistol with the Russian markings. Lying beside it on a shop cloth was a full magazine of fresh ammunition. After ignoring it for nearly three years, only two weeks ago I cleaned it carefully. I could not remember when last I had fired it or if I ever had. As a rule, I could never hit much with a pistol at any distance but up close it might be a different story. With trembling hands, I inserted the magazine, pulled the slide back and chambered a round.

Hearing wood splinter shortly thereafter, I heard the intruders making their way from one room to another, cautiously working downward in my direction.

"Hey old man," a voice called. "Where you at? Tell us where you keep all that money and we'll go. Yeah. Show us the money!" Then nervous laughter from them followed this remark. I wasn't laughing. "Almost forgot, we want the keys to that sweet cherry Desoto in the garage and we'll take the keys to that new Taurus in the driveway too. You hear that? You know Leon here wants to drive that old Desoto real bad. C'mon you old geezer, where you at?"

I heard the floor creak just above me. "Stay back, I warned them, "I'm armed and will shoot!"

"That's a lot of crap. Whatcha got, a BB gun? We know ya sold all those guns long time ago. You better give it up smart guy, we got guns, real ones. This here is a .357 Magnum, go right thru your bony old butt without stopping. You get what I'm saying?"

I was tempted to tell them my savings was in the Old Kent Bank, but thought better of it. How did they know about my guns? Well, all the neighbors knew, lots of people did, it was not a big secret. Oh God! It sounded like they had made it into the kitchen now.

"Hey Leon, tell him what kind of gun your carrying, maybe he will wise up and get us the money he has in the house. Betcha it's in that special room down there with the standup gun safe. Huh, don't you? Say something you dumb old fart! Here Leon wants to talk to you."

Leon giggled nervously before he spoke. "I got one of them Glocks in nine millimeters just like the cops! Found it in a house on 8th. street when nobody was home. Shoots real nice."

Then in a sing-song voice he called, "Come out, come out, where ever you're hiding."

They were in the kitchen for sure now. The refrigerator door popped open. I heard it make the familiar sucking sound it always does.

"Hey old man, no beer, no wine, no pop, but what's this stuff here? So... I see...its insulin. You must need that stuff huh? You know my mama has to take it too. So, if you need it now I'll send you some special delivery air mail – here it comes."

I heard something whiz down the stairway, bounce off the wall and hit the concrete floor. Soon afterward another one came, then another. I don't remember how many were thrown down the steps. I could see them lying by the wall, bursting, leaking their precious contents on the floor.

"Hey old man, here comes the last of the bottles. You're going to see my fast ball-watch this!"

I saw the white box hurtle downward, hitting the last step, bounce upward, hit the wall like the others, no doubt spilling its fluid as it came to rest. Then a thought came to me. I hurried to the laundry room, opening the circuit breaker panel and began flipping switches. Seconds later the house was in total darkness. Maybe they wouldn't be so brave now, I thought.

"So you're a smart ass now, aren't you? Too bad. You see, I always carry a little flashlight with me. I never leave home without it." He played the light up and down to make his point.

"See what did I tell you? Have you wet on yourself yet?"

"Go home boys, while you still can. Don't be stupid. Someone is going to get hurt if you continue like this." I replied.

"A.., I know who that's going to be. Are you ready for this you old B…"

In the darkness, I found the basement flashlight by the furnace. I heard the stairs creaking with the weight of two people descending. Just why, I'll never know, but at that moment, he was not using his flashlight. When I thought he was halfway down the steps, I flicked my light on. Oh God! It was blinding! In that fleeting instant, I saw the silver revolver of his come up, and I pulled my trigger. He fired too. In that brief moment, the muzzle flash lit the area. With both guns going off in a closed space the report was deafening. He missed by a mile. I did not. With heavy thumping my uninvited visitor was sliding down the stairs, headfirst, his pistol bouncing across the cement floor. I had pointed at his chest. With my ears ringing from the discharge of both weapons, I held the light on him, where he came to rest. He was jerking some and I knew I had hit him hard. Upstairs I heard the back door open and close and footsteps running away.

He was making gurgling sounds and trying to get up. I kept the light on him until he stopped moving. It did not take long. I went over to him with the pistol still aimed, touched him lightly and rolled him over to see what I had done. Damn…I had pointed at his chest and hit him in the throat. It was a gruesome sight. I was not proud of this, just happy to be alive. The damn kid had wasted himself on bad information.

With pistol still in hand, I stepped around him and hurried up the stairs. I pause briefly at the back door to find no sign of the other guy. Satisfied, I took off running for the street. I went directly to Marcie McTavish's and began ringing the bell and pounding on the door both at the same time.

"Marcie, Marcie, wake up! I just shot somebody that broke into my house." A light came on and I heard footsteps coming.

©*Author's Footnote: This story had its basis with a nightmare. In this unsettling dream I am a victim of home invasion. With references to the gun collection, I was once a collector. (I also know what it is like to be insulin dependent.) D.K.*

The Easy Button

by G. Otto Fanger

Part I

Tom Johnson loved his EASY button. It was positioned on the right side of his desktop, just above the remote mouse and mouse pad. He was the only one at International Register that had one. Habitually, while he was considering the right word or phrase to use in his latest report, he moved his hand up from the mouse pad to the button, and caressed its smooth bright plastic surface.

Tom sat back in his armchair, and smiled. He remembered the events leading up to the acquisition of the button. He had seen it in a display at the office supply store. It was there to promote their motto of being able to supply ALL of your office supply needs. Tom had coveted it immediately. Then he had an extended talk with the office store manager. Tom explained how much it would mean to him to have that button on his own desk. After some hesitation, the manager promised Tom could have it in two weeks when the display came down.

The manager was aware that Tom was an employee in the offices of National Register, and had been a good customer, even referring other Register employees to the office store. And, let's face it...it was just a simple, non-functioning plastic button. It was of no further use to him. If the company wanted it shipped back, he would simply say it was in too bad a shape to save.

Two weeks and one day later Tom picked up the button in an after-work trip. The next morning Tom had installed the button on his desk. (Actually he simply placed it where he wanted it on his desk. It was not yet connected to anything)

Arnold Sweet his supervisor, saw the button the next day, and asked Tom about it. After Tom replied with such enthusiastic jubilation concerning the addition, Mr. Sweet decided that there was no harm in his employee having a non-functioning button on his desk. "Tom, said Arnold, under no circumstances are you ever to hook it up to any of the company's phone or computer lines. Is that clearly understood? This button is strictly 'show only'."

Tom was intelligent enough to follow Sweet's suggestion. The only apparent change he made to the button was to attach a gadget called a 'Decision Module'. These were readily available from Electronic House. It consisted of three colored lights: red, yellow, and green on a display panel. Not showing, inside the panel was a triple C battery, and a one inch square circuit board holding electronic circuits that when given an outside input command (pushing the EASY button), it randomly sent power to one of the panel lights, allowing it to blink out its color. The ratio of selection was adjustable as an additional outside input could be added. Even without hookup, Tom's productivity almost immediately increased. The button quickly became indispensable to him. EASY was the key to keeping up with his heavy workload. (Tom never refused work, or to stay late to finish a project. He was regarded as the "workhorse" of the department. Whatever you needed, Ole Tom would be happy to do it for you.

Tom was the only manager at International with an EASY button on his desk. It was not that he was so high up in the company organization. That fact was obvious to anyone by simply looking around his small windowless office. His desk was the same size as the other technical managers, but it was the only one adorned with the bright red button. No, it was the fact that with the EASY button close to his right hand he was so much more effective in his job.

I suppose it was Clancy Turnabout that started the snowball rolling. Clancy had just returned from a vacation in Jamaica. On his first day back his hard-nosed boss, "Pink' White charged into Clancy's office and demanded that he finish the new two year key panel model design plan.

"I want that design plan on my desk by Thursday morning, or you'll regret being in my group!" Pinky said, with a little deeper red in his usual deep pink face. He turned and walked out.

Clancy knew he was in trouble. After a few minutes puzzling an idea popped into his head: how about his buddy Tom? Tom would help him again this time. But could he? This was a Herculean task to accomplish in a minuscule of time.

Clancy hurried down the hall, turned to the right, knocked on the door, quickly, and walked into Tom's office. He looked at the desk, and saw the EASY button.

"What the hell is that?" he asked.

"That, my good friend," said Tom, smiling, "is the EASY button!"

"So, what does an EASY button do?" questioned Clancy.

"It, bragged Tom, provides an easy answer to complex problems."

"O.K. buddy, I just happen to have a very complex problem!"

Clancy grabbed onto the top of a plain, worn, wood chair in front of Tom's desk, flipped it around, and sat down. He laid out the details of his problem. Tom and the EASY button listened.

When Clancy was finished explaining, Tom waited a moment, then looked at Clancy and said, " Watch!" with authority, he pressed the EASY button.

Clancy watched…a moment later a small green light flashed on.

"You are in luck, my friend, EASY has the solution to your problem!" Now listen closely. You may want to write this down".

Clancy sat and listened; taking notes as Tom relayed in detail the message from the EASY button. When Tom finished, the green light went out. "Any questions?" asked Tom.

"Jeez, not now, let me get this in presentation form. If something comes up I'll be back to you. Thanks Tom… you saved my job!"

"Think nothing of it. Tom replied…that's what the EASY button is for! Oh, by the way you look great. That Jamaican sun really suited you. Maybe someday I'll be able to afford to go there."

"Thanks again Tom," Casey said, as he went out the door whistling, "The Girl From Ipinima."

On Thursday morning, to the amazement of Pinky the two- year plan for key-panel model design from Clancy was center front on Pinky's desk. Pinky immediately skimmed through it. The detail and quality of the design amazed him. The plan was incredible. " Best thing I've ever seen that goof-off do," he growled gruffly still amazed.

"Hot Damn," he chuckled. This would save him from doing this labor-intensive task. He buzzed his secretary in her adjoining office. After she came in he handed her the plan, and told her.

"Here Marlene, retype the report headings, and replace Clancy's name with mine and, have it ready in 15 minutes, it's urgent!"

As she scurried back to her office, he rationalized, "No goof-off deserves the credit for this, but I do. After all, I'm the one who initiated the request!"

With that off his desk, he picked up the phone and began calling his golf buddies. Now he could keep his golf game date. It was turning out to be beautiful day.

There are no secrets in an office. The word quickly got around the department that Pinky's report, coming through Clancy, actually originated in Tom's office, and was inspired by his EASY button! The whole department staff was amazed.

Anyone could have predicted what would happen next. It was office business-as-usual. No one wanted to do much work, so everyone started frequenting Tom's office, even with the most trivial problem.

The easy button quickly remedied that situation. It selectively chose to green light only the most important and financially significant company-related problems to solve. It relegated the others to yellow or red light delays.

For instance there was that incident with Janet 'the mink' She was the sexy secretary of George Tyler, another technical manager down the hall. She had softly knocked, and with his invitation stepped into Tom's office a few minutes before the day closed.

She strutted over to his desk and leaned down. Her deep cleavage under her low-cut blouse cried out for attention. Tom could have counted the freckles on the top of each breast.

"Tommy honey, please help me out on this report, if you do I'll make it worth your time!"

She began showing him papers and asked Tom if he would look over the new regulations that she was supposed to make ready. Regulations that the supervisor wanted all the managers to read and provide they're input, before they were given to the general staff. Normally, this would be a perfect task for Tom to handle. Oh, no, he thought, not this time. She wants me to help her again; I've got to stop this nonsense right now!

She pleasantly presented her story, but as she fumbled with the new regulation, his right index finger executed down pressure on the EASY button. The red light flashed.

"Sorry, Janet, he said, regretfully, EASY says that you'll have to wait on that. "EASY Rules". With that he went back to writing his report.

She looked startled, then wheeled around toward the door, cattily snapping, on her way out, "Well, I never thought the day would come when you would not help out a lady in distress! What is this place coming to!"

Then there was the time when Harvey Click, a top salesman at International whom Tom often collaborated with on technical matters came barging into Tom's office in the middle of the afternoon.

"Tom, 'ole' buddy, ya gotta help me out! The Simpson account needs information on the G303 product. Please, would you get that together for me, so I can present it to "Sly" at a sales meeting tomorrow morning? I'd do it myself, but I'm swamped and, good buddy, you're so talented with technical things like this."

Tom smiled at Harvey, and said, " Well let's see what EASY says."

With that statement, Tom pushed the EASY button. The red flashing light appeared.

"Oh, that's too bad Harvey, but it's out of my hands. There's no way I could do this myself, maybe next time. Tom picked up his red Parker pen, and for all practical purposes no longer recognized the presence of the salesman. Tom did not hear Harvey mumble, "But ya did it for me before," as he exited the office.

The fame of Tom's marvelous EASY button spread further through the company corridors. It was the subject of almost all of the coffee breaks, even replacing the usual tidbits. Even Janet's latest sexual exploits were now passe.

Inevitably it was not long before Internationals VPs were sending their managers into Tom's office for answers to decisions they had been asked to make. Then, after continued success, the VPs came in themselves to visit with Tom, and see the marvelous EASY button in action.

None of the managers or VPs even considered asking for the unsure advice from the marketing division. Data from the Strategic Sales Forecasting department in the Sales division were now irrelevant. The same thing was true of Advanced Design in the R & D division. Instead, when a question came up needing an answer, they all made a beeline to the EASY Button.

It was only a matter of time before the members of the Board of Directors were sending their VPs to the EASY machine office, or what was now called, company wide, the' EWIT', an acronym for Tom's EASY button.

From there is just a matter of a short time, before the Board found a loophole that would allow Tom and his EASY button to sit in on the company board meetings.

During all this time, the Country Club was hosting the highest attendance on record on the fair lanes, and amassing record profits! Business at the bordello strategically located above the Office Bar was also outstanding.

At the quarterly technical meeting the technical VP, Dr Very Smart, presented with the Productivity Award. It was given to whomever the supervisor decided had made the highest impact on increased productivity in that quarter. There was no question in anyone's mind that anybody but Tom should receive the award. After the presentation, some of the staff jokingly told him, he should be nicknamed, "Mr. EASY Button."

Part II

However, Tom's EASY button was not greeted with rejoicing in other parts of the corporation, far from it. Members of the, marketing group, who were once the guiding stars of the corporate ship, now discovered that their duties had been taken over EWIT.

They reasoned it would just be a matter of time before management realized that a marketing department was no longer necessary. The same fate was inevitable for the future sales forecasters in the sales department, as well as the concept designers in the product design departments of R&D. All of these people soon would be out of work because their duties had suddenly been usurped by Tom and his EASY machine. They decided in unison that EWIT had to go.

These department heads called an informal meeting of their upper staff. They held the meeting at the Office, where many of them often stopped for a few drinks and relaxing conversation, as well as other available amenities.

The meeting was called to order by the most verbally affluent present, Jack 'The Rat' Swiftie, VP of marketing.

"Ladies and Gentlemen," he announced. We have a crisis to deal with. We are in danger of losing our jobs because of some ridiculous button on some former minor manager's desk. We need to eliminate this threat to our right to work and return to the way things were before that damn EASY button! Does anyone have any ideas on how this could be accomplished?"

Johnny Wet Behindears, A brash young salesman spoke up, "That miracle EASY button might just disappear some day and accidents can happen to people…it's a dangerous city."

There was some anxious eye searching among the surprised audience.

The Corporate controller, "Slimey" Sandy Schemer, calmed the conspirators. " Putting aside any bodily harm for the time being, let's consider the disappearance of the red button. As I understand it, the button is unconnected. These marvelous things happen because of what power and understanding this Tom person has with the button on his desk. So, if that button disappears, what's to stop him from just going out and finding another one?"

The sly old fox running corporate sales, 'Slick' Charlie Oils, said smoothly, " It seems to me we need to attack, and destroy this person's confidence in his button!"

Then corporate gadfly, Darlene Backstabber spoke up, "We should use the political ploy developed by Clever Cole. It completely destroyed his candidate's opponent in the last presentational election: Attack your enemy's strong point. Destroy this and he has nothing! Use whatever we have to lies, bribes, deceit, whatever! Like they say, Politics is not fair. If you want to be fair, then get into another line of work!" (Darlene exemplified this policy in her own day to day actions. She was infamous for causing trouble, especially spreading lies about her "good" friends)

"Or, man" broke in Don Wonderboy, the VP of design, speaking in a rhythmic beat, as his Willie Nelson pigtailed hair bounced on his shoulders, "Or, like, convince de big boys, man, that the button that has done lost its pazass, it ain't no account, no more cool, man, that's coap.. a..setic!"

"And that it can no longer be relied on for key decisions!" broke in Darlene.

That idea stirred a buzz of comments, and initiated their plan of action. They diligently began to plan, in detail, their infamous plot to destroy the trust of upper management in EWIT.

Part III

A moment later, there was a tentative knock on his office door, and Mrs. Pleasant, his new secretary entered the office. "Yes, what can I do for you, Maggie?" he spoke out pleasantly. (He was now on a first name basis with her.)

As she was closing the door, she announced," Mr. Johnson, I knew you was busy writing on ya aw re port, soes Ah reconed I'd order you all lunch in. Ah has all the foods y'all like: a hot cup ah ham und pea soop, ah burger the ways yaw likes it, ah glass ah cold milk, and ah slice of yall's favor ite desert.....strawberry cheesecake! Now yaw just leaves dat ritin, and eat yall's lunch, ya hear me?"

"Well, thank you, Maggie" he said, as he moved his papers over to make room for the plastic tray.

He gazed at the feast before him. The whole meal was there, just as she had described it, along with the familiar, well-worn silverware. The milk was even in one of his favorite Red Wing glasses! But, most important, the catsup was present on the tray. Maggie Pleasant was one of the few people that he would never push the EASY button on, to make them go away.

On the other side of the one-way mirror in Tom Johnson's 'office,' Nurse Darling was talking quietly to the resident Doctor." Mr. Johnson is still completely delusional. He's living in what he believes to be his own little office at work. At least 5 times an hour he will stop inputting meaningless data into his computer program, and look up as if someone had come into the office. He will then raise his voice in an argumentative tone and reach up and deliberately press the EASY button. When he does, his angry mood immediately changes to an attitude of triumph. Then, after a short pause, he either resumes typing meaningless words in an illegible report or creates another one of those free verse poems he keeps writing. Of course once a week, while Mr. Johnson is outside or in the recreation area, our computer technician goes into his room and deletes out all new files from his program as well as defragging his computer." "Doctor, she emphasized, he is truly and deeply delusional and has shown no improvement since he arrived. However, he is quite tranquil, and seems to enjoy the fake office we set up for him at his son's request. He even travels down 'his' hall to his bathroom and often puts money in 'his' Pepsi machine as he passes. He is much easier to control now than when he arrived in a straitjacket just after he was sent here for attacking some of the other company employees. Evidently, he was set off when they tried to take away his EASY button. However, your decision to reinstall it in his room certainly helped calm him down. He so enjoys it!"

"Absolutely, the doctor answered, positively, you are handling the situation very well. However, we will keep up the medications, and the physiotherapy. However, I don't see much chance of change for Mr. Johnson, in his deep delusional state especially with his constant audio and visual hallucinations. But, he seems to be harmless enough and not outraged against his fellow employees, or suicidal. He obviously really enjoys sitting at his desk typing and pressing his EASY button. Keep me informed of any changes in his condition." He paused, and smiled, saying, Maybe all of us could use an EASY button. What do you think?" He laughed, and turning, walked down the hallway with authority, carrying his patient folder under his arm.

Nurse Darling thought a minute" What would she do differently if she had an EASY button on her desk?"

On the other side of the mirror, Tom Johnson was typing away. He had a leather brace on his right hand. It was placed there to reduce the inflammation on the ligaments controlling his finger motion, especially his index (EASY button) finger. He had been diagnosed as being afflicted by what is known medically as carpal tunnel syndrome. He was just pressing down too often and too hard on the EASY button! ©

56

The Admiral's Kite

by Dan Kent

The war in the Pacific had ended nearly a month previously, when an ocean going tugboat, the K. Sullivan engaged in engine trials came up an American made flying boat adrift some seventeen nautical miles south of the Japanese Naval base at Yokosuka.

When viewed from a distance aided by binoculars, no sign of life was evident. As the tug drew closer, the crew noted the aircraft had sustained damage form gunfire and on board fire in the port engine. The entire propeller to the damaged engine was missing. It appeared the machine had been struck multiple times by gunfire in the wings and tail section. The tugs' Executive Officer was quick to note a further discrepancy and alerted everyone at hand.

"Hey, what gives with this? Aside from its odd greenish gray paint job, it looks like a genuine Navy PBY Catalina, but notice it bears no markings whatsoever. This might be trouble in the making. Tell the radioman to report our findings to harbor authorities and I will be along shortly, as soon as I brief the skipper on this." He barked.

Response was quick from headquarters ashore.

"Do not bring your vessel in close to the derelict machine. This could be a ruse of some kind. Stand off at a safe distance and send a small boarding party to examine the aircraft. Tell them to exercise extreme caution."

Within the hour Chief Engineman Brimley and another man were returning to the boat. Brimley was clearly agitated and eager to talk to the captain.

"Well Captain, why that damn thing didn't blow up, I'll never know. It is still leaking fuel and that ain't all, they are all dead aboard. They are all dead on board. I counted eight bodies, the two in the cockpit apparently died from wounds, blood all over the place. Others probably killed in an exchange of gunfire as we found a number of spent cartridges cases by the defensive waist guns. It also looks like some then apparently died from self-inflicted gunshot wounds. It's crazy. I found one man that seems to be an Admiral, sitting in this little compartment in full dress uniform complete with all kinds of medals and the ceremonial sword. That whole plane is loaded to the gunnels with explosives. It beats me, as to what they were up to. I'm certainly no expert on explosives but all those wires leading everywhere are enough to scare the living hell out of me. We need somebody else to look things over and tell us what's going on. Every man on that plane is dressed in a Japanese Naval uniform. As you said, that airplane bears no markings anywhere. By the look of salt water stains on the hull, it has been drifting quite some time. Most, if not all of the bodies are in an advanced state of decomposition. If you want me to go back on board, I'll need some kind of breathing device. The stench is so bad; it is a wonder that you cannot smell it from here."

With nightfall upon them, the tugboat crew was advised to put a line aboard the derelict and maintain position until daylight. A Navy destroyer with explosive technicians would rendezvous at dawn to assist. Authorities feared the plane might drift ashore with increasing wind and sea conditions and had no desire for the plane to be brought into the harbor either, with questions concerning the explosives aboard. Without difficulty, a line was secured to the bow of the drifting flying boat and the tug remained on station throughout the night.

At first light, the man on watched looked out to the plane astern and in horror saw that the mysterious machine was no longer there!

The Captain and Executive Officer were understandably at wits end over this development and wondered it the plane had taken on water and sunk during the night. When the tow line was brought aboard it was evident the line had been cut and not parted under strain.

The perplexed man on duty, Seaman Nigel Larkins, thought he heard engine sounds on his watch, but the with the boats own diesel engine noise combined with the wind and wave action, it was difficult to distinguish anything in the direction of the Catalina.

The service conducted an extensive search for the plane without success. Nothing was found to prove it ever existed other than the photos taken by Petty Officer Shaffer. Months later, intelligence learned that the remains of revered Admiral Munakata had been laid to rest near his birth place in a secret ceremony.

Signed/Yeoman First Class
Augustus E. Thompson USN

The Red Lake

by Elaine 'Elle'Cousino

Slowly Kate walked into the bathroom and turned the shower on cool. The heat and humidity of an August night had left her sleep deprived and exhausted. Drying she slipped into an old white shirt and cut offs, leaving her feet bare, except for an pair of well worn tennis shoes.

Walking down the long dock to the little wooden rowboat, lights were twinkling here and there as cottages slowly came to life. Kate settled in the seat, adjusting the oars as she looked at the green, silky water, and then pushed off towards the center of the little lake. Working the oars, she could feel the shirt already sticking to her back. Her dark hair formed tight ringlets where it escaped from the ponytail. As Kate rowed further and further she saw other boats already fishing. Lights sparkled bouncing on the still water.

"This is my favorite spot." She said as she slowly slipped the anchor down into the inky water with barely an splash or sound. Kate had been coming to the lake since she was a child, first with her grandparents then with her parents. Yet the little lake held secrets and places of mystery. Kate set about baiting the hook as she had been taught and cast the line gracefully across the water. It landed with a soft plop, then she settled down, waiting, then reeled it back and forth. Her mind was not here. Fishing was a time for thinking, sorting things out, relaxing enough to put situations into proper perspective. As the little boat bobbed in the lake, she focused on the morning sunrise.

Angry dark clouds scudded along the horizon. As she watched, the pink burst into flames of orange framing the black and gray clouds with crimson. The sun, a sizzling orange ball rose majestically, promising one more hot August day. Sudden thunder clapped, Kate jerked the line, at the same time feeling a strike, not a gentle one, but one that demanded attention, right now. The fight began. The fish ran with the line, Kate returned the pull, but not too strongly. "Don't want to lose this one." She muttered through clenched teeth.

Sunrise had turned the water blood red. Silver lightening slashed through black clouds. Wind howled, rain pelted Kate, the white shirt billowed out into the wind. Her black hair came undone and streamed out behind her. The tiny boat, helpless in the storm protested loudly, squeaking, creaking, oars clanking in and out of their sockets. Nothing mattered to Kate. They continued to battle, the big fish for its life and Kate to win.

The entire sky was now shades of red, touched with black clouds moving swiftly, propelled by the wind and rain that poured angrily down. Kate was oblivious to the storm. "Nothing else matters!" she screamed into the wind, "I cannot let him go!" The boat broke free from the anchor and she knew that she was drifting wildly. The fish pulled once more, then Kate felt the line go slack.

The boat knew the fight and its life were over. It drifted towards the rocky cove that practically ate old wooden boats. Angrily she pulled at the oars. Waves lapped over the bow into the boat. Between strokes she bailed out a few coffee cans of icy water. Then there came a terrible screeching almost human-like screaming of a sharp rock hitting the boat's bottom. Kate lost one oar trying to guide her boat away from the rocks. Then another rock caught, the boat disintegrated around her. She splashed into the cold water, falling and parting the red waves. Kate watched, fascinated as the rock formations passed by.

Survival instincts kicked in and suddenly Kate found herself swimming upwards to the surface. Jagged lightening pierced the water as she rose. "It is like being re-born!" Kate mused as she saw the red waves, velvet clouds and lightening brighter than anything she had seen before in her lifetime. She swam to the rock, higher than all the others and with great difficulty pulled herself up. Water streamed from her clothes and amazingly enough she found she was still wearing those old tennis shoes. Kate was crying. Raw emotions surfaced during the storm. "Was it the storm or the storms of life?" she mused, tears cutting down her cheeks as plentiful as the rain. It no longer mattered who was right or who was wrong.

How long she sat on that rock no one knew. They only knew that the little blue wooden boat had sunk in the rocky cove. Why had she gone out in the storm? They did know she had a husband and family in the city, and that she had left them while she stayed that summer at the lake. They knew she was kind of an odd-ball. Kate knew what they thought and it didn't matter.

Kate felt the pull of the water now that she had regained her breath and strength. "No, you can't have me quite yet," she said to no one in particular as she nimbly jumped from rock to rock then finally to the shore. Kate then began the long trek home, lake water squirting from her shoes with each step. ©

Slice of Life Opinions and Essays

"The trouble with the future is that it usually arrives before we are ready for it." Arnold H. Glasow

50 Words or Less

by Elaine 'Elle' Cousino

There is no other way to say it. Mom was a contest junkie. After working at hard manual labor for many years, in addition to raising seven unruly children on her own, she decided there must be an easier way to make ends meet or perhaps have a little extra cash.

So that's how our living room desk and kitchen table became a mailing depot for contest entries. Mom was determined. Her small figure was there at the desk, sitting up late with her ancient Remington typewriter writing rhyming verses for everything from soup to nuts. There was the laundry soap powder, Duz. "Duz, does everything!" Men's hair tonic, "Wildroot, a little dab will do ya." Scouring powder, "Babo, it floats the dirt right down the drain." "Rinso, Rinso white, happy little wash day song!" All these winners were just trivia to her. She wanted to compose an entry that would knock the judges dead in their tracks!

When employed at Ford Motor Company, they sponsored an employee monthly slogan contest and she never failed to participate. Finally after many entries, hers was selected. "The Ford I'm making may be the Ford I'm buying." Her boss handed her the $50. prize check and told her, "Quit your job and write a book."

Our family thought this was a strange slogan from her as Mom never drove a Ford or any car for that matter in her entire life! With the winnings, she took us on vacation, renting a cottage in the Irish Hills for a week. My brother-in-law transported us there in his old Dodge. She of course took the typewriter with us on vacation. While we enjoyed the lake and sun, she sat on the little screened-in back porch filing entries of 50 words or less. ©

The Unbreakable Soul

by Beverly Lee Bixler

The trip to Russia in 1975 heightened my awareness of the suffering of Jews in the Soviet Union. With this new awareness I became a member of the Union of Council for Soviet Jews where I learned more about the struggle of the "refuseniks" (Jews who have been denied the right to emigrate.)

Eleven years after my visit to the USSR, I chose to wear a bracelet with the name Ida Nudel. I had asked for the names of two women, Inna Meiman and Ida Nudel. As Inna was dying of cancer from a tumor on her neck, I was only given Ida's name.

Who is this woman Ida Nudel, and how did our lives cross paths? The following information is taken from the book, <u>A Hand in the Darkness</u>, by Ida Nudel. (Quotes are indicated by italics.) I have selected just a few of the many incidents in her life as she struggled to be free.

Ida was born in 1931 and grew up during the time when Hitler invaded the Soviet Union (June 22, 1941). A day later her father, a reserve officer left as a volunteer for the front. His few letters described the conditions in which Jewish officers were shot in the back by their own soldiers. This is how deep antisemitism was felt in Russia.

The enemy began to bomb Moscow and in October 16, 1941, the family was given a ten-minute warning to get ready to leave. Her mother and sister and Ida were loaded on the train as it was being bombed and traveled beyond the Ural Mountains to a small Siberian town. They returned to Moscow in 1943.

Meanwhile, the family learned of her father's death. He died near Stalingrad and a friend wrote, "You can be proud of your husband, if he were not a Jew he would have been a hero of the Soviet Union." A few weeks later they learned of the death of her grandparents and her entire family. They were annihilated in a mobile gas chamber alongside the road leading to the dump where the Nazi murderers threw the corpses.

Then January 13, 1953, Stalin decided to try to annihilate the Jewish community and concocted a terrible tale about Jewish doctors murdering Soviet people. The doctors were declared guilty. Friends no longer offered handshakes or smiles to fellow Jews.

November 1971, a month and a half after she had submitted her application for an exit visa, her departure was denied. The reason for denial was security. They stated, "You might have overheard something." She was to be detained for five to six years. She was now a "refusenick"…a Jew who had been denied an exit visa.

December 1972 ~ There was a hunger strike at a telegraph office where thirty people were arrested during the night. An inner-city bus took them away. They were kept busy throughout the night with interrogation and filling out forms. They were then loaded into cars and taken to People's Court. The charge for Ida was that she insulted the honor and dignity of a policeman. She got fifteen days in isolation.

Upon returning home, she found a hole in the ceiling for the bugging devices of the KGB. Now she was trailed every time she went out and they disconnected her phone.

On June 1, 1978, there was a demonstration at six locations in Moscow. It was International Day; a day set-aside for the protection of children's right to have a peaceful and happy life. The demonstration was at the homes of Jewish women. There were five to six women in each apartment with children behind closed doors. They put up posters that read, "KGB – Give Us Visas to Israel…Let Us And Our Children Go To Our Homeland" in windows or hung them from their balconies. This was done one after another in forty-five minute intervals.

Ida took a piece of wallpaper and made a sign that read, *"KGB Give Me a Visa to Israel,"* and also wooden pieces with nail protruding outward to place on her balcony. When the police began lashing her poster with flexible metal rods, she began to douse them with water.

A crowd formed and began crying, "Hitler did not finish the job…Where is Hitler?"

The next day the apartment was raided and Ida was charged with malicious hooliganism. According to criminal code, a crime under this article can be punished by and up to five years imprisonment.

There was a mock trial which ended by her joining a new social caste, that of criminal offender. It was off to Siberia to the village of Krivosheivo, a small settlement of about two thousand people. Here were nine months of winter and three months of summer with winter temperatures between 5-40 degrees Fahrenheit, occasionally dropping to -75 degrees Fahrenheit. There was a thick, constant fog covering the ground. In the summer the temperature ranged for 75-105 Fahrenheit with mosquitoes crawling into ones mouth, nose and ears, making life unbearable.

Upon entering the village Ida had fifteen days to find work. She found no one who would give her work so the police assigned her to a small colony three miles from the village. Here she worked as a draftsman in the office of the land reclamation project. She was assigned a room in a barrack where the other sixty inhabitants were men and former criminals. After several incidents of men coming into her room uninvited, she went to the police station and told them she refused to live in a male dormitory. She was told that there was no other place to live and that nothing would happen.

In the summer of 1979, Ida moved out of the dormitory with the help of three good friends that had come from Moscow. With her savings and money from friends she bought a small peasant log hut. She was now doing guard duty at night. Completely alone, she fought on, comforted only by the collie, Pizer, who was give to her by friends from Moscow. She was guarding the trucks and cars alone in the yard of the road department. For four years she had lived, going from hardship to hardship.

In March of 1982, after spending one thousand four hundred days and nights, she took a seven-hour bus trip to Tomsk and transferred to a plane for Moscow. But upon arriving, she learned she was forbidden from staying because she lacked the most important thing for any Soviet citizen…a stamp on her passport which certified she was registered to live in a certain location. Without this little stamp, she was automatically considered a criminal. She had seventy-two hours to leave Moscow.

Ida left Moscow and headed to a friend's home in Tattu in the Baltic Republic of Estonia, but police hounded her and she was not able to get permission to stay in that town. She then went to Bendery in the Moldavian Republic where in October 1982, she got that precious stamp on her passport! She lived in Bendery until October 1987 when she was finally granted a visa for Israel!

On November 18, 1987, my parents and I were watching the news on television when they showed a picture of Ida Nudel landing in Jerusalem. We were so exited and had a grand celebration, lighting all the candles symbolizing the light over the darkness. I immediately wrote Ida the following welcome home letter and poem.

Dear Ida,

Welcome home to Israel. What more is there to say? Home says it all. Who am I, a stranger to be writing? I am Beverly L. Bixler, from Waukegan, Illinois. The town is located forty miles north of Chicago. I am a teacher of reading and writing skills for those who are attending our community college.

Yes, I am a stranger in personal relationships, but very much connected to you in acts of prayer and speaking out on behalf of Soviet Jews. In 1975, I was in Moscow with several Jews from Michigan State University. This university is located in East Lansing, Michigan. Like Moses, each time I see the suffering of people, it awakens in me another level of consciousness. This awareness has linked me with the Soviet Jews since 1975.

My wrist bracelet with your name inscribed on it arrived about a year ago. I have been wearing it continuously and thinking of you.

In the Soviet Jewry information, I read that you had a sister in Jerusalem and that you had been struggling for seventeen years to immigrate to Israel. This information also I tell you because these three pieces of information were all the news I have had.

Every day I read two or three newspapers looking for one sentence that was about you. In the year's time, I saw only four separate lines of hope. Your visit with Imma and the Sakharovs, the first word that you may go free the confirmation of immigration to Israel and then your picture in Israel.

May you remember that there are Jews and a few non-Jews who love you. You are truly a faithful one. May your life overflow with blessings. I am filled with joyful thanksgiving.

Your wristband friend,

The following is the poem I wrote for Ida:

(to the tune of "Somewhere out There")

Somewhere out there, beneath the Moscow sky

Ida, were thinking of you and loving you tonight.

Somewhere out there, someone's singing a prayer

That you'll find freedom in this big dream of yours

And even though I know how very far apart we are

It helps to think we might be following that same Bright star.

And when the night winds start to stir the lonesome

Fears again, it helps to remember that there are friends

Somewhere out there Gd's love, has heard your plea

And now you're together with all Israelis

In Jerusalem where dreams come true

May your light shine for all the world to see

That one more Jew has be rescued from the plight.

Somewhere out there if schedules can see you through

Then we'll be together and another dream will come true.

My parents and I moved to Ann Arbor, Michigan (1988) just in time to greet and tutor some of the first Russian immigrants. I was thrilled to be given the opportunity to teach English to our new future citizens.

Then the moment arrived! It was announced Ida Nudel was coming to the USA, I was filled with joy and happiness. She had written a book titled, "A Hand in the Darkness," and was touring the country at Jewish Book Fairs. She was to be at the Jewish Community Center of Metropolitan Detroit in West Bloomfield, Michigan, during the week of November 10-18, 1990 or 22 Cheshvan 5751. Hot Diggide Dog!! I was finally going to meet Ida!

The night of 22 Cheshvan 5751, my parents, Mirra Ginzburg, Mikhail Kogan and Yevgenia Ganelina, my new Russian friends traveled by car to West Bloomfield. There she was this tiny, little woman, standing so tall giving us a talk on some of her experiences in Russia.

After her talk, we went to the room designated for the book signing event.

When it was my time to be with Ida, I took my arm, showing her the bracelet. I asked her if she would kindly remove the bracelet from my wrist. I handed her a rose. She smiled and slowly removed the bracelet. Pictures were taken of her removing the bracelet and her signing the two books I purchased. I had met the unbreakable soul and she was finally free! ©

Chocolate!

by Sally Wu

As I was walking in the supermarket, I came to the aisle with all kinds of candy. I wandered along to find out what kind of candy they carried. Then I saw the Hershey's dark chocolate bar. It drew my attention. Lately I have learned to eat dark chocolate and like it. It is not too sweet and melts in my mouth quickly. I told myself not to buy it. I walked away and looked around for the things I had come to purchase. Without realizing it, there I was back in front of that dark chocolate again! "It is no big deal to have chocolate once in awhile." I told myself. So I bought it.

The moment I got into the car, I could hardly wait! I took the chocolate bar out and bit a big piece off from it. I was driving, eating chocolate. Yum, it surely tastes good! I remember when I first came to the United States; I did not like chocolate at all. "It is too sweet," I used to say.

My dear friend Jean who arrived in America the same time as I, loved chocolate dearly. In just a few months, she put on lots of weight eating everything made with chocolate. Ever since that, I seldom touch chocolate, let alone buy it.

On my way home, I looked in the rear-view mirror to make sure there was no chocolate stuck on my face. I was surprised to find myself smiling. Hmm, why was I smiling? Was it the taste of the chocolate still lingering on my tongue making me smile, I wondered.

For the first time in my life I discovered that chocolate could lift my spirits and make me happy. What a great discovery indeed! From then on, I had a good excuse to eat it without guilt. Surely it was a great discovery! ©

Thunder in Avignon

by Joanne Savas

The coach came to an abrupt stop at the TGV rail station in Avignon, the GARE. From the window I could there was a sea of faces, high school students protesting poor conditions in the school system. "Allegere, Allegre," was their chant. The students were primarily dressed in black and white, a strange sight for the Province that is know for its brilliant Vincent Van Gogh colors of yellows and blues and the sunflowers more vibrant than heaven itself.

And this was not all, the students, dressed in mourning had unique hand drums, recorders and musical instruments to make their presence known. "Allegre, Allegre," resounded through the streets.

Our group was visiting Avignon for the day, the Pope's Palais and Avignon City life. Lawrence, the petite small-framed guide hurriedly guided us through the narrow cobbled streets ahead of the protest. "Our destination is the bridge," she kept repeating. Some of the group could not resist the smells of the bakery and stopped to sample the baked good. It was wonderful how Lawrence took to our group and we to her. As we paused in the square at the Palais Ouvert, she gave us further interesting tid-bits of centuries gone by, but we could not help but feel the immediate needs of the students, taking over our thoughts as the repeating drums and singing were heard in the distance.

I decided not to make the climb to the Rocher des Doms Gardens that overlooked the Rhone River and the Pont d'Avignon. I agreed to remain the square as our rendezvous point. I watched them depart. The square was virtually empty except for a mime clown that Jack had befriended. (Jack was our ace photographer who would from time to time leave our group for those special shots.)

Within moments the thunder arrived. Students stormed the square from everywhere. Thunderstorms arouse our sense of awe and wonder. This certainly was a similar situation! It is said that Thor, the God of Thunder, rumbles his chariot and strikes storm clouds, that was the belief of the early Norsemen. With a howling roar, the students advance like thunder and lightening ripping the sky. Signs went up, voices raised as the students made their feelings known.

I was overwhelmed with feelings of support for the students. Their sincerity and fight impressed me. The staging of this thunder was charged with electricity like a thunderstorm that makes several cells in a row, a squall line, and the line of students resembling new cells, replacing the old ones. Strange that I would think of this now. From a distance thunder sounds like a growling noise. Determination was written on the painted faces of the students but violence was absent. "Boom Boom Boom" was heard and it was saying, "We are here, and we want changes." As I walked through the throng, feeling very much a part of it, I spotted a man in a Georgia Bulldog's sweatshirt taking notes. He stopped suddenly.

I offered "Bonjour."

Cheerfully, he replied in English, "Hello Madam."

We chatted as best we could over the drone of the students. He was reporting for Radio France. He questioned the approach of the U.S. to teaching obstacles. As if he didn't know! I found the French extremely informed and knowledgeable about the U.S. and life itself outside their country, unlike Americans who sometimes barely know what is going on in their own country. The crowd was thinning, some students sat cross-legged on the old stones and the red Mc Donald's boxes swayed to and for providing nourishment American style with a bit of frivolity. I observed them and they in turn observed me. We smiled at each other.

Thunderstorms cleanse the air. They carry life -giving water from seas to lakes and dry land. I hope this happened to these students who wanted and needed change so badly. Would this demonstration make an impact? I thought to myself. Thunderstorms are powerful. In twenty-five minutes they can drop 125 million gallons of water and give off more electrical energy than is used in a large city during an entire week. Nearly 30 minutes had passed, my rendezvous with the group was nearing. I glanced to the top and recognized with comfort the familiar faces approaching the square. Lawrence was holding up that unsightly sign, "USA, Lyon Travel." The students saw the sign and broke out in a cheer. We cheered back. It was a warm moment. A memory I take away with me of a trip to a beautiful region of France.

Thunder can be loud. Thunder can be frightening and uncertain, but these young students who came from Avignon knew their thunder could bring lasting results to the school system of France. Bravo! ©

My Love Affair with the Blimp!
by Elaine 'Elle' Cousino

Many of my long lazy days of summer in 1946 were spent at the top of Murray's Hill outside of Mooreville, gazing at the bright blue Michigan sky, trying to see which cloud shapes formed pirate ships and which formed angel wings. One of those glorious childhood summer days while in my usual repose, a shadow fell over me and to my wonder was the Goodyear blimp, directly overhead. Its' silvery whale shape glided soundlessly in the sky, perfectly at home with the angel wings and summer sunshine. Bounding up on bare feet, I ran racing after the heavenly ship until it slipped away above the woods and Saline River, where I could no longer follow it.

Our weekly Friday night trip to Milan in my Aunt Jane's Oldsmobile, I immediately went to the library and looked up all the books and dirigibles. There were two precious volumes available! However, because I was only ten, the rule was one book to be checked out a week. Choosing the thicker of the two, I happily climbed into the back seat and read it completely, by street light while Aunt Jane completed her weekly shopping at the C.F. Smith store.

I just could not wait a whole week to learn more abut dirigibles, so I walked three miles back to Milan the following day. The librarian was surprised to see me back so soon toting the book I'd taken out the evening before. She carefully stamped the other book that I'd selected on that topic, stamped it and handed it to me with a quizzical look.

Walking home along the dusty dirt road, I branched off to follow the cow path along the Saline River. I sat down under a crooked branch of a wild apple tree, sun dappling off the glossy pages, engrossed in the history of blimps, as the afternoon slipped away.

That summer I spent a lot of time gazing upward, hoping to catch a glimpse of the blimp, but never saw it again. My interest however, never waned and in my dreams I rode like a queen in that silver sphere. I was dressed in white flowing white chiffon, silent, part of the floating ship itself. As childhood passed into adulthood, the blimp floated in and out of my life, in reality, in imagination and in dreams.

Author's Footnote:

To my delight in 1997, while commuting to the University of Michigan, tethered earthbound was the Goodyear Blimp at the experimental airport on S. State Street. Signs down the bumpy dirt road indicated that visitors were welcome.

Without a heartbeat of hesitation I turned down the drive. Walking across the dusty field, a ghostly child took my hand, leading me unfaltering to my destiny. The bubble ship gleamed in the late afternoon sun as I caressed the tethers and those yellow ribbons trailing from her belly. I saw her ribs and seams that held her together. I felt her breathe, her airiness and once more I was in summer love with that Goodyear blimp. ©

Bridge of Friendship

by Beverly Lee Bixler

In 1968 I received a gift from Marie Louise Jongen Bonnemayer. It was a sketched picture of a bridge over the Maas River in Maastricht, Netherlands. The bridge is important because it connects the city to the route to Achen, Germany. In the history of Maastricht, the bridge had to be blown up three times to protect the people from a German invasion. The sketch was of the new bridge that had been completed after World War II.

During World War II, Aachen, Germany and Maastricht, Netherlands were important in the life of a young man named John Daniel McCabe. The following is the story told to me by his sister Charlotte McCabe.

John had a scholarship to St. Joseph's College in Rensselaer, Indiana, where he studied accounting. He started his freshman year in the fall of 1941. The bombing of Pearl Harbor took place in December 1941. During his sophomore year John left school for the service.

He had a choice, which included naval officer training, but John chose the army. He processed through Camp Grant, Illinois and took basic training near Texarkana, Texas. Because of his high testing results, he was placed in the Army Specialized Training Program (ASTP) and sent to Hunter College in New York City.

During the early part of the 1944- the ASTP training was cut short and he was transferred to the infantry in Camp Carson, Colorado. In August of 1944, his unit left New York for Europe.

John's unit was a part of General Ted Allen's Timberwolf 1st Infantry Division. He was in Company C. 415th. Infantry Regiment. His rank was Private First Class when he landed at Cherbourg, France.

The unit worked their way towards the German border through the Dutch territory. John's unit had a few days of rest in the city of Maastricht, Netherlands. The families in Maastricht had little food but they could provide housing for the soldiers to have a better place to sleep than in barns or open fields. An Army mess tent was set up in the nearby area. John was sent to the Jongen family home. There he met Edward and Louise Hugigen Jongen and their children, Louis (Lou) and Marie Louise.

Mr. Jongen was an engineer and had been taken to a German Camp in Poland where his full head of black hair turned completely gray. Mrs. Jongen spoke French, and John had his high school French, so they were able to communicate somewhat. John had a life magazine with him and showed them a picture of Oak Park, Illinois, and told them he lived near that town. He went on to say that he had parents and three sisters. After a few days of rest, John returned to battle lines, but not before promising the family he would return. On February 23, 1945, John's unit was at the Roer River. In the information that the army had, the river was a tributary. A small stream approximately six feet wide and three or four feet deep, but when the unit arrived they found the river was six feet deep and very wide for a dam had been blown up by the Germans further north. The men had to cross by boat.

John had gone on a scouting mission over the Roer River before the pre-dawn attack. His group had seen where an enemy machine gun was set up. So in the wintry, pre-dawn hours, boats were launched to get over the river. Many boats overturned because of the waves and the German soldiers firing into the boats. During the battle, John's lieutenant wanted to go right toward the machine gun and John advised him to go to the left, away from the gun. To prove his point, he stood up and was immediately wounded. By exposing himself to the enemy, he may have prevented his unit from more harm. John experienced a chest wound.

He was taken to a nearby shed where he was placed on a shelf to await further medical assistance. From pre-dawn until late afternoon, John waited for medical care. When Medics did arrive, they wrapped him in a khaki army blanket to transport him by boat back across the Roer River, probably to a Medical Army Surgical Hospital.

As the small, inflated rubber boat reached the opposite shore, the earlier battle area, a medic leaped out to steady the boat containing wounded soldiers. He stepped on a land mine and was thrown back into the boat, tipping it over. The following account was told by one of the medic's who was John's friend. He stated that he grabbed for John's blanket, thinking that he had John, working his way to land, only to find that all he had was the blanket. John was reported missing in action as of February 23, 1945.

When John did not return to the Jongen family, Mrs. Jongen sent Lou on his bike to ride to Magraten- an American cemetery outside of Maastricht to see if John's name was on the list of soldiers that were buried there. After finding the name, the family took care of John's grave and placed flowers there.

Sometime later, Marie Louise wrote a letter to the Burgemeister (mayor or head magistrate) in Oak Park, Illinois. She included John's service number from the cemetery cross and stated they wanted his family to know where he was before he was killed.

In 1945 there were about six McCabe families living in Oak Park. The letter was thought to have been forwarded to each family. One of the families had family member who worked for the government in Washington, D.C. She wrote to him with John's service number to find John's family.

On a Sunday in July, this McCabe family drove to Harvard Illinois to deliver the letter from Marie Louise. After this, John's mother began communicating with the Jongen family. She sent parcels of food, clothing and many letters.

In 1966, I went with John's sister Char, to meet this wonderful family. Mr. and Mrs. Jongen drove us across the border area in Germany to the site where John's unit was believed to have been on February 23, 1945. The area still had warning signs about the possibility of unexploded mines. The Roer River was once again a small stream.

John had joined the Army, passing up the opportunity to become a Naval Officer because his parents had a fear of the water and he did not wish to worry them. Yet his death was probably due to drowning. The Bronze Star was given posthumous.

In 1962, at the YMCA in Chicago, Illinois, I was a swimming instructor and it is here that Char learned to swim.

The sketched bridge over the Maas River is a reminder of the friendship between American and Dutch families. I remain in touch with Marie Louise Bonnemayer-Jongen to this day. ©

Medium Rare Steak

by Sally Wu

I went to a joint 80th birthday party of three friends. It was a very nice party at Weber's restaurant. Each of us has a choice of steak or trout. I took the steak. As the entree came I got a big juicy pink steak. How have I become accustomed to eating half-cooked beef?

That was in the early part of 1970s when we were living in Los Angeles, California. My husband Paul went out for lunch with a few co-workers to a steak house. He liked the steak and the steak house very much so he took our three children and me to that restaurant for dinner. It was a steak house where you had to cook it yourself on a grill with all the needed seasoning provided. The lighting in the restaurant was very dim, giving us a very peaceful and tranquil atmosphere.

I have never liked meat that much let alone a bloody steak! The Chinese always stir-fry or pot-roast the meat. They do not eat half-done beef. No, definitely no bloody meat for me on the dinner table. It was beyond my imagination. I heard people said that the medium rare steak is very tender and juicy while the well done is somewhat dry and tough. In spite of that I still want to have my steak well done.

I had never grilled steak in my life. I had no idea how long should I grill it and when should I turn the steak over. The room was so dim I could not see the color of the steak; I was kind of lost while I was watching the steak cooking on the grill. Paul came over to rescue me. He finished the cooking, put the steak in a plate and took it to the table. I just followed him back to our table. I sat down and ate the steak. It was dim I could not really see the color of the steak but it was very tasty and juice. So I just kept eating. "Is it well done?" I wondered, but it did not matter as long as it tasted good. So I enjoyed my steak. At the end of our dinner Paul asked me: "Do you like your steak?

"Yes, it was very delicious." I said.

He said to me "Do you know the steak was medium rare?"

I was speechless. I was realized that I'd been tricked! From then on I always order medium rare steak. ©

Patriotism Extends Beyond Independence Day

by Carole M. Hendrickson
*(as published in the Ann Arbor News
"Other Voices")*

July 2008

The July 4TH celebration is over but patriotism should remain. The weather was perfect at the lake we shared with family and friends on the holiday. The country was decorated in red, white and blue, as usual. Food, fireworks, and singing were a part of the day along with parades. It is a celebratory day with folks flying their flags. Once I even made a platter of nibble food from cherry tomatoes, cauliflower flowerettes and blue berries in the shape of a flag.

This year I feel moved to write about patriotism. I can't get past thinking much of the parading, flag waving and decorating, though nice, is superficial. It even smacks of consumerism and may lack the real essence of patriotism.

Do we remember what it is all about? Do we read the Declaration of Independence or recall the struggles our future country had in the 1700's? The heated debates and battles fought? The time our founding fathers devoted to our freedoms? Do we realize the Second Continental Congress really voted on the Declaration of Independence on July 02? That independence and the efforts of the Second Continental Congress had been hard fought, using both weapons and words? Family ties were often strained if not permanently severed. Do we read that fine document with its well-edited, poetic language so full of passion and meaning?

Think how we fuss over and make laws against dishonoring a piece of cloth known as our flag. How we march in political parades or are disgusted at those who protest wars. Even suggesting they are unpatriotic. Do we really think and strive as those founders did how to best defend our country while protecting it?

Perhaps patriotism should be evidenced by how we live all year. Not by how we dress or enjoy parading. Nor by how well we sing those beloved songs associated with July 4TH.

Perhaps it should be self-evident in how we study our history for the lessons it offers. How we seek to protect human rights. The importance we place on following laws and insisting on non-violent protests, discussion and diplomacy to accomplish conflict resolution whenever possible. How we fight for freedom of speech. How we value the right to be heard through our voting. How we defend and try to understand our constitution. Do we choose candidates for office by the substance of their platforms more than by the untruths of many ads against opponents? Do we assess the truth in sound bites and sift through media sensationalism? Do we measure candidates by the long measuring stick of history and current events? Then realize those candidates are human and we serve them well when we provide oversight. Do we expend energy on what is best for our country as a whole? Yes, wave that flag, never to diminish or dominate others, but to bring out the best in each of us. ©

The Birth of a Legend

by Tom Torango

In the early spring of 1958, I was working as a draftsman in the Engineering Department at Wyandotte Chemicals Corporation in Wyandotte, Michigan. I had been working there for almost three years. The department had a shortage of projects going at the time. Rather than layoff any personnel, the Chief Engineer contracted with Great Lakes Engineering Company of River Rouge to perform drafting services for them in our offices on a contract basis.

Great Lakes Engineering was a ship building company with ship yards in River Rouge and Ecorse. I didn't have any experience with ship building drawings, but that wasn't a problem as none of the draftsmen in our department were familiar with shipbuilding. All we had to do was make inked drawings on cloth from sketches provided to us from the designers working at the Great Lakes office in Ecorse. It was a fascinating experience for a young draftsman and very different from the work that I had been doing for the past several years. I learned that ship building has a vocabulary all it's own. I became familiar with terms such as camber, shear strake, tumble home, gudgeons, etc. I was assigned to draw the shell plating drawings for hulls #301 and #302. Before a ship is christened, it is known by its hull number, a sequential number assigned by the builder.

Drawing with ink was a new experience for me also. Wyandotte Chemical's practice was to make all their drawings on cloth using pencil. I had a drafting table in the front of the drafting room near the coffee machine. One day after returning from lunch, I discovered that someone had apparently set their cup of coffee on my drawing board and that it got knocked over and spilled down on the inked hull drawing that I had been working on for a week. No one ever owned up to the incident, but the tracing wasn't salvageable, and I had to begin again. Valuable lesson learned. Never leave your drawing board uncovered when leaving for any length of time.

Hulls #301 and #302 were lake freighters. Hull #301 was owned by and being built for Northwestern Mutual Insurance Company of Milwaukee, Wisconsin. Her keel was laid on August 7, 1957 and was scheduled for launch on June 7, 1958. In that ten month period her hull was completed and boilers and mechanicals installed. She would be launched and sail to a Great Lakes Engineering Company shipyard in Ashtabula, Ohio for final outfitting of the galley, heads, officer's quarters, chart room and staterooms.

We were invited to attend the launching of hull #301. On June 7, my very pregnant wife and I drove to Ecorse and parked our car in the parking lot near Jefferson and walked into the shipyards with several thousand other people to witness the launching of the largest great lakes freighter ever built as of that date. It was to be a side launching. I had brought my 8mm Bell and Howell home movie camera to record the event.

There she stood, her immense hull cradled on underpinnings next to the slip. She was longer than two football fields, 711 feet long and three stories tall. She was 75 feet wide and weighed 13,632 tons. She was less than 100 yards away from our vantage point. Too close to be able to take in the whole spectacle.

A platform had been erected on which the ship's owners and other dignitaries were to stand for her christening and launch at noon. Shortly before noon, crews of workers began to drive the wedges from the underpinnings, which would allow the ship to slide sideways down into the adjacent slip. On signal, as the crews drove the final wedges from under her, the owner's representative stepped up with her bottle of champagne tied on a ribbon tether. She aimed for the 5 foot tall letters on the bow of her hull which spelled out her new name. As the hull began it's slow slide into the slip her voice could be heard through the P.A. system proclaiming, "I christen thee, Edmund Fitzgerald."

It was an amazing sight to see the controlled movement of the gigantic hull as she began her unstoppable slide into the slip. The displaced water made a huge wave on the opposite shore of the narrow slip with the ships lines pulling tight under the strain to hold her in the channel as she bobbed back and forth. Whistles were blowing and the roar of the crowd was thunderous. It was truly a moment I'll never forget. Little did we know at the time that we were witnesses to the launching of a legend.©

That Moment

by Sally Wu

The nurses and doctors were rushing and running in and out of his room as I was watched in the waiting room down the long corridor. Something very urgent and critical was going on inside that room, I told myself silently. I felt uneasy but I just sat there idly, patiently waiting, nobody seemed to notice my existence.

Waiting, waiting quietly, holding my breath like a "scardy cat," not daring to make a sound. A nurse was passing by so I asked her:

"What has happened?"

" His heart has stopped for a moment. They are still working on him." She told me and went away.

Seven-years, it was not short, yet not too long. In and out of the emergency and ICU quarter. Finally that moment was here, I knew.

Something had to be done. I drove home (only one mile away from the hospital) to call the kids in San Francisco area and some close friends, then back to hospital waiting.

At the end of the eternally waiting, a doctor came.

"His heart has enlarged too much that it cannot pump any more. A machine is hooked on him. I am so sorry. You can go in to see him now." Then the doctor left.

Walking into the room quietly, where he was lying in the bed with eyes closed, tubes inserted in his mouth, his chest moved up and down violently as the machine was hammering along. He was in coma I believe. I kneeled down by the bed and prayed: "Please give us one more chance, Lord."

God did not wait. "It is too late, child."

All the work needed to be done had been done. Finished at last. I stood next to his bed watching intently as his chest moving up and down and the machine hummed along. Both of us were waiting in silence.

Suddenly, his chest stopped moving. I yelled: "Nurse, nurse!" People rushed into the room. A nurse took me outside. In a short moment they let me in. The nurses and doctors rushed, running in and out of that room as I watched in the waiting room through the long corridor. Something very urgent and critical was going on inside that room, I told to myself silently. I felt uneasy, but I just sat there idly, patiently waiting, nobody seems noticing my existence.

The machine had stopped. There was the immense quietness. Only he and I were in the room. The machine was at last silent. There was the immense quietness. Only he and I were in the room.

A nurse dropped in.

"What should I do?"

"Nothing." She told me and walked away.

So I just sat on a chair next to the bed. What am I waiting for? I didn't know. A huge empty space filled in my mind and heart. I did not feel anything. Did not know what to do, just sat there. I remembered that people said when a person is dead his body becomes cold. Is that true? I got up, went to his bed and felt his body temperature. "Not cold yet." I went back to the chair and sat down again. I did not remember how long I have been doing that until my friends Emily and Tongpo came to the room. Suddenly I came back to reality and started to cry for the first time. He has gone forever, but I am still here.

That was twenty years ago. Time has rushed by but that moment is still so alive as if just happened yesterday. ©

Edna's List

by Edna Massey

Having a good attitude all the time may help someone that has a bad one.

Change your bad attitude to good, and it will give you a better life.

When you let someone anger you, you've lost, they won.

It is not what you leave for your children that counts. It is what you leave in them that really counts.

If you pose long enough it will turn to poise.

You can see the tree, but you cannot see the roots.

If you want a friend, be one first.

If you believe, then you will receive. Be in doubt, and you will do without.

Every closed eye is not sleeping. Every open eye is not seeing.

We might get knocked down, but not knocked out.

Misery loves company, so I am not keeping company with you today.

Can you see the light at the end of the tunnel? If you do, make sure it is not coming at you.

Let's take time to smell the roses now, for when we leave here, we will be just pushing them up.

Keep exercising our mind, body and soul. If you don't use them you will lose them. ©

A Refugee In My Homeland
by Sally Wu

In June 2007, I went to China with my daughter and her family. At the end of our trip we came to the city of Guangzhou on the Southeast coast of China.

Standing on the sidewalk across the busy street, I looked at Dr. Sun Yet-Sen Memorial Hall. It is an auditorium in memory of the founding father of China. Dr. Sun was a medical doctor in Hawaii. He left his medical practice and joined the Chinese revolution to overthrow the Ching dynasty and founded the Republic of China in 1911. It is an ordinary memorial hall but very special to me, because I lived inside the auditorium for two months before I left Mainland China for Taiwan in the fall of 1949. I was then only 16 years old.

After the World War II my family was relocated to Wuhan. I attended the local junior high school and really enjoyed life there. Everything went along so well. It seemed that we had a very peaceful life. But the civil war between the Chinese Communist party and the ruling government had been going on ever since the end of the World War II. In a short three years, the Chinese Communist occupied many places and their military strength was growing stronger day by day. China was in turmoil.

People wondered: "Is this another revolution like those we had in Chinese history? Should we move? Where? The new government might bring stability and prosperity to us." But most people were just confused and bewildered. I was in 10th grade then. My mother was worried. She had five children scattered all over different places: England, Shanghai, Nanjing and Guangzhou; only three daughters and one orphan grandson were living with her in Wuhan.

One morning, Sister Ming and her boy friend Pei came home from Wuhan University. Pei told Mom: "I just learned from my friend working for the Central Intelligent Agency that the Communist army is approaching Wuhan and the government decided not to fight but retreat to Guangzhou. There is a government retreat train leaving tonight to Guangzhou. I would like Ming to go with me. Whatever you plan to do is up to you."

We were all shocked. Just like a tornado coming in from nowhere on a bright sunny day. There was no time to plan or think of details. No time even to pack our essential belongings. But we had to make a decision now... right away. Finally, Mom decided that I would go with Ming and Pei with whatever we could pack that same afternoon. Mom would leave Wuhan with sister Gung and nephew Wai next morning. We would meet in Guangzhou at my sister Guan's place.

Before nightfall, we boarded the train for Guangzhou. It was an open top cargo train. There were no passengers except people like us who were related to the government retreat plan. We just climbed onto the open top flat car and sat on the boxes. Ming and Pei were sitting next to me giving me a feeling as if we were going on an adventurous trip. It was a very beautiful full moonlit night with a few stars scattered in the sky. The trees and houses rushed by the train in the darkness looked very spooky and fascinating. When I was tired I dozed off. That was the first night. One day it was raining. We had only one umbrella between the three of us. Luckily the rain was not heavy. After the train moved out of rain clouds the sun came out again.

When we reached Hunyang, a city between Wuhan and Guangzhou, the train stopped. There was an announcement that the schedule of our train had been changed. It would not go to Guangzhou as originally planned. We had to get off the train to take the next train from Wuhan if we wanted to go to Guangzhou. We took our luggage, got off the train and waited on the platform. Then we heard the news that the Communist army had occupied Wuhan.

Where was my mom? Had she caught the last train from Wuhan in time as we planned? Would there be a train coming out from Wuhan? We had no idea and nobody knew what had happen.

The night came in slowly. The station was somewhat deserted. No vender was in sight selling food or anything. People became agitated and filled with despair. We sat on the cement platform hungry and tired. I forgot when I last had food or water but I dared not to mention it. I sat on the floor, leaning against the luggage and dozed off.

I heard a whistle from far away. Suddenly I woke up. Was it a dream? I listened carefully. Yes, I heard a whistle from a distance, definitely a train was coming. I heard the whistle come closer and closer, louder and louder. "A train is coming, a train is coming!" Everyone on the platform shouted. We were all excited. There was hope, hope at last. Then I saw a train moving slowly into the station. Instantly I became energized. Everybody was getting ready to board the train. Sister Ming handed me the small briefcase to carry and took care of the big luggage.

The train did not come to the platform. It stopped in the middle of the tracks. All people on the platform rushed down toward the train. It was midnight and dark. Walking on the tracks was difficult. Which car was available for us? No one knew. All the passenger cars were full, occupied by people stuffed all the way to the doors. It seemed there was no room even for the air. We just ran along the train, checking one car after another until we found an empty cargo boxcar. People pushed each other to get on it. The opening was so high, almost to my chest. I had to push myself up with my two hands to get to the opening. So I put down the little briefcase on the floor of the car right in front of me and pushed myself up. In that split second I got on the car and the briefcase had disappeared. Sister Ming and Pei got up behind me. But the briefcase was no where in sight. It was pitch black and crowded. Where could I find the little briefcase? I started to cry but my voice just sank into the darkness. All our money and the important papers and personal documents were gone. What should we do? I knew Ming and Pei were upset, but they did not say anything just hugged me and comforted me. I hated myself. I never even dreamed things like this would happen. How could I allow this to happen? Now we were left without any money or identification. What should we do?

The train was moving forward steadily under the dark sky while we were sitting on the floor inside the crowded boxcar. We cuddled on the crowded floor and had a moment of peace and quiet time together. Nobody had the energy even to talk.

Day finally broke and the sky was bright. It lifted our spirits. We learned that this train was indeed from Wuhan. Was my mom on this train? We decided to try our best. Whenever the train stopped at a station we got out of the boxcar and walked along the train on the platform looking for my mom. Every car was as full as a can of sardines. We called my mom loudly as we walked one car after another. Could she hear us in the noisy and crowded car?

Suddenly we heard an answer. Oh, my mom was in one of the passenger car and my sister too! We burst with joy and the tears kept running down my checks. "We found my mom! I found my mom!" I was jumping up and down with joy. But how could we get into their car? The doors were jammed with people. My mom asked some people sitting

86

next to the window to move away a little from the opening so we could climb into it. After we got into the car we hugged and cried happily. We were united on the train finally!

On our way to Guangzhou, my mom told us that after we left the Communist army was approaching Wuhan. They could hear the gun shots in the distance. So they packed a couple suitcases, went to the train station and left every thing behind. Nobody knew whether there would be a train going out of Wuhan. They just had to wait there on the platform. Meanwhile the sound of the gunshots were getting closer and louder.

The night inched in and the sky was getting dark, it was silent except for the sound of the gunshots whistling through the clear night air. People waiting on the platform were getting quieter, so quiet that they practically whispered to each other making one felt suffocated. We spent the night at the platform waiting.

Next morning, at the crack of the dawn a train finally came. People were excited and rushed and pushed to get the train. My mom, sister Gung and my nine-year-old nephew could not get near the train doors. At the moment when they felt great despair, suddenly through the train window they saw a friend in the train. Finally he helped mom get on the train through the window. How lucky we were that we reunited on the train to Guangzhou! From then on time went by quickly and we arrived at the city of Guangzhou on a beautiful bright sunny morning of May.

Before long my sister Guan and her husband came. They had just relocated to Guangzhou two weeks ago with the government from Nanjing and were waiting for the instructions of the next move. Their temporary home was very tiny. There was no room to accommodate us. They heard that the government had arranged some kind housing for the people who came to Guangzhou. We reported to the government agency. They arranged Sister Kung and I to stay in the Dr. Sun Yet-Sen Memorial Hall, and mom, Ming and Pei in an elementary school.

We went to the Memorial Hall. It was a very big auditorium with chairs scattered all over inside. Some people were there already. They made beds on the floor and arranged the chairs as partitions around their territory. So we followed the suit and made our "home" in the auditorium. Our "next door neighbor" was the Mung family of four, one brother and three sisters from Nanjing. The big brother was in the same grade as Sister Kung and the big sister in my grade. Their two little sisters were in eighth grade. Instantly we became friends and family too. We did everything together as if we had known each other for a lifetime.

The government gave us daily allowance for meal expenses. We made our stove with three pieces of bricks outside the auditorium and made fire with tree branches, twigs or anything that we could get hold of to make a fire to cook a simple meal. Once in a while we bought some fast food from the street venders. One morning, I bought some famous Guangton style sweet bread. It was very delicious indeed. I was eating the bread alone while walking on the terrace in front of the auditorium under the bright morning sun. What a wonderful treat! I always remember that happy moment to this day.

The only source of water available in the memorial hall was from the fire hydrant at the right side of the auditorium. We used that water to wash every thing including ourselves. Of course there was no enclosure around the water hydrant. The water shot out from the hydrant like a mad giant dragon. We just ran into the water with our clothes on just like the kids in modern United States who play in and out of the water fountain in their backyards in the hot summer day.

Without any grownup looking over our shoulders, we were living a carefree life, doing things as we please. Most of the times we were on very good behavior but sometimes we were full of mischief. For instance, on Sunday mornings, there were free movies showing in the theaters for the veterans and the soldiers. Since it was free and there were so many of the soldiers, we just went to the theater entrance, hid between them, and got in the theater to see free movies. Ordinarily, we would not do this kind of thing. Somehow as teenage we were a little bit wild once in a while. At that time it was fun indeed and the only kind of entertainment and recreation we had. Since there was nothing for us to do, we roamed around the city with our new friends day and night.

Gradually more and more teenagers moved in. Some of them came from northeastern part of China. Some were from other provinces like us. They had left their families behind and traveled away from the Communist occupied cities. On their road to Guangzhou, they met other students, and traveled further down south. They lost contact with their parents. Finally they were ended up here in the Memorial Hall in Guangzhou.

At the end of summer, the government setup a temporary middle school in Zhungsen County, a small town near Macao. At that time Macao was ruled by Portuguese just like Hong Kong by British, and moved us to the school, so we left the Dr. Sun Yet-Sen Memoriam Hall.

Fifty-eight years has passed. For the first time I stood across the street from the Memorial Hall. The street was much busier then before. So many people and cars were on the street. We had to use the pedestrian bridge to cross the street.

The Memorial Hall looked much smaller now then I remembered. The grounds were well maintained with beautiful landscape, flowers, bushes, trees and a splendid water fountain. Oh! I saw the red water hydrant that we used to play in and wash things. Just like an old friend, it was still standing there on the right side of the building welcome me. Suddenly, for the first time in my life I realized that I had been a refugee once, living inside of that structure. I always took those days as an interesting adventure in my growing years, even though I did not have a place to call my own. No money to live a comfortable life. I did not know what was ahead of me in the political turmoil.

I turned around seeing my daughter, her husband and their two girls standing behind me watching a group of policemen doing their routine exercise. I was so happy and grateful that I had a chance leaving China in October 1949, leaving all the political turmoil and mental torture behind. ©

Segregation

by Elaine 'Elle' Cousino

L et me tell you a story about segregation, no not the capital S̲ segregation but segregation of another nature, (only a lower case s needed for this one.) For the first nine years of school, I attended a two-room brick school, as did all of us in our neighborhood. Then in the very early fifties, we entered the high school, which was three miles away. At first there were no busses so we found our way to school anyway we were able, walking, running or hitching a ride with a neighbor who had a car going in that direction. (The Ferrington Clan, of which I was the youngest member, did own an automobile.)

Once in town, we as incoming freshman were directed to go to the gym were they segregated us alphabetically then handed each of us a daily class schedule. We were all petrified at the notion of finding ourselves around to the different classrooms. (The first day I ended up in a Latin class where I wasn't assigned and the kind teacher quietly showed me where I belonged.)

We were quick learners however, and after a week we all became rather accustomed to the building and changing classes and floors. Since our high school was a two story affair, we had an up and down staircase situation. The segregation part rears its head again about here.

After attending for about two weeks, a general assembly was held where only freshman attended. The "Townie" freshman all sat together and the "Country" freshmen did the same. Townie's had cashmere sweaters and white bucks. Country's had jeans overalls, work-shoes, homemade dresses, penny loafers or saddle shoes. Townie Girls had shiny, smooth pageboy hairdos (ala Breck shampoo.) Country Girls had barrettes, ribbons, and some hair dos made curly by rags and homemade haircuts. Townie boys had soft hands with trimmed nails, their longer hair held in place with Vitalis or Brylcream. Country boys sometimes had dirt under their nails, due to last minute chores, or maybe a stray fish scale on their thumb, smelled of fresh air and sometimes of Dads stolen Old Spice.

So it began, the segregation of the freshman. Townies laughed at us, thinking that the Countries were dumb. But Country girls had learned to can and preserve fruits and vegetables, to cook and sew, how to milk cows, slop hogs, feed the chicken, assist in the birthing of calves and colts and how to tell stories to amuse younger sisters and brothers. Meanwhile the Townie girls had learned to play tennis and golf, play piano and read classics like Jane Eyre, knew geography by travels with parents on vacations, unknown to Country kids. Country boys knew how to drive tractors and trucks, fix them if they quit running, bail hay, thresh wheat, which fences were electric which were not. Important if one were taking a short cut! Townie boys wore their Levi's low hanging on flat butts, and soft pastel, either blue or pink nylon sweaters and went swaggering into Harwarney's soda shop to get a cherry coke after school, if they were really cool. Country freshman hurried home to help with fall chores, late harvests, finishing up the butchering, getting supper started or working in any way they were assigned.

Very slowly, integration took place between the Townies and the Countries. First one gorgeously stellar country girl was nominated and voted to be Homecoming Queen. Then a Townie was invited by a Country to come out on Saturday to target practice for the upcoming hunting season. Several Country boys fell smitten at the feet of the amazing Breck shampoo pageboy Townie girls. Then Band, where both Townies and Countries tooted, drummed and marched, finally finding that their love of music could be realized, playing their favorite instrument. Football and Cheerleading try-outs were held. The fellows and girls who milked cows and pitched hay were both strong and graceful. Summer lawn mowing for cash paid out in more than one way for Townies as they found they could run fast and long distances on summer legs that had been strengthen by that exercise.

Eventually we all became sophomores, juniors then finally seniors. Taking our senior trip to Washington, D.C., on one of the first air conditioned trains, touring, walking and seeing sights that we in our naïve small town eyes thought we would never see. By the end of that trip, before graduation, we knew each other better than family and by graduation day, we were a force to be reckoned with…The Senior Class! No longer Townies and Countries, but graduating seniors, some ready for college, some going directly into the armed forces (the Korean conflict), others entirely ready to go into farming that had subtlety become a sophisticated business. Now we knew friendships and loves. We, tender buds that we were, semi-realized the responsibilities of becoming adults, making choices and decisions. Some say that high school was just a waste of time, but I disagree. Those very early socialization skills, some of which, painfully taught were important to a Country person such as me. ©

~ Memories ~

"You know you're old when you've lost all your marvels." Merry Browne

The Refugee

by Joanne Savas

This recall was hard, painful and disconnected; so Kalliope shut it out of her mind. Whenever the subject came up she dismissed it. Kalliope, my mother, was a refugee. As I grew up, I thought the flight of refugees would make an excellent report for school. I tried unsuccessfully to talk to my mother about her village, her experience. Perhaps, I thought I had the name of the village wrong.

She would tell me, "I can't remember what you are asking. Just leave me alone!"

Kalliope would sit very still, refusing to talk. She was a grown woman when she became a refugee. Then magically one day, fate came in the answer in the Shaman Drum Bookstore, in Ann Arbor, Michigan.

It is customary for the author to read from their works at the store. I was unaware of the subject matter; I only attended, as it was a fellow Greek author and speaker. His reading caught me by surprise and the emotional aftermath was cleansing. It was Kalliope's story! My mother came from a village named Athramete in Asia Minor, Turkey. It was not on the map and no one that I knew had ever heard of this place, until I met the Pulitzer-prize winning author, Jeff Eugenides. I had stopped thinking of my mother's stoic demeanor whenever I mentioned her village.

But he knew. "In the year, 1922 on the slope of Mt. Olympus in Asia Minor, the view was impressive. He said, A thousand feet below lay the Ottoman capital of Bursa, like a backgammon board spread across the valley's green bottom. Red diamonds of roof tiles fit into diamonds of white washed buildings. What a sight! Here and there the Sultan's tombs stacked up like bright chips."

Eugenides continued with his story. (I was still unaware of how his story would intertwine with my search.) He told us that Bursa looked pretty much as it had for the past six centuries. It was a holy city, a center for the silk trade, and the Greeks living there had a good life. Cypress trees were everywhere and along the streets, abloom with minarets. The people in the bookstore listened intently.

It seemed the Greek Army encouraged by the allied nations invaded Turkey in 1919. They reclaimed the ancient Greek territory called Athramete. I sat up in my chair. Did I hear correctly? The tears began to roll down my face. Could this be happening? That I would find the answers now was incredible! Greek troops occupied Bursa for the first time in their lives and Greeks were out from under Turkish rule. What a celebration!

There was more to the story. The next night, the moon like a Turkish crescent on the country's flag shown bright. Mustafa let it be known that the battle was over. Then he tricked the Greeks. He burned every house, every store to the ground. People scrounged for food. The Greeks were expelled from Athramete with nothing but the clothes that they were wearing. The refugees could be seen running between the flaming trees. "Running on foot, two hundred thousand of them," said Eugenides as he closed his reading. I could only think of Kalliope and how she must have felt. The visitors at Shaman Drum were silent and motionless. The refugees left by boat, many drowned, many were shot, and some managed to reach the shores of Greece.

The past stayed buried in my mother's life. She was never free. She was cheated of her ability to feel happiness. Now I had the answers! I remember how, even in 1950, she was still an imprisoned refugee. Refugees have tortured lives. They live in grief. Never knowing if they will ever see their loved one again, they become suspicious and haunted. Many have deep fears that keep them from a productive life, unable to enjoy their own children's love.

As I studied psychology, I learned the behavior is better defined as cumulative trauma disorder and is very difficult to overcome. When my mother arrived in Athens, she was encouraged to marry. (Of course women did not work outside the home in those times.) Life and her family brought her a husband and abundance in a new country, America. Her life was well lived but there was no magic pill that could make her torment go away.

Refugees are like trees without roots, wavering back and forth. Their moods are scattered, and unpredictable, Kalliope personified. She was black and white, with no gray area. She was a petite woman with green/gray eyes that had lost their sparkle. I had answers that fateful day in the bookstore. My curious nature about the refugees at last satisfied.

When I was ten years old, I tutored Kalliope for citizenship. I wanted my mother to 'belong.' I wanted my mother to be a proud American like my father. She studied and took the oath. Kalliope voted with her husband until his death in 1951, then never voted again. She smiled when I reminded her that Einstein was a refugee.

Never returning to Asia Minor, Kalliope was fortunate enough to make several trips back to Greece. Of course her family had changed drastically. Brothers died that she had not seen since 1936. She found that refugee wounds changed lives in her family but with weary hearts and troubled minds they managed to survive. ©

My First Job
by Tom Torango

It was in the fall of 1953. I was a 15 year old junior in high school. In desperate need of money for my dates, I needed a job. At 15 I didn't have too many options. I had worked sporadically delivering newspapers as a substitute for a buddy of mine, but nothing steady enough to keep me solvent. Bus fare on the loop bus had just gone from 5 cents to 10 cents, cigarettes were 25 cents a pack, a cup of coffee or a coke cost a dime and the movies were 70 cents. After the football game or a movie like Dial M for Murder or On The Waterfront, we'd go to the Loop, a "greasy spoon." The Loop was our usual hangout while waiting for the bus to come. We'd have a soda and a hamburger for 75 cents and feed the juke box nickels listening to the Crew-Cuts singing Sh-Boom or Rosemary Clooney singing This Old House. We liked to play Cross Over the Bridge sung by Patti Page over and over again. It became our song for some long forgotten reason. Yes, it all added up. It was tough entertaining a steady girl friend. You see, I had been smitten by a cute little girl, Gerry Cullen who was also a junior at Roosevelt High School.

Dad suggested that I go down to the Wyandotte Chemicals Club formerly called the Michigan Alkali Club, were he was a member to see if they needed any pin setters in the bowling alley. He'd put in a good word for me. So I went. Seems they always needed pin setters. I wondered why. Little did I know what I was letting myself in for.

The Wyandotte Chemicals club house was located on Biddle Avenue at the corner of Mulberry. Its membership was limited to employees of Wyandotte Chemicals Corporation and it's subsidiaries, Wyandotte Transportation, Wyandotte Terminal Railroad where dad worked and the J.B. Ford Division. It was a nice facility that had been around since the turn of the century. There was the bowling alley consisting of 12 lanes, a bar with lounge, billiards room, gymnasium and a sitting area with a natural fireplace, real cozy. Downstairs were the showers and locker rooms. Not cozy!

It was all set. I'd start working on Saturday when business was light. Some of the other guys who had been around awhile would show me the ropes. The procedure was to return the ball by placing it on the ball return track and give it a push to send it on it's way. Then you had to pick up the pins four or six at a time, depending on the size of your hands, and place the spent pins in the rack leaving space for the pins that were still standing. At 5'-6", 119 lbs. with a 28" waist, I could only manage to pick up 4 pins at a time. Next you had to sit on the bulkhead between the pits and wait for the second ball. After the second ball, you repeated what you did after the first, but then pulled down on the rack's reset bar to lower the rack and reset the pins.

Saturdays and Sundays were limited to open bowling and the pace was easy. There was a maximum of 12 pin setters ideally, one for each lane. It wasn't uncommon for two or three setters not to show up. This wasn't a problem on weekends when business was light but it proved to be a big problem on Tuesday nights when there were two men's leagues and on Thursday when there were two women's leagues. If the pin setter who was assigned to the alley next to yours didn't show up, you had to set pins on both alleys! I'm telling you, you're busier than a cat covering poop. Double the work, but double the pay!

Smoking in the work place was no problem back then. What's smokier than a bowling alley? We'd go into work with our cigarettes rolled up in the sleeve of our T-shirt almost as a badge of our manhood. Of course the T-shirts eventually came off back in the pits. But that didn't stop us from lighting up.

On Saturday, we were required to clean the alleys and repair the pin racks. Since we were paid only for setting pins, we did this work in exchange for the privilege of bowling for free so long as there weren't any patrons. Of course we had to set pins for each other without pay. We could also horse around in the gym or play pool.

On league nights, I'd get home from school around 4 o'clock and have supper. Dad would normally drive me to the club to arrive at 6:30. The first league started bowling at 7:00. Getting there early allowed us to "set spares" so the bowlers could warm-up before league play. They would pitch nickels, dimes or quarters down the gutters to us in the form of tips. The second league started at 9 o'clock with not much of a break in between. One of the fringe benefits of the women's league was being able to look down the front of the matronly women bowlers'dresses as they bent over to throw the ball. One woman rolled her ball so slowly, that you could time it with a calendar. Bump, bump, bump down the alley it would go. When it hit the pins they seemed to fall over in slow-motion. Or there was the macho guy who'd throw his ball so fast that when it hit the pins they'd fly into the next pit. This could be a dangerous job!

By the time the last league was done after 11 o'clock, I'd be drenched in sweat. My Levis would be soaked. In the winter months it wasn't uncommon for ice crystals to form on them as I waited for the Loop bus to take me home. After a two block walk home from the bus stop, what a welcome sight was the warm glow of the porch light which mom always left on. She'd be sleeping on the couch waiting for me to come home. "Don't forget to set the night lock and turn off the porch light", she'd say as she staggered off to bed.

I don't remember most of the fellows that I worked with. Some didn't stay too long and we didn't become too buddy -buddy. I remember Dominic Palazzolo the "dago" with his black hair slicked back into a duck tail. He thought he was a 'stud'. There was Stan a big 18 year old "pollack" who had quit school and worked very hard. He could set pins on two or three alleys and never complain like the rest of us. And there was Freddy who had a crush on Roxanne Goodney, the shop teacher's daughter. Roxanne. Sounds as sexy as she looked. But she wouldn't give Freddy the time of day in spite of what he claimed. The braggart!

Now, you may wonder, how much money did I make for all my efforts? Well, that depends. Bowling cost 50 cents a line. The club got 35 cents. The pin setters got 15 cents. So on a normal week when everyone showed up and I only had to work one alley. On Tuesday and Thursday evenings, that meant 5 bowlers per alley times 3 games per league times two leagues per night times two nights per week works out to $9.00 (not including tips) plus maybe $1.50 for setting pins for 10 games on the weekend. Ten dollars for 20 hours of back breaking work comes to 50 cents an hour. Not even minimum wage at the time. Oh, the things we do for love!

We were paid in cash on Saturday morning. An incentive to come in. It came in a pay envelope with nothing deducted for FICA or state and federal taxes. I even managed to save some of it.

I worked there setting pins from the fall of 1953 until the spring of 1954 when school let out and the bowling leagues stopped for the summer months. I didn't go back in my senior year. I worked in a hardware store where my brother-in-law worked. I swept floors and did stock.

When my sweetheart Gerry and I graduated from high school in 1955, our all-night dance was held in the club house gymnasium. We married two years later.

In 1990, I was working as an estimator for an asbestos abatement contractor. We were invited to bid on the removal of asbestos from the clubhouse as a preparation for its demolition. I toured my old haunt. The electricity had been turned off. It was dark. It was quiet. It was ghostly. It held many memories for me, both good and bad. I could smell the sweat, the smoke. I could hear the pins exploding in the pits, and oh, the laughter, and the curses! I went into the pits. There were still some bowling pins back there. I told my story to the project superintendent and asked him if I could take one of the pins home for old times sake. He said, "Of course. They'll only be part of the rubble anyway". The club house saw the wrecking ball in 1990 after almost 100 years. But I took home a souvenir. Sadly, I don't know what became of it. It probably got tossed when we cleaned out the basement or had a garage sale. ©

Close Encounter

by Sally Wu

If I had become a prostitute at the age of 12 when I was newly graduated from elementary school, what kind of life would I have led and what would I become? I wonder!

It was 1944 in China during the time of the Japanese invasion. We lived in a small village called New Bridge far away from the outskirts of Chungching, the war time capital of the Republic of China. Life at the New Bridge village was very quiet and peaceful because Japanese fighters or bombers would not be bothered to come this far to drop the bombs or to sweep their machine guns to kill just some unimportant innocent Chinese citizens.

That was the year I graduated from elementary school. The nearest junior high school was in Sandy Plain, a village where many universities and high schools were located. Those schools were moved from their respective provinces that were occupied by the Japanese army and relocated at the village of Sandy Plain. Sandy Plain was located somewhere in the middle between Chungching City and New Bridge village. Due to the underdeveloped transportation system at that time, it would take about two hours by horse carriage to the town called Little Dragon, from there it took over half of an hour walk to Sandy Plain. The school I was interested in attending was Central Middle School (combined the junior and senior high school in one.) I signed up for the entrance examination. On the day before the examination, my two friends from my elementary school and I left home and went to the horse carriage station. At the station we met another girl named Sue who was also going to the Central Middle School for the entrance examination. The carriage could accommodate only four people at a time. So we had the entire carriage for the four of us.

It was an adventure for all of us going on the horse carriage to a place away from home and staying there over night. On our way to Little Dragon we were singing and talking, as if we were grownups going for a vacation. After we got off the carriage at Little Dragon we walked to Sandy Plain and found the Central Middle School. It was a very nice school with beautiful buildings and gardens surrounding it. The school did prepare a couple classrooms to accommodate the out of town students for the night. It was an empty classroom without the bed or bedding, just the flat clean cement floor. I did not bring anything with me to sleep on the floor and I could not imagine that I could lie down on the bare cement overnight. What should we do? My friends decided to stay there but Sue and I wanted to go back to the Little Dragon to find a hotel because there were no hotels at all at Sandy Plain.

It was almost supper time. We decided to find a hotel first before having supper. When we got back to Little Dragon we discovered that every hotel we found had no vacancies. We were getting tired and frustrated. Should we go back to Sandy Plain to stay overnight in the school? Bare cement floor or not, it was better than staying on the street overnight.

Just at that moment a woman came along. She told us that Sand Plain is a university town and all the universities and high schools were having entrance examinations at the same time. That's why all the hotels in the Little Dragon area were full. If we don't mind we could stay in her place. I was skeptical about her kindness. I heard my elder sisters and brothers talk about some terrible things people did to innocent people.

"Why she is so kind to us two strangers? I don't feel safe about it." I said to Sue.

But she insisted we go with the woman. Without Sue I was a little lonely and scared to walk back to school all by myself. So I just went along.

By then it was getting dark, I felt anxious, weary, frustrated and hungry. I was trying to find some excuse for not going or at least to delay it.

I whispered to Sue, "I am worried about her kindness. Can we tell her that we want to go to a restaurant for supper before we go to her place?"

Sue replied, "If you want to go to a restaurant you can go, but I am going with her." I could not do anything but follow the woman. She seemed very nice and asked us some questions about our families and ourselves. I didn't know what Sue was thinking, but deep down inside me, I felt very uneasy and miserable.

As we walked a little while we were walking away from the center of the town. There were less buildings and houses. Then we turned into a side street. The street became narrower and narrower; then we walked into a small footpath leading up into a hill. Along the footpath I saw some shabby shacks and run down huts scattered on the hill. I have never seen anything like this in my entire life. I asked myself: "Where are we going? Why does she live in this kind of place?" It was quite dark by now. There was no streetlights whatsoever on the footpath. As a matter of fact, there was no electricity up there on the hill. I could not see the surroundings very well. I had to follow her closely. Finally we came to a shack and stopped. She let us in.

We went into the shack and she lit a kerosene lamp. It was a living room, with a square table and chairs. Then she brought us into the adjacent room with a bed with comforter and chairs. She told us to lie down on the bed. Then she left.

I did not feel good at all. It was very hot and stuffy under the heavy comforter. I was hungry and most of all I sensed that something was not quite right.

I whispered to my friend: "Something is strange, let us get out of here."

But she said to me: "I am going to stay. If you don't like it why don't you leave?"

How could I get out of this place? I did not even know where I was. I felt that I was trapped there. I did not believe that I could fall asleep under these circumstances. As I was lying there I heard some noise from the other room. It seemed some people came into the living room, lit the lamp, moved the table, talked in whispers, put out the lamp then went out. The whole business was strange to me. I was constantly on guard waiting for something to happen. I prayed to God to take good care of us. That was all I could do.

I don't know how long I had been in bed. It seemed forever. Then I heard the steps outside of the shack. The people came into the living room, and the lamp was lit. I became very alert and tense. The hairs on my neck stood up. The woman who brought us there came in the room with a kerosene lamp and a man followed her. The man told us politely to get up. He said that he was a policeman and asked us our names, why we came to Little Dragon and why we were in this place. We told him that we were students coming here for entrance examination and could not find a hotel room. This lady invited us to stay with her. The policeman told us to gather our belongings and went with him. The woman went along with us to the police station. The policeman was very kind to us. He told us nicely to sit down on the chair but ordered that woman to stand there at the counter. After he finished his paper work he told us that the owner of the hotel that we visited last reported the incident to the police office. They were willing to let us stay in their own living quarter in the hotel. So another policeman came and walked us to the hotel.

When we arrived at the hotel it was late at night. The owner's wife was very kind to us. She told us that the woman who took us to her place was a prostitute. She was sold to the madam many years ago just like what she did to us today. When they watched that woman approaching us they realized what she was trying to do. They could not let two nice innocent young girls get sold into prostitution. So they called the police. Because the hut was on a hill and it was very dark out there it took the policeman quite some effort to find us.

Wow! What a night! Somebody up there had been watching over us. So we two went to bed again in a nice comfortable hotel room with empty stomach. It was midnight. ©

Revealing the Secret

by Beverly Lee Bixler

It all began in the summer of 1954, at the age of thirteen when my grandfather said "Come my child with me to the vegetable garden to help pick some beans, tomatoes, and corn. It was a great honor to be asked by grandpa to help him for he was sometimes gruff. He had been a widower for 19 years, but today he was in a good mood. We began to pick. This was the perfect time to ask him all my longing questions.

"Grandpa, where did we come from?"

He replied, "We came from Bavaria Germany outside of Munich and after that from Maryland. Three brothers John, Absalom and Christian traveled together with the Mennonites. They came to Philadelphia where John and Christian remained and Absalom went to Virginia."

My next question. "Did grandpa and grandma speak German?"

He replied "They spoke what was called high German. He went on to say, our name is spelled Buechsler. This is very important because it ties the family together so remember… " s l e r." We have a family secret that I don't want revealed until after my death." He paused and looked at me tenderly.

I asked no more questions. I took all this information and tucked it into my heart. I told no one what he had said.

In 1957 my grandfather died but no research was started because my father's three brothers said "I don't want the secret revealed until after my death.

After the funeral the four sons were discussing what city in Germany did the Bixlers come from. One brother said "Nuremberg", another said "Pforzheim" and another said "Munchen." The debate went on. Finally I spoke up and said "grandfather told me outside of Munich," This stopped the debate until December 28, 2008, when I telephoned Eugene M. Bixler (Buechsler), the great, great grandson of George who was my great, great, grandfather's brother Fredrick.

He said in the Trinity Lutheran Church records in Lancaster, Pennsylvania, Volume 1 (1730-1767) page 248 was recorded Jacob Buecksler, single, from Engelsbrand (Anglefire- in English) near Pforzheim in December 1755, married Maria Barbara Schweickart, a widow.

The discussion continues because I found in April 14, 1999, in the International Genealogical Index 4.01 – Germany in 1768, 1770, and 1792, Buechsler living in Baye which is Bavaria. This research was done at the Family History Library in Salt Lake City, Utah. More research is needed to see which relative was from Bavaria. The brother named Christian came from Engelsbrand and he is our line of Buechsler brothers.

The next big event was my journey to Europe in 1959 with the Teen Overseas Program. It was a program provided by a Methodist minister and his wife. For a year once a month 15 teenagers got together to share what they were studying about the 14 countries we were to visit. We studied the culture, the educational system, the governments, and the arts in preparation for our three month journey.

Germany was one of the countries we would visit so my father asked me to check the phone books to see if our name appeared. I knew nothing about World War I or World War II history because my history teacher was an Afro-American man who spent most of the time teaching about the Civil War. (I did visit Nuremberg, Pforzheim, and Munchen but I did not find our name in the phone book.)

In the city of Gottingen I stayed with the Elsner family and I asked Mrs. Elsner if she knew what my name meant. I told her we were German. She and her husband whispered back and forth and later she told me they did not know. I learned nothing on the trip about the family.

I went to Berlin to visit my two German friends. One friend Helke Koch was an exchange student at my high school and the other friend Gaby Voight was a neighbor's niece who with her mother had come out of the war torn city of Berlin to our town. They both had returned to Germany and were my inspiration to come to Europe to visit them. In Berlin I saw the results of the War. Throughout my European tour no one spoke of the War. I was still in darkness.

A return trip to Europe was made in 1966 and this time I was traveling with a woman whose brother had been in World War II. We visited cemeteries and in Paris visited the deportation memorial where I learned the terrible acts of war against the Jews. I was struck by the cruelty and hatred of the Nazi German people. I was told that each little light in the memorial represented 1,000 people. There were 100's of lights. I was moved beyond words of expressing my sorrow. My Jewish consciousness was awakened

While traveling in Russia in 1975, I met three Jewish women who were on the trip. They asked "Do you know that your name is Jewish?"

I replied "No, but thank you for telling me." Was this grandfather's secret?

My Jewish awareness was heightened and I now began to pay close attention to the Jewish way of life and the people. The next step in this awareness was in 1978 while acting as assistant dean of students a Jewish family asked if I would see that their daughter was able to attend High Holiday services. I promised them that I would see that their daughter attended services. I immediately began to locate the nearest synagogue.

I telephoned the office and asked if I could bring a student to the services. They said yes. The student and I drove 25 miles to the synagogue and together attended the service. When it was time to go a member of the congregation said "Come again."

The early 1980's found me living in the Hyde Park area of Chicago where I was studying for a Masters of Divinity at Catholic Theological Union a Seminary. I was symbolically preparing myself for the priesthood since women were not to be ordained. (This is another story!)

My Jewish conscious was again awakened when I met a woman who worked with me in the bank. She asked me if I would go with her to the High Holy Day services. She had two tickets and thought it would be of interest to me since I was studying theology. I accompanied her and was so inspired that I began to question what I was studying. At the same time I met a young Jewish man who was extremely kind to me. We would have meals together at the shores of Lake Michigan. We sat on the rocks and shared the moments together. He later went on to Rabbinical School in Cincinnati. His name was Ernest Rubenstein. He invited me to a Shabbat service and again my heart was warmed. Again I asked myself, was this, the secret grandfather kept in his heart?

In the meantime Soviet Jews were suffering. The Jews were protesting on behalf of the refuseniks (a person denied the right to leave Russia). I attended the gathering and received information on how to support the Soviet Jews. I ordered a wristband with the name of Ida Nudel. I wore the band until Ida Nudel removed it from my arm at a book signing event in Bloomfield, Michigan in the fall of 1990. I was at one with my first Russian Jew.

During the winter of 1984, I began to get ill. I had been working three jobs and taking 4 to 5 courses per semester and only eating one meal per day because I had little money. This chemical change in my body forced me to leave school and return to my parent's home. Here I continued my Jewish journey. I would drive to Skokie, Illinois where the largest number of Holocaust victims live. It was my little Israel. I would buy food from Israel and records by Sol Zinn and take them home. I would sit by the Holocaust memorial and meditate on the suffering of Jews. I was learning for the first time about World War II and the horrible murdering of Jews. It was my first understanding of the plight of Jews throughout history. I had known only the story of one Jew who had suffered at the hands of the Roman government but now I was learning about the 6 million murdered because of lies told by religious leaders and antisemitism. I was appalled. How could they murder gentle, kind, loving, gd.-fearing people. People who were talented, intellectually gifted, conscious raising people against oppression of any kind. I wept for the House of Israel.

In the meantime my parents were on their own awakening journey. They had traveled to Israel in 1980. They had toured Jerusalem by car with two Jews so they were able to learn about Jews and their stories as well as see the Christian sites. When I returned home my parents were open-minded and eager to learn along with me. We drove to Evanston, Illinois to hear Elie Wieizel speak. I bought a Menorah and we began to celebrate Chanukah each year by lighting the candles and playing with the dreidel.

The year 1988 was important to the family for my parents and I moved from Waukegan, Illinois to Ann Arbor, Michigan. While reading the Ann Arbor News, I spotted an ad asking for a volunteer for the Jewish Community Center. I was elated. I went and spoke to the Director Nancy Margolis about volunteering. I told her I was not a Jew but I would like to work at the Jewish Community Center. She said "okay I could answer the phone". At first it was a little difficult because I am dyslexic. I have trouble pronouncing names for I don't hear all the letters correctly. She was kind and patient with me. I was now on the road discerning whether or not I was a Jew. I began to take classes at Hillel (a Jewish House of study). I went to Israel with eight people from the Beth Israel Congregation on December 17, 1989. The Israel trip was the highlight of my Jewish journey.

After the trip to Israel, (which again, is another story,) I began to attend Shabbat services on a regular base and one day the Rabbi asked if I would like to join the Jewish community. Without hesitation, I said, "Yes." He went on to ask "What will be your Hebrew name?"

I replied "Peaceful Dove" to connect my Native American and Jewish heritage. My great-great grandmother on my mother's father's side was a Cherokee maiden.

He went on to say, "Your name will be Shlomit Yona. The date of the ceremony was set for December 20, 1990 which is 3 Tevet 5751. The day I claimed my birth-right.

It was a bright crisp sunny December day when my parents and I drove from Ann Arbor, Michigan to Southfield, Michigan to Beth Achim Congregation for the Mikva. My parents sat in the lobby while Rabbi Robert Dobrusin I and went into a room where there was a table and chairs set up for the interview with the bet din. The three Rabbis entered and the discussion began. It was for the purpose of ascertaining that I had prepared for the ceremony. I was asked questions about specific details of Jewish tradition and my personal thoughts relating to the conversion. This was not a test but rather an opportunity for me to discuss the studying I had done.

After the bet din, my father went with the Rabbis to a place outside the door of the Mikva while mother and I entered the Mikva. Inside I was greeted by a middle age woman attendant. She was to accompany me into the mikva to assist during the immersion. After taking a shower I was ready to begin. I asked if the water would be cold.

She replied "Oh no, it will be warm." I was delighted.

In the mikva I walked down into a pool of warm water where I listened for the Rabbi to say the blessing in Hebrew. I immersed myself and repeated the blessing in Hebrew, then immersed a second time and repeated the second blessing and then immersed a third time. I then showered and dressed and met my parents and the Rabbis in the chapel where I stood on the bimaha and read from the prayer book. The ceremony took about 40 minutes.

I was so excited to be reunited with the House of Israel. It was one of the happiest moments in my life. After the ceremony, we drove to a Jewish restaurant where we had our first Jewish meal (blintzes) with the Jews of Oak Park. Unbeknown to them I was the newest member of the community. We then went to the Jewish shops and looked at the various items. It connected us to Israel.

Later we drove home to light the many candles and receive the bouquet of flowers from friends and relatives. We celebrated the new light in my life.

My father's last brother died in August of 1990 and after the funeral of my uncle his daughter Janna brought out a small old stationary box and gave it to my father. The box contained papers that were 100 years old. It was a jewel for with the knowledge of the story my grandfather had told me and the letters, receipts, and other papers; now we could begin to research our family history.

In the old card box we found two important letters. One letter was written from Manchester, Maryland. Now we had a town instead of just knowing that they came from Maryland. The letter was written by a friend of my great grandfather. He and my great grandfather (John) had attended the Old Academy in Manchester. In the letter he mentioned the name of great grandfather and great grandmother's last daughter Ida and the name of great grandfather's father-John Frederick. The second letter was written to Elvina S.A. the name great grandmother used while living in the West. The letter was from her mother. She had remarried and her name was now Mrs. Finefroch or Finekoch. The letter was mailed from Blackrock, Pennsylvania. In the letter she mentions great grandmother's brother-Oliver.

A receipt from great grandfather's brother Henry gave us the name of the town where he lived. It was Wooster, Ohio.

With eager anticipation and high energy my father Reyno and my mother Frances and I on August 6, 1991, began the journey to Manchester, Maryland. We traveled by car.

I had written a letter to the Historical Society of Carroll County informing them that we were coming and the information we were seeking.

We arrived in late afternoon at the Comfort Inn just outside of Westminster, Maryland. We had come to Westminster because that was where the County Courthouse and the historical society were located.

Early the next morning we went to the Historical Society and checked church records for births, marriages, and death. We found nothing but we did learn that nested in the farm area of Manchester was a church named the Bixler Church.

We then went to the Westminster Branch Library where we located on micro film the 1860 census track. We had all the names of my great grandparent's children so we knew we had found the right John Bixler.

Now it was onto the county Courthouse. In the Vital Records we located the book that contained the signatures of those people requesting a marriage license. John Bixler and Elvinia Egolf had signed on March 29, 1855. We also saw John Frederick's will. In the will it stated the names of John and Henry of Wooster, Ohio. Thus once again we knew we had the right family line.

After our visit to Westminster, we drove to Manchester which is 18 miles from Gettysburg, Pennsylvania and 10 miles from Westminster. We asked in town for directions to the Bixler Methodist church. By lefts and rights and winding farm land we found a little church with an iron rod archway reading Bixler Methodist Church. The church is still very active even today.

Inside the church we found that most of the stain glass windows were dedicated to a Bixler family member. The graveyard had primarily Bixler family members with dates on the gravestones being mainly from the late 1800's and 1900's .

It was now time to drive to York County Courthouse in York, Pennsylvania. At the courthouse we saw papers with the crown of England on them which John and Christian had signed to an oath to the King. The papers were missing when I returned in 1998. We also found John's will of 1765 which at the end of the will was a large circle and twelve little circles. This signature was taped over when I returned in 1998.

After York we went to Lancaster Mennonite Historical Society to see if the three brothers were Mennonites. No information was found.

I later wrote them to ask them to do a thorough search in their records of Mennonite meetings to see if the names of John, Christian, and Absalom Bixler were in attendance. Their names did not appear in any record and the reply reads "although we are not certain that "your" John Bixler was a Mennonite". This was the first hint that the brothers traveled with the Mennonites but were not of the group.

On the way home, we stopped at the Wayne county Clerk of Courts in Wooster, Ohio. We looked at the naturalization books and discovered that there were many people who were changing their name to Bixler regardless of the spelling of their real name. Thus, the large number of Bixlers in Ohio in the census.

After the trip out East, I received a letter from Agnes Bixler Kurtz who got my name and address from the Historical Society from the letter I had written. She was writing a book entitled <u>John Bixler Pioneer, Immigrant, Farmer and His Descendants</u>. She had added my father and my name to the family tree in her book. We had connected with the Bixlers of the East. It was very rewarding to know that our research was meaningful.

The Rabbi went to Israel again in December of 1991 and brought back the information about my last name. I learned that the name Buechsler meant People of the Book or People of the Torah. The name was a variation of Buch. The family name could be derived from Baqi/Bokij, the Hebrew for "knowledgeable man." Moreover, it could be an abbreviation of Bukki. The Bible identifies two men bearing the name: Bukki, who was the son of Jogli and Prince of the tribe of Dan (Numbers 34:22) and Bukki the Levite, son of Abishua and father of Uzzi (Ezra 7:4) This information was gathered at the Nahum Goldman Museum of the Jewish Diaspora.

After visiting the Holocaust museum in West Bloomfield, Michigan, I have learned that at least 27 family members were murdered in the Holocaust and that 100's of Jews with the derivative of our family name also perished. No Jew was spared from this atrocity. May we never forget.

Yes, the secret was I am a Jew. We have been hidden since 1723 because of hatred and antisemitism. The seeds of antisemitism were brought with the first immigrates. According to the Jewish Encyclopedia, in 1634 Catholic Propraetors in the Colony of Maryland established a ruling that, "no person who professed to believe in Jesus Christ should in anyway be troubled, but further provided anyone who does not believe that Jesus Christ is the Son of Gd. Should be punished by death and forfeiture of land." By 1723 the ruling was changed to read "the first offender was to have his or her tongue bored, the second offends was to have the face branded, and the third offends was put to death.", thus we were hidden Jews.

When my great-grandfather (John Bixler) and his wife Melvinia Egolfstein registered for a marriage license in Manchester, Maryland my great grandmother wrote Elvinia Egolf.

They traveled West with great grandfather's brother Henry to Wooster, Ohio and then John and his family went to Indianapolis, Indiana where he established a rope factory on 6th Avenue. The industrial revolution took place and replaced rope with metal cables. Thus my great grandfather moved. He bought a farm near Anderson, Indiana where unbeknown to them was the Imperial Wizard's headquarters of the Ku Klux Klan. Still to this day is the headquarters of the Ku Klux Klan. Once again the Jewish identity had to be hidden.

You might ask the question "Have you experienced antisemitism since coming out as a Jew?" The answer is yes. I live in a housing complex where there are several Arab families. When recycling my newspapers, I recycled the Jewish News (which is mailed to me) and therefore had my name and address attached to it. A few days later in the middle of the night I heard teenage children outside my apartment window. I discovered the next morning that they had taken an instrument to try and make a Star of David and along with the star read "sucks." This inscription appeared on the sidewalk in front of my apartment. Later they threw a large rock at my bedroom window cracking it. I relocated to another apartment in the complex.

The second incident took place at an interview at Adrian College a Methodist College. During the interview the man said "I don't know if you will fit into our faculty." I was puzzled for I did not know what he was referring to I had been raised a Methodist forgetting for a moment that I was a Jew. Later after reflecting on the experience I realized that my former boss at Washtenaw Community College had told them I was a Jew. I had asked her for a reference.

The seeds of antisemitism are trying to take root once again, especially in Europe and other parts of the world. It is up to the American people to protect itself from antisemitism and any hatred towards another group of people so that no one has to be afraid to express their religion, their ideas or beliefs or go into hiding.

At this time of globalization we must learn the difference between a spiritual life and religious ideology. A spiritual journey is a life time quest that keeps asking the question "What is the kindnest choice to be made." The spiritual life does not pit one religion against another but calls the individual to become more loving each day. Religion is to be the mold wherein the spirit can grow.

This writing is dedicated to my loving family and to all the people who helped me find my way back home-especially Sister Agnes (Eleanor) Sheehan, C.S.J., and Rabbi Robert Dobrusin. ©

President Kennedy and President Bush

by Bonnie Branim

I can always count on something different happening when I am showing someone around the infamous Las Vegas strip. My brother and his wife were visiting me. I took them to the huge Venetian Hotel primarily to see the gondolas floating down the river on the second floor. Cary and Dorothy were amazed by that.

Our next stop was the new Wynn Hotel next door. We walked in the front door and viewed the beautiful flowers and waterfalls. When we went back to the front door to leave, there was a large security guard there. He told us we couldn't go out that door. Upon checking several other exits, we received the same response. We couldn't get out! We finally asked a finely dressed employee how to get out. He was gracious and showed us the back way out. We went down a long hall and out the back door.

When we walked around to the front of the building facing the Las Vegas Strip where we observed men in suits, sunglasses in a hot 80 degree day, all talking on cell phones. The busy strip was completely shut down and blocked off. Closed! The whirring of helicopters filled the air as they flew overhead. Crowds of people lined the street and catwalks. We edged our way out into the crowded street to see what was going on. Just then President George W. Bush's entourage drove by swiftly. He was on the way to a benefit dinner for Senator John Porter. Many of the car windows were darkened. They wasted no time driving immediately into the Venetian Hotel driveway as the crowd watched and cheered after long anticipation. It was all over very quickly. My company was thrilled with their trip to Las Vegas.

They saw something they had not expected, the United States President's entourage!

This incident brought back memories to me of the spring of 1962, when I was in Washington, D.C. I had just stepped off the bus and was walking down the street. Suddenly a man in a suit came rushing by and asked us which we would like a small U.S. flag or an Iran flag. I opted for the U.S. flag. Shorty thereafter, President Kennedy's bubble top limo came slowly creeping down the street. The bubble top was down. We could clearly see the President, Jackie Kennedy and the Shah of Iran. They were all waving and smiling.

The next year, I saw the President and Jackie on TV riding down the street with the bubble top down. I have seen the famous car since then at the Imperial Palace in Las Vegas and then at the Henry Ford Museum. How times have sadly changed. ©

Dreams

by Janis Schuon

There's an old song I associate with early childhood memories that begins, "...a dream is a wish your heart makes, when you're fast asleep." But I've discovered dreams are more than just wishes; they are revelations. They are guideposts. I haven't given dreams much priority lately and I have missed the unequaled surprise of discovering my own solutions that are buried deep within the subconscious.

Several months ago, I had a very disturbing dream. My dream included a car that looked to be straight out of the Al Capone days. I was alone in the street and the car was circling with someone at the wheel firing a gun at me. Then I looked down at my feet and there were shards of glass imbedded in my ankles. The pain was horrible and I was bleeding, not knowing what to do next.

After thinking about that dream for several days, I realized the dream actually represented deep emotional pain from a long time of being treated badly. The dream was something like reading a child's book— the kind of story meant to entertain but if you care to listen carefully there's another story woven underneath -- complex and meaningful. It was emotional pain that had kept me immobilized and unable to move ahead in my life. The dream was an important insight about where I was going emotionally.

So in recalling that dream now I realize I need to dream again. I need to listen for what is revealed from the deepest part of me. I am again at a crucial crossroad of my path. I don't always know how to get there but I am beginning to know more about where I want to be. It has more to do with who I want to be than where really. There have been some unexpected turns in my path recently and I need to know, to be sure, that I'm still on course.

I have heard that the heart is the seat of all wisdom and will always know the difference between the things we can and cannot change. I have some choices to make in the days ahead; some changes to make. It's a chance to listen to my heart and my dreams—for they are the same. ©

Once Upon a Time
In the Canadian West

by Carole Hendrickson

O nce upon a time in the Canadian West, the Rasmussen Homestead in Alberta, Canada, lay under the purple gaze of the Sweet Grass Hills of Montana. Those hill that preceded to the Rocky Mountains in time.

Here in 1909, Richard Jul Rasmussen found pacing out the boundaries of the N.E. quarter of Section 4, Township 7, and Range 6 exhilarating. It is the land my Pop, as I called him, settled, proved-up and made his life's work.

To my Mom, it was her home. To her and Pop it was a place to raise their ten children. To me, Carole, it is a place on the prairie that reminds me of a life that few of my peers experienced. This piece of land provided ten children freedom to roam while imagining distant horizons. It is the land that calls me back every few years to reunite with family, friends and the place where I "took root."

In 1889 Pop was born in Hornsyld, Denmark. At the age of fifteen he immigrated to Minnesota. He had followed three older brothers to the U.S. Pop soon realized the Midwest had been settled by the 1890's. Three years later, enticed by ads for free land on the Canadian prairies he crossed the border into Saskatchewan, finally locating in Southeastern Alberta. He set to work proving-up the land. (I'm sure the ads did not mention the area was drought prone or that many ranchers left after the severe blizzard of 1906-07.)

It must have been a struggle, although I have never heard my father say that. His strong body, good work ethic, Danish cooperative spirit, and everlasting optimism served him well. In those early years he travelled by wagon. The wagon was pulled by a team of horses. (Actually, that was how I travelled, as well, until I was six years old.) I can imagine him following the narrow trails that knit prairie and coulees together to go the thirty-five miles for supplies.

The nearest town was Seven Persons. It would not be until after the bumper crops of 1916 that Orion would spring up eleven miles away.

Like most small towns, it faced the new railway which gave it its life blood.

In 1913, Minda Bakstad (my Mom) her mother and four brothers arrived from Kuam, Norway, by way of Minnesota. Mom benefited from going to school in the Starbuck, Minnesota area. Mom and Pop had, as I recall, ten years of schooling between them. Mom likely made it to the sixth grade. The Bakstads homesteaded near my Pop's farm and lived with Great Uncle Ole for a time. Ole moved back to Norway. I had the good fortune to meet him there, just one week before he died in 1966.

Mom and Pop married and Lloyd was born in 1926. After a few good years they were able to buy a tractor, a radio and a car, as well as to build a two-story house. Good crops and good times were short lived. The "Dirty Thirties" were stressful enough but in 1934 their new home burned. It left my parents and six of my older siblings with only the clothes on their backs. By this time, Helen, Ruth, Gordon, Gladys and Violet had joined the family. Pop's hands were burned when he went back into the house to look for Lloyd. Fortunately that was the only injury and the mercy of Mom's family and neighbors helped them make do.

A two-room house was moved fro the abandoned Gotfried Anderson place. My oldest sister remembers five sleeping cross-wise on a bed at the time. I had it easier in my earlier years; it was just three to a bed!

Walter and Margaret were the next additions to the family tree. Then I was born in that little house on the prairie in 1942. One of earliest pictures of me is of a tow-headed, diapered child standing on a wooden block in front of the house. I have often joked that my siblings were trying to auction me off! Then four years later, Dick completed the family. He arrived home from the hospital and was tucked in a dresser drawer.

We enjoyed few amenities. The house had been enlarged. The unfinished back bedroom was lined with heavy blue paper that moved with the winter wind. The house was heated by a wood and coal cook stove and one heater. My Mom made graham bread in large loves to our delight. The cows provided fresh milk and cream. The ice house preserved ice for use in making homemade ice cream in the summer. We raised horses, cattle, pigs, turkeys, geese, and chickens.

Pop was frequently called on by neighbors to butcher animals. He was also good at salting down pork. My Gramma was known for her blood sausage. "Waste" was not a word in our vocabulary. We picked berries and canned fruit to eat in the winter. Only once do I remember having to eat boiled wheat. Our two-room cellar had one room full of coal and a second with a huge potato bin, a sand pile with buried carrots, and shelves of one and one-half gallon jars of fruit. Our planting and hoeing provided the vegetables. Boxes of fruit from British Columbia provided our one luxury. The tissue wrap replaced the Eatons and Simpsons catalogues in the outhouse!

I learned to milk cows, churn butter, gather eggs and bade cream cakes and jelly-roll cakes. I stoked oats, shoveled wheat, and cleaned the chicken coop, helped make pillows from goose down, washed wool socks on a washboard and learned to darn them. Of course, first you had to carry water from the dam. I went to the well too. I learned to iron with a flat iron heated on the old cook stove, took out the ashes and chopped wood. But most activities were shared and somehow made fun because of the company. I can't remember that many orders were even given.

At mealtimes, we laughed, teased and shared, enjoying my mom's stories and the tales of older siblings' adventures. We roamed the prairies and badlands. The games we played seldom required any equipment. Most of all, our character was shaped by loving parents and a Pop who believed all people were hatched from the same basket. Also, that you always had something to give away. Once he put in a widow's crop before ours. The reason he gave to a protesting older brother was, "Lars never treated her very well." I don't recall any undo consequences. Mom enjoyed being a Mother. Thank God! Through it all she never lost her sense of humor. Neither did my older sisters. When they went fifty miles away to high school they told classmates, "Pop raised Great Danes." Living off the land gave us an appreciation of creation, and a sense of independence tempered with respect for interdependence.

After my parents died in 1954, my brother, Gordon took over the farm. He and his wife, Joyce built a new house and sheds, planted four hundred trees and received a farm beautification award. Now their son Duane and his wife Janene own the farm. As the homestead approaches its one hundredth birthday, we learn they may be the last Rasmussen's to own it. Still I know I remain connected to that homestead through memory and ever so grateful for the love experienced and the lessons learned there. ©

Store Closes – End of an Era
by Jack Hinshaw

The recent (2007) closing of Purchase Radio Store in Ann Arbor, open for 77 years, from 1930-2007, brought to mind memories of early radios, broad casting stations and their various programs when I grew up in the late 1930's. The following is just to say "good-bye" to that perfect place and the owner.

"Hi Ho Silver, Away!" and as he rode away in a cloud of dust, you could hear an old timer asking his friend, "Who is that masked man?"

It was sometime in the late 1930's and I hurried home from school to crouch down in front of the family's big zenith radio console to hear the latest adventure of the Lone Ranger. I lived in a small southern town in Kansas. This program originated from radio station WJR in Detroit, Michigan, remember? This was perhaps followed by Little Orphan Annie, Jack Armstrong, The Green Hornet, all on various days of the week.

These were all live performances with sound effects so realistic they would raise big goose bumps on the back of a little kid like me. Of course, they all had free prizes available in jars of Ovaltine, breakfast cereals and other foods.

Live radio programs and most of the stations had not only their own sound effect people but also a live house band and orchestra. Later in the evening, my parents listened to various news programs but they were not as interesting or exciting!

Some of these stations were known as a clear channel station, meaning their frequency on the dial was some distance from any radio station, making it less likely for interference. Then it was all AM radio, with its ear splitting static caused by a bolt of far off lightening or even a stiff wind. It was not until the 1940's that FM became available with superior sound fidelity, but with the disadvantage of a signal that only carried fifty miles or so.

Competition was stiff between radio manufacturers, each making beautiful cabinets in many lavish styles. Many of the early radios such as RCA, Philco, Arbor Phone (made right here in Ann Arbor!) Spartan (made in Jackson) Atwater Kent, with its big horn speaker, are presently selling for several hundred dollars. All radio sets needed long antenna wires, high in the air, clear of any buildings. These had insulators at either end, then led down to the house on a lightening arrester, and back into the house to the radio.

About this time I became interested in building radios, starting with simple crystal sets using Galena Crystals. What a thrill for a little kid like me to hear a program or two on a set that I built! Most stations were nearby, but at certain times I could hear classical music from Interlochen Music Camp, way off in upper Michigan. My most pleasant memory is lying in my bed late at night enjoying this enchanting music.

There was a powerful signal sent out by Doc Brinkley on the Texas/Mexican border. I heard him speak of his "goat-gland" operation for men, never understanding what he was selling, but he did have a strong signal. (I found out much later that he was a millionaire crackpot who had been run out of the country for a number of reasons!)

This interest in listening to radio programs made it necessary for me to have radios that were more powerful in order to bring in signals that were weaker and/or stations that were farther away, also to obtain a higher quality signal. I began to learn about radios with more complicated components. This led me downtown to obtain parts I could not salvage from old radio sets.

Walking into the store completely changed my life. The owner put me completely at ease, making me feel very welcome. It was the beginning of a wonderful friendship. He answered all of my questions, sold me a few parts I needed and even gave me a few I did not need. He was a ham radio operator and stimulated my interest in amateur radio. He taught me the Morse code, sending and receiving, using a practice key.

When I visited Purchase Radio at the closing in 2007, it was as if a door opened back into the 1930's. A mixture of antiques, a repair shop, a ham shop with all those familiar old odors. Small radio parts all around the store, some in bins and others scattered on tables. I could almost see my childhood mentor, Mr. Davidson, smiling at me as I looked around. Lots of ham gear (I was sorry that I never got my license). About a dozen people milled around, picking things up, then putting them down to look at something else. One couple was looking at a small plastic AM radio just like those of my youth, asked a few questions, bought it along with a few other items.

Leaving the shop and seeing all the parking meters along the street was a shock. They looked so out of character. This sight brought me back to 2007 in a hurry!

My early mentor, Mr. Davidson's encouragement in my youth led me to a career in electronics in the Navy in World War II, then to a very interesting job at NASA in Greenbelt, Maryland, and at Cape Canaveral, Florida. I'll never forget walking into a beautiful government equipped electronic lab in Greenbelt, remarking to my boss, "Wow! You've got some really neat radios in here!"

Well, back home to my little transistor radio, with some push buttons and six different frequency bands, to listen to jazz music or perhaps to some radio station around the world. Thanks to Mr. Davidson and shops like Purchase Radio!

About the Author

Jack Hinshaw is a WW11 veteran, widower with one daughter living in Virginia. He grew up in a very small town in south central Kansas, where his mother taught him to read at an early age and to love books passionately. Jack is a resident of Saline, Michigan.

He has always loved reading but never though of writing until becoming acquainted with the Creative Writing Group facilitated by 'Elle' (Elaine Ferrington-Cousino).

"Writing," says Jack, "is bringing back memories from the days long gone by, that I didn't even know I had, and perhaps will stir a memory or two for you."

The Word Game – One of the exercises we use to loosen up "writer's block" is to choose a word or phase from the basket and write on that topic as the prompter. The following short, short story evolved in just that manner.

End of the Affair

by 'Elle'

Two men played sad Greek songs on their mandolins as they sat sipping sweet wine in the late summer sun. The fountain in the center splashed quietly, soothing, sparkling water fell gently into the pool below.

A perfectly beautiful couple sat nearby, sated by the rich dinner, the wine and romantic music. They were made lazy by the warm glow of summer, this peaceful afternoon, just before sunset. Anyone could see that they were lovers, fingers intertwined across the table, eyes filled with happiness, intent on each other.

"Come away with me." He whispered, kissing her fingertips gently.

"Darling, you know I cannot." She answered quietly. His eyes pleaded with her. "Jerry, you knew what my limitations were from the beginning. Please don't ask me again. It hurts too much. Let us enjoy the moment, that is our theme…Remember?"

"Anita, I need more than moments. Become my wife. Please, Please! Yes, I'm begging. I cannot go on without you." He finished hoarsely.

"Jerry," she sighed softly placing cool hands on his back.

He faintly heard the fountain splashing in the background as she spoke in that tinkling voice of hers, blending with the water sounds. Tears filled his eyes as she walked away. She paced back and forth along the pier, near the edge, gazing westward toward the setting sun that was glowing crimson, turning the water to red. Anita's long shapely legs peeked out of the slit skirt as she became more agitated, pacing faster and faster. The thick white marine rope was the only obstacle.

Jerry could not fathom the pain that was to come of ending their affair. Anita turned to him slowly, undoing the long blonde hair, letting it escape into the summer wind, her blue eyes shone with tears, then smiling slightly, she raised her hand to her lips, sending him a kiss. Then turned toward the sea, deftly stepping over the fat marine rope, slipped off the skirt, kicking it back on the dock floor. Unbuttoning the blouse, she wiggled out of the silky bra, tossed with the skirt, and without hesitation, she dove, splashing water on the gray boards of the old pier and was gone, tail fin shining silver in the red sea. ©

Tiki ~ The Amazing Amazon
by Bonnie Branim

At one time I had a blue-front Amazon parrot, Tiki, who caused me some embarrassing moments. Four particular anecdotes come to mind.

I'll start the countdown with number four. Tiki could do a very nice trick to amuse his audience when I had company. Similar to Clint Eastwood shooting the orangutan in "Any Which Way But Loose," where he would fall flat on the floor. Tiki would perch on my finger, I would shoot him with my other finger-Bang! He would fall backward and swing underneath my hand. He would drive the people watching wild.

He embarrassed me with the number three on my story list when we went to the doctor. He had to have an exam slip signed by the veterinarian every time he flew on an airplane. When I put him in his 12x122 travel box, he would know exactly where he was going. He didn't like going to the vet. I strapped him in with the seatbelt and away we went down the road. It was a nice day, so I cracked open the window. We stopped at the traffic light on the way. A car pulled up beside us. Tiki started yelling, "Help, Help! Let me out!" The driver in the car was looking at my truck with a very alarmed expression on his face. Fortunately, the light changed to green and we moved on. Tiki wowed the receptionist at the doctor's office with a greeting, "Hi Cutie!" Luckily she showed us right in because I was sitting there with a bird in a box and a cat was on one side of me and to my other side was a very large bird dog. The doctor came into the room. I opened up the back door of the box and Tiki came running out with his beak wide open. He charged up the doctor's arm. I stopped him just in time by putting his long stick in front of him and he hopped on. The doctor quickly signed a pink exam slip for him agreeing he was healthy enough to go on an airplane!

Number two was when we went to the airport. The security officer confiscated my stick for Tiki and threw it in the box with the nail files, scissors and knives. He said, "What do you have in that box?" I replied, "I have a bird and a ticket." "Well you have to take him out of that box so we can run the box through the metal detector." (I surely didn't want them to send Tiki through the metal detector!) I said, "You just took my stick away that I do that with. He has become quite nippy, but if you would like to stick your hand in that box and take him out, go right ahead." So Tiki, in his box, was given to a special agent to examine. She determined that he and his box were both safe to fly. So we made our way through the airport with several wide-eyed travelers curious to see what was in that little screened in box that I was carrying. Inside the airplane it was too noisy for passengers to hear, "help, help…"

O.K. The number one top event happened when we needed to paint the dining room in our house. Birds have a very small respiratory system. They should not inhale a lot of bad smelling chemicals or paint odor as it could be fatal for them. Therefore, I moved Tiki and cage into the bedroom way on the other end of the house. In a couple of days the dangerous paint smell had subsided, so I moved him back to his corner in the dining room. I covered him up for the night as usual, so he could go to sleep. Then I turned on the TV and sat down. My daughter came over that night to visit. "What's that strange noise?" she asked. It came from the corner of the dining room. I walked over and quietly and carefully lifted up one corner of the cover on Tiki's cage and peeked in. There sat Tiki on his perch, hunched up, feathers all ruffled, eyes closed tight, and snoring to beat the band. A perfect imitation of my husband!©

512 Ash Street
(Waukegan Illinois)

by Beverly Lee Bixler

The little white stucco house on Ash Street had a screened-in front porch and a green lawn divided by the sidewalk leading to the steps to the front door. Entering the front door one was immediately in the living room, then the dining room, and then the kitchen. Finally there were two bedrooms that were separated by the bathroom. My sister, Barbara and I shared the big double bed, where we slept at night and played "paper dolls" during the day; the other bedroom was occupied by my parents and my brother, Bob.

Inside this house was a deep appreciation of music. The harmonious and not so harmonious sounds came not only from the radio, but also from the piano and cello as both my sister and I struggled to please my mother, a music major. We practiced each morning before school then after school while my father was away. He didn't have the patience to listen to us practice.

The dining room table is where we did our homework from 7:00 p.m. to 9 p.m. We were to be in bed at 9:30, before my parents returned from teaching night school.

Our kitchen was a family room, where everyone participated. We each had a chore and everyone helped with the dishes. Doing the dishes was a time for fun as we listened to Bing and Bob Crosby, the Lone Ranger, the Shadow, and on weekends, Buster Brown, Archie, George Burns and Gracie

Allen and of course…Jack Benny!

In the morning it was my job to pump the gas stove, but that was all I was permitted to do, besides set the table. Mother was afraid of fire so she did not allow us to do any cooking.

We had a big basement where we played when we could not go outside. My father was the head of the business department at our high school so he taught us business skills at a very early age. In one section of the basement was a corner set up like a store with shelves which held cereal boxes, fruit and vegetables, cans and pairs of old shoes. Cardboard boxes were set up for the counter.

Another part of the basement was for roller-skating. We had a ball suspended from the ceiling. It was from there I learned to bat the ball. My father would squat down behind me and release the ball. Once my father was practicing with me. I hit the ball so hard that it went flying. My bat hit my father's head and I knocked him out. I went screaming up the stairs to my mother and told her that Dad was lying on the floor. She came running but by the time she got there, Dad was coming out of unconsciousness.

In another part of the basement were the washing tubs and the wringer washer. My mother occasionally got her arm caught in the wringer while wringing the sheets. She would call me and I would come and release the wringer by pressing on the release bar. Also we had an old icebox which we used to make homemade ice cream. We bought ice in twenty-five pound blocks from an ice store not far from our home.

Around the corner from the icebox was the old coal furnace that kept our home warm and cozy. It was one of my chores to shovel ashes out of the furnace and put them in a wooden basket. I learned to stoke it for the evening and keep it burning until my parent returned.

The basement was also where I showed 16-mm movies. The neighborhood children would pay a nickel for an hour or two of movies and 3 cents for popcorn. Abbott and Costello movies were the favorites for I would first show them forward, then backward, then upside down! The children would respond with cheers and laughter.

Our other play place was the garage. Here was a loft, which was reached with the help of a ladder. Two wooden orange crates were used, one to store the play dishes and one for the table. We entertained kings and queens and neighborhood friends.

The floor of the garage was piled with newspapers and old comic books that were collected by my brother and I. My brother was only big enough (age five) to lie on the newspapers so they wouldn't blow away while I went into houses to collect more papers. We went to house to house to pick up old papers to sell them for forty-five cents per 100 pounds to Johns Manville.

The collected comic books were a special joy for we were not able to buy them. We would sit on the piles of newspapers and read for hours from them.

In the back yard there was a jungle gym and a vegetable garden. In the winter was a small ice pond.

These early memories from 1946 to 1955 of 512 Ash Street still linger on as the years pass. ©

On Giving Her a Japanese Garden Tool for Valentine's Day

by Michael Andreoni

If another civilization of semi-sentient life were detected living microscopically in the residue at the bottom of our coffee cups, would we find them more difficult to understand then our own kind? A caffeine-based race of aliens from a coffee bean galaxy, the Starbuckians (well, what would you call them?) could at least communicate to us, without much in the way of argument, how they like their coffee. We might easily understand their preference for, say, a large Double-Mocha with extra froth, over the Petite Espresso taken black, by simply counting how many were swimming around in each cup.

I find myself envious of such easily achieved communication this morning. Of straight-forward demonstrations of "I like this, I don't like that." Gazing into the bottom of my cup of cold comfort, I'm keen to initiate First Contact with the Starbuckians, to pry out their alien wisdom for the good of my species.

"Oh my little friends," I murmur, hoping none of the other café patrons enjoying their magic elixirs overhear me talking to a paper cup, "How go your lives, and do you marry? Have you ever, completely innocently (or completely unconsciously), given your partner anything that caused her eyes to blaze with a fell light, to pierce you with their baleful glare? Has, just for example, the phrase "Clueless Lummox," ever been applied to you in a pitying tone? And how did you get out of it?"

I need answers on this cold winters day, a plan of action for escaping the regretful pall weighing heavily on me. If I can piece together exactly what went wrong, if I can list my errors as a warning to others, then perhaps something could be salvaged from last nights' horror. When I fell from grace over what is already permanently imprinted on my cerebellum as "The Unfortunate Hori-Hori Incident."

The Starbuckians might tell us that love among humans is an odd phenomenon, a too complicated dance, performed blindfolded, compared with the matter-of-fact romances of the rest of the animal world. They could cite the example of Trumpeter Swans, which mate for life, but so far as anyone knows do not feel called upon to present their darlings with thoughtfully romantic gifts every fourteenth of February. They build their nests and raise their fuzzy little swan-lets without losing any feathers over whether a bit of dried seaweed is or isn't the most affectionate symbol of undying devotion. If they give gifts at all, any old thing would seem to do just fine.

It might require a more sophisticated race then our own to point out that a finely made gardening tool can be romantic, and I wish a Starbuckian would jump out of her coffee cup and tell her so this morning. I wish it would whisper that the Japanese do not mess around when it comes to garden tools that all the latent skills of a people who once equipped the Samurai with the finest swords in the world went into the Hori-Hori she rejected violently last night.

No overgrown tangle of vegetation could frustrate its ten inches of forged surgical steel, mated for life to a handle precisely milled from the hardest hardwood to be found on the Asian continent. A blade that makes short work of irritatingly deep-rooted dandelions, but is also fully capable of giving the North Koreans something to think about should they be foolish enough to invade while an avid gardener is stabbing weeds.

That said, it must be admitted that love expressed through gardening tools is risky. There was a certain amount of doubt in my mind as to what she really meant when she presented the catalog and proclaimed "It's wonderful! It's just what I want!" I took a look at the picture, and was properly skeptical. I had learned, I thought, that usage and context are everything in these matters and that connecting "Wonderful" to something which exists to root around in mud could be perilous.

"Oh come on," I scoffed. "You don't really want me to get you this, do you?" I knew she couldn't be serious for I had history on my side—my history, unfortunately. The memory of the chilly reception given to a barbecue grill presented on the auspicious occasion of her fortieth birthday was still very fresh, as was the contempt shown for my agonized plea of "You said you wanted one!" As well, the bitterly regretted Dim Sum cookbook, an unwelcome ghost of a decidedly cold Christmas past, warned of the penalties for guessing wrong again. No, I wasn't to be fooled this time. A romantic something would be found—I could never be stupid enough to give her, on Valentine's Day, a fancy weed-digger.

It's a funny thing (though not quite so amusing this morning), the way that ideas which are laughable a month before a deadline become more and more appealing with each passing day. I sneered at the catalog straight through the last days of January, confident that something better would suggest itself. It wasn't as though I'd never achieved the complex alchemy of the right gift given at the right time. I bolstered my self-esteem with memories of her beautifully twinkling eyes reflecting light from the glittering jewelry of years past, her joyful squeals over surprise vacation trips. No man can be wrong every time and expect to go on claiming half of the marital bed. The logic was comforting: I was still married; therefore I'd had a few victories and was at least as good as other men. Which, as it turned out, meant exactly squat.

The problem was that yesterday's brilliant success is hard to copy. No one can stand in the same river twice when it comes to presents, which, like nuclear weaponry, are a perpetual quest for the newest, the biggest, and the best. The gold bracelet that delighted her last year would not work again unless this year's selection sported diamonds. And should I choose to live really dangerously, next years gold bracelet had better be adorned with jewels looted from a Pharaoh's tomb. I knew all that. I also knew my credit cards would not stand that level of escalation. Biggest and best were out, newest would have to do.

All through that first week of February I searched. I remember it only dimly now as an increasingly frenzied montage of flash-edited scenes of my hands pawing through catalogs of every description. They Googled countless variations on "Romantic and Affordable Valentine's Gifts She's Never Heard Of And Will Worship You For." There really weren't any results returned that met all the criteria, though some of the x-rated products were interesting, and if I had been able to believe their manufacturer's claims, would have come close.

By Sunday afternoon I was a wreck. Confidence gone, avoiding eye-contact with my wife, I complained, around seven o'clock, that I was really, really tired and slunk off to bed. There to mull my options and avoid, as best I could, thinking about the Doomsday Option: "Dear, I couldn't find anything good enough for you." A moments' unguarded prescience revealed the direction my life would take after such a gambit and I lay shivering in terror under the blankets, my life-force ebbing away. Anything would be better then that. A few tired looking grocery store roses, twin ferrets on a leash, chocolate covered balloons-- all infinitely better then appearing before her empty-handed.

It was time for honesty. I'd struck out big and there wasn't much time left to do anything about it. I ran through the dozens of possibilities

I'd rejected as too expensive, too clichéd, too this, too that. Was there anything I'd nixed too quickly? Anything I'd never given her before that didn't cost a fortune? Well, yes. Yes there was.

I'd never given her a Japanese garden tool. The logic of it was revelatory. In the history of the world, probably no one had ever given a Japanese garden tool for Valentine's Day—even in Japan! I would be the first. That this seemed a good thing to me is illustrative of the distant and dark place my reason had fled to during that stressful week. I had lost my way in the quest for a perfect gift and there, in the gloom of my darkened bedroom, this most feeble glimmer offered hope of rescue. I just wanted... needed the ordeal to be over.

That my wife had put the idea into my head was most appealing. She'd placed the catalog before me and asked... no, demanded a garden tool. She had done this several weeks before Valentine's Day, which, I was proud of being smart enough to recognize, was a hint that she wanted it for Valentine's Day. I'd be doing what she wanted, wouldn't I? And, I asked the ceiling, if that wasn't the essence of romance, what was?

I was suddenly giddy and had to get up and walk around the room to burn off the energy surging through me, rejuvenated by the knowledge that I'd cracked the code. I flicked the light on and spoke aloud into the mirror: "To hell with the ferrets! I spit upon stinking ferrets. I spit upon wilted grocery store flowers and inedible chocolate balloons." I would bask in my wife's admiration by giving her the perfect romantic gift. The bedroom could no longer hold me. I had an order to place.

The Starbuckians have failed me. What is the use, I'd like to know, of inventing an alien race if they won't do what I want? I've sat in this café (and really, the décor is quite ugly, greens and browns—ugh!) all morning, pleading for their help. People are looking at me and I don't know if I can stay much longer. An overly officious manager-type has gathered a protective screen of baristas around her, pointing them toward me like attack dogs. And still the Starbuckians refuse to answer! I wave my cup around to shoo away the coffee clerks and stir up the stubbornly mute aliens. Maybe a good shaking will make them understand I'm not playing.

I've told them my sorrows and now I want the use of their greater wisdom to answer a few questions: I would like to know how everything went wrong so quickly. I want to know where the hori-hori landed when she threw it out the back door into the garden. Most of all, I would very much like to know if I can go home yet. Her birthday is less then two months away and I'll need every minute. ©

Cruising on the Penobscot Bay

by Thomas Torango

O ver the years I have traveled to many places. Germany, Switzerland, Austria, Italy, Australia, New Zealand, Fiji, Mexico, Ontario, Quebec, British Columbia, and thirty eight of the continental United States plus Alaska and Hawaii. Of all the vacations that I have taken I think my most memorable one was taking a six day windjammer cruise off the coast of Maine. Perhaps it is the sense of adventure that I felt as we embarked on this new experience that has stayed with me all these years.

It was in August, 1980. We were 42 years old and almost empty nesters. Son Paul was married, daughter Pam was a senior at Western Michigan University. Daughter Melanie had her own apartment. Only youngest daughter Amy at age 16 was still at home. Wouldn't it be nice if just the two of us could take a very different kind of vacation? We saw an article in the travel section of the newspaper regarding windjammer cruises out of Rockland and Camden, Maine. It sounded exciting. Just the thing I was looking for. Gerry, being a good sport was always willing to go along with whatever I came up with.

After sending for some information regarding the cruises, we settled on booking a reservation on the Stephen Taber. The Stephen Taber was and still is the oldest documented sailing vessel in continuous service in the United States and listed in the National Historical Register. It was launched in 1871. It is a two masted schooner, 68 feet long. Her sleek, black wooden hull and tall masts belie the fact she had spent her years in drudgery, hauling bricks, pulpwood and oyster shells. Her oak beams creak like the old lady she is, from decades of bucking the Maine surf. She had never lost a season. She had never had an engine in her. She's never been decommissioned. The schooner was owned by Ken and Ellen Barnes, two former college professors from North Carolina. Ken was the captain and Ellen was the cook. They were the parents of four children who all took part in the family operation, although they didn't sail with the clients.

Adding to our sense of adventure, we packed all our belongings into duffle bags. We carried these bags over our shoulders looking like Santa with his bag of toys. At the time I was even sporting a full bushy beard although it was near black, not white like Santa's. I felt like a latter-day hippie! We were warned not to pack too much as space on the boat was very limited.

On Saturday, August 9, 1980 we left Detroit Metro on a Northwest Orient flight at 7:55 in the evening. We were headed for Boston. The airfare for the two of us, round trip, was $318.00. We arrived there at 9:15 and got a room at the Logan Airport Hilton Hotel for the night. The room cost $60.25. The next morning, Sunday, we took a taxi to the Greyhound station in Boston and boarded a bus headed for Camden. The round trip fare was $83.30 for the two of us. We traveled on US-1 up through New Hampshire and into Maine stopping in Portland to change drivers. We continued along US-1 following the coastline. We traveled though many small quaint towns, arriving in Camden at 3:20 in the afternoon. Camden, Maine is a very small fishing village with a population of about 3,500 inhabitants. Ay-uh, it was Maine all right. It was about as Down-East as you could get. The view of the cove where all the ships were moored was as picturesque as a postcard. The tall masts of the schooners Timberwind, Roseway, Mattie, Lewis R. French, Isaac H. Evans, Mary Day and Stephen Taber stood out in the crowd of smaller sloops, fishing boats and motor boats that were riding at anchor there. The weather was very warm and sunny.

We boarded the Stephen Taber at 4:50 and were checked in by Robin Barnes, the captain's daughter. She showed us to our cabin. Being a married couple we were afforded one of the private cabins, measuring no more that 6 ft. wide x 6 ft. long. It consisted of two berths, one above the other and a 3 ft. wide aisle next to the berths with a small sink at the far end. That's it!! We stowed our gear then went on deck and introduced ourselves to our shipmates as they arrived. There were five couples, Stephen and Lesanne, newlyweds, rode their motorcycle from Quebec to Camden. There were seven single girls, one 70 something widow, one bachelor and a married man in his 50's whose wife didn't share his sense of adventure and stayed home. In all there were 20 of us. We were given an orientation by Ken, our captain and Ellen, his wife, the cook. In addition to Ken and Ellen, there was a crew of three, Matt, Neal and Robin, Ken and Ellen's daughter. Our itinerary would be at the caprice of the wind. The windjammers skirt the ragged coastline sailing an average of 15 to 40 miles a day. But five miles could seem like 50 when you're bucking gusty winds and rolling fog. There were no showers and no full voltage electricity on board. We would get a little gamey. We could always dunk a bucket of frigid water over ourselves and wait a week for the goose bumps to die down. Privacy is an illusion on board, we were told. Those who were not traveling as a couple were assigned curtained berths along the length of the hull in the galley area. There were two heads, or toilets, on the quarterdeck that worked when they felt like it. Ken told us that we were welcome to loll around for six days or help crew, learning sailing, navigational and knot-tying skills. Three volunteers are sought after each meal for dishwashing. Ellen would do all the cooking on the wood-burning stove! After this orientation, we went ashore to tour Camden's boutiques while we digested all that we were told and to ponder what we had let ourselves in for. Back on board, we settled into our cabin for a good nights rest after a very long day, anticipating the start of our adventure tomorrow.

On Monday, August 11, we left Camden harbor at 10:15 after a delicious breakfast prepared by Ellen. It consisted of melon, blueberry pancakes, bacon and coffee. The weather was very cloudy and by 10:30 it was raining. It rained for a very short time, but it remained cloudy and cool, approximately 65 degrees. It was very calm. We could not get to open water under sail. Ken pushed the Stephen Taber to open water using the ship's motorized yawl, a small boat bigger than a dinghy. Once in open water, we set sail and cruised Penobscot Bay. At 5:30, we dropped anchor between Babbage Island and Calderwood Island. We all helped take down the sails, pleated them and tied them down for the night. We had a dinner of chicken, rice pilaf, peas, home made bread, iced tea and strawberry shortcake. After dinner we boarded the yawl and motored to Calderwood Island and hiked. Returning to the Stephen Taber, we bedded down for the night.

Next day, Tuesday, August 12, we were up at 6:30 to a very gloomy, windy and damp day. After breakfast we weighed anchor, hoisted the sails and set out for Castine. The sailing was very good but the weather was very ugly. It started raining. It rained hard all the way to Castine. We were able to dock there along with a couple of other Windjammers. We tied next to the Mary Day and had to cross her deck to get to shore. After exploring the town we took advantage of an opportunity to shower at the Maine Maritime Academy. The ladies were glad to have the chance to wash their hair. We spent the night docked there in Castine.

Wednesday, August 13 proved to be a beautiful sunny day when we awoke. After breakfast we sailed Penobscot Bay passing by

Cape Rosier, Green Ledge Beach, Butter, Eagle, Porcupines, Shepherd, Babbidge, Calderwood, Stimpson, Fox, Thorofare and Widow Islands. We dropped anchor at North Haven for the evening.

Thursday, August 14 greeted us with an overcast sky. The weather looked threatening but eventually, it passed over. The sun came out. We dropped anchor in late afternoon and took the yawl over to Warren Island. We were about to enjoy the gourmet treat of the week, a lobster bake on shore. This is a cruise tradition. While we gathered driftwood for the fire, Matt and Ken procured the main course from a nearby fishing village. Two lobster for each of us. The crew threw the live lobsters into a great tub of boiling water. Soon they were bright red and ready to eat. We were made to crack open the shells with a rock. We also enjoyed corn on the cob, fruit salad in a melon basket, chocolate chip bars, 's'mores' and John Wayne coffee.

Returning to the Stephen Taber, we laid on deck staring up at the stars in an ink black sky. There were some shooting stars. We sang to the accompaniment of Ken on his guitar until 11 o'clock then went below to our cabins. All in all, it turned out to be a beautiful, fun filled day.

Friday, August 15 started with dense fog but while we were eating breakfast the sun came out. The sailing was great. It was a very warm day. We dropped anchor in Gilkey Harbor. John and I went over the side for a dip. The water was near frigid. Back on board, I dried off but instead of feeling refreshed, I felt salty. After dinner we took the yawl over to Idleboro Island Inn and had Black Russians.

Saturday, August 16 was to be our last day at sea. We awoke at 7:15 to a very cloudy, windy day. The waters were very rough with temperatures quite cool. We wore our sweaters and windbreakers. Neal hoisted anchor, raised the sails and got us out of Gilkey Harbor before 8 o'clock to beat the threatening weather. We were heading back to Camden. We arrived there in mid afternoon feeling clammy, salty and generally uncomfortable but glad for the experience. After saying goodbye to our host and hostess and the other shipmates we headed for the Town Motel in Camden where we had made reservations the previous Saturday. We showered and changed into fresh clothes, then made our final rounds of Camden after dinner in a local restaurant. Back at our motel, we went to bed to rest up for our trip home tomorrow.

The next day, Sunday, August 17, we boarded a Greyhound bus for the return trip to Boston. Once there we put our baggage into a locker at the bus terminal. We had time to spare before heading to the airport to catch our plane home. We decided to tour Boston on foot. There were several walking tours within easy walking distance from the bus terminal. We saw artists drawing pictures in chalk on the sidewalks of Boston Common. We saw Paul Revere's house and Old North Church. Took in Boston Cemetery and saw Paul Revere's grave. Soon it was time for us to collect our baggage and take a taxi to the airport where we boarded our plane back to Detroit Metro.

Arriving home, we were proud of the fact that we were able to get to Maine and back without the aid of a travel agent or the use of a car. The result was an experience never to be forgotten. ©

SOMETHING TO STAND ON

Janis Schuon

It's just a plain little stool. Sturdy and square with two coats of paint competing to be the one showing. Nothing fancy, no extra trim, no carved detail; just a plain sturdy little stool.

Dad built that stool for Christmas in 1978. I could not have imagined then the number of times I would step up on it to get something just beyond my reach or sometimes to sit on it for a task down low.

All these years gone by. So much has happened. None as I imagined it would be. Some better, some not. I wonder if Dad had ideas of what my life ahead would be like. I wonder if he felt he had prepared me for whatever life brought. We never talked about things like that. I don't remember that he ever told me how I should live my life. But by example, he was honest, dependable, trust-worthy, and reliable; traits you could count on. He was always there, always ready to help a neighbor in need.

He was probably the least hypocritical person I've ever known. Honesty was the core of his character traits. He wasn't sophisticated, pretentious, or flashy--kind of like that stool he built; just plain and sturdy. Something to stand on, something to count on holding you steady when you reach for something. Who knew a plain little stool could say so much for so long? ©

The Accident
by Tom Torango

It was a beautiful October morning. The sun was shining and it was dry and clear. The temperature in the mid 50's. This would be a good day to ride his motor scooter to work. His wife needed the car to run errands while the children were in school and it would save her the seventeen mile round trip to drop him off at his office so that she could use their only car for the day. Besides, there wouldn't be many more nice days for taking the motor scooter to work with the last days of fall fast approaching.

He had attached a plastic milk crate to the back of the motor scooter as a place to carry his lunch and any other items that needed to be stowed. With a kiss before leaving, he bid his wife goodbye and said he'd see her around 5:30. He donned his helmet and off he went. It was 7:15. He left the subdivision and headed east on West Road heading for the river road which joined the neighboring communities along the river. He was riding into the sun which was rising in the east. Too bad he didn't think to wear his sun glasses. But it was too late to turn around to get them as he would be late for work. When he reached River Road he turned left at the traffic light and headed north, through Monguagon's downtown shopping district with its still sleeping storefronts, awnings rolled up in the early morning hours.

Leaving his home town of Monguagon and entered the community of Brownstown. Past the ugly black buildings of the steel mill on his right with their yawning transoms full of broken window panes, greedily monopolizing Brownstown's waterfront. Across the thoroughfare to his left, a scrap metal yard followed by a string of company rows houses, each one giving the steel mill a blank stare with their sooty faces.

He stopped for the traffic light at Sibley Road where only one car reached the T intersection and made a right turn while he waited patiently for the cycle to complete .

The light changed to green and he continued on his way toward the city of Fordville. Traffic was light. He was thinking of what the day held in store for him.

He left the community of Brownstown and entered the southern outskirts of the city of Fordville, the city where his offices were located. To his right rose the chemical plants that provided him his employment. But his offices were located at the north end of town and he continued on his way. As he approached the central business district, he observed that there was construction taking place up ahead at Eureka Avenue on the east side of River Road to his right. Putting in new sewer lines and repaving perhaps. Barriers had been placed in the right hand lane funneling traffic to the left hand lane. As he approached the intersection of River Road and Eureka he checked his rear view mirror to look for traffic in the left hand lane behind him. All was clear. Up ahead, there were but a few cars. One was approaching from the opposite direction and was moving into the left turn lane with it's signal blinking. "Where does he think he's going with Eureka blocked off?" he thought to himself. He check again to his rear and to the left as he entered the intersection. After that he remembered nothing.

When he regained his senses, he found himself sitting on the pavement, dazed. What happened? Where am I? He looked down at his left leg which seemed to be pointing off at an impossible angle from the knee on down. He couldn't look up. All he could see was a worms eye view of a woman's legs from the knees on down. White open toed shoes. The hem of a flowered house dress. Nylon stockings rolled down below the knee.

"Where did you come from?" the flowered dress asked.

"What in the hell are you doing?" he replied.

Where was she going? Where was she coming from? Why hadn't she seen him? A voice from out of nowhere.

"Don't worry about your motorcycle buddy. The police gave me your address and I've loaded your bike into my truck. I'll take it to your house for you. I ride a motorcycle too."

"Thanks" was all that he could mutter.

He began to realize his predicament. Police cars with lights flashing. An ambulance with stretcher awaiting, someone was placing an inflatable sleeve over his leg. When they inflated it to straighten and immobilize his leg, the pain was unbearably excruciating. He lost consciousness once more.

When next he regained consciousness, he was in a hospital. Doctors and nurses milling about. His friend from work was there.

"How are you doing?" he asked. "Bob Miller was on his way into to work and said he saw you had been in an accident. I though I'd come to see if there's anything that I can do."

"Where's my wallet?" he kept asking.

"It's OK his friend replied. They have your things at the nurses station. I called your wife and told her what happened. She should be coming anytime now." Then he faded away again.

The diagnosis was a severely crushed knee, a comminuted fracture of the tibia plateau and a simple fracture of the fibula. An orthopedic surgeon called by his family doctor and wouldn't be able to schedule surgery until the next day. Until then he was kept sedated.

From his hospital bed in the days that followed his surgery he asked for details of the accident. He was angry.

"Who was that crazy bitch?" He ranted. "Didn't anyone get her name? Hasn't she called to inquire about me?" he wanted to know.

"Get a lawyer," his brother-in-law advised. "I know a good one."

And so he did. His attorney sent an investigator to get the police report and to interview the woman and take photographs of her car and the accident scene. Only then did she call her insurance agent to tell him she had been involved in a personal injury accident. And he came running to the victim. Due to an error in copying his birth year, the police report gave the victims age as twenty, whereas he was really a month shy his thirty-first birthday. Her insurance agent thought he'd be dealing with a minor. When he came a calling, he was surprised to learn that the injured was a family man who told him it was too late for a statement. He'd have to deal with *his* attorney.

Seven months later, both parties assembled to give their depositions as to the events surrounding the accident to their respective attorneys. The parties involved did not come face to face. Ever! When he later read her deposition, it was the first time that he heard her version of the incident. ©

Oppression Then Freedom

by Beverly Lee Bixler

"The surest way to corrupt a youth is to instruct him to hold in higher esteem those who think alike than those who think differently."
Nietzsche

While a student at Michigan State University, I was invited to join a group of educators on a visit to the Union of the Soviet Socialist Republics (USSR). It was called the Winter Festival Tour. I traveled with approximately one hundred and sixty people, mostly educators from all throughout Michigan. In the group were Jewish teachers hoping to learn more about the plight of Soviet Jews. We were only given permission to visit two cities, Leningrad and Moscow. These two cities are the showcase for the Russian government.

December 22, 1975 ~ We began our twelve hour flight to Moscow. The pilot informed us that we would be circling many times to get rid of the fuel and to remind us we were under the control of the Russian government. This was just the beginning of experiencing the Russian use of control of darkness and oppression.

Upon landing, there were about forty military personnel around. We arrived late in the afternoon and it took us about an hour to pass through customs. (Détente was still working for we were told that sometimes it takes hours to be checked.)

After boarding buses, we were taken directly to the Hotel Russia, where we were assigned rooms. The room assignments were scattered throughout the hotel, and there was no list for us to locate each person. We of course quickly made our own list for there were six thousand rooms.

In the hotel on each floor there were three checkpoints in which to stop and state where you were going. At the last checkpoint you were given the key. We were required to follow this procedure each time in our coming and going.

Upon entering the room, the first thing you would do is turn on the light, which turned on the microphone. We had been instructed that all rooms would be bugged.

My first day in Moscow, I chose to visit a school for the mentally challenged. I was searching for the value system. At the school I was surprised to find posters four feet by five feet with children's pictures and stories. I asked the tour guide to explain the posters. Without hesitation the guide explained proudly that these were mentally handicapped children that had helped during the war.

One young boy had carried grenades and had blown up a bridge, another boy had carried weapons to the men in the forest. There were twelve pictures and twelve stories, each one telling of the children's heroic acts of war. I could not understand how retarded children could be used in such a way. I just could not understand.

While contemplating this moral situation, I began to reflect upon this morning's event. All those people lined up in the cold, cold early morning. I asked the guide, "What are they buying at the stand?" She replied, "One or two eggs is the ration for the week." "But there are so many eggs on the table, what does that mean?" I muttered to myself.

As we drove around the city, we saw huge propaganda signs the size of two billboards connected together which pictured Lenin, and a saying about how much the Soviet Union was doing on behalf of the people. We also saw other elaborate signs declaring future goals of the party. The signs were just so big that one felt very small both inside and outside. The signs just overwhelmed one by their physical size.

December 23, 1975 ~ A day to remember! That was the day we attended an "open" forum with the publisher of Soviet Life Magazine and the Chairman of Propaganda. They both recited their speeches and then asked for questions. I started, "Could you please explain the emigration procedures?" The gist of the argument was that everyone was free to go but the elderly parents wanted their children to stay.

Hands started coming up and the more questions asked, the more ridiculous became the answers. The Jewish Community had prepared for this meeting and questions answered by lies were flying left and right. Even though truth was not to be found in this encounter, the life of the Soviet Jewry and the life of the refusenicks had not been forgotten.

On December 27, three of us decided to be a part of the everyday procession by Lenin's Mausoleum. We had read that the Russian people began to pass-by starting at 9:30 a.m. People are required to line up in neighborhood blocks around 9:00 a.m. After we turned in our camera and bag to security, we went to the back of the line and began the very long slow procession. For some reason having Kleenex and sunglasses in my pocket gave the guards a reason to harass me.

Ten people moved forward we came to another set of guards and each would ask me to empty my pockets. I was grumbling about this harassment when a young man in line spoke up in English, "Don't worry, they do this everyday." In about one and one half-hours we viewed Lenin's body. It reminded me of the wax figures in the Wax Museum in London. I thought about how this figure was being used to reinforce, to motivate and control the people's ideology.

The entire experience was depressing. As we slowly walked along we experienced the constant reminder of control. The slow steps of the people emphasized the dragging of time and the feelings of hopelessness. Would Russia ever be free? Did they even want to be free?

After lunch, two students asked if I would go with them to see Gum's Department Store. I agreed to go. This store looked like an old enclosed European market place. There was a place for men's shoes only, and a different section for women's shoes. The color for shoes this day was black. If I understood correctly, you gave the clerk your size and you received a pair of shoes. There was no place to try them on and no conversation about the shoes. It was like buying those eggs I mentioned earlier. You got what they had and that was it!

The next day, December 27, 1975, I journeyed with two other students to a Russian Government tourist shop. We boarded the bus. It was so crowded that I go stuck at the ticket taker's position. For the next ten minutes everyone gave me their ticket or two small coins. I continued at my post until the crowd thinned out. I moved forward to where my student companions were seated. I asked, "Do you know where you are going?" They replied, "No, we lost our count." An elderly woman motioned for me to come and sit by her. I was still able to speak with the students and sit with the woman. We continued to talk. A young man came forward to speak and everyone glared. (It seems the rule was don't speak to foreigners.) He said, "I am a university student and after I get off...you go four more streets." We thanked him when he departed. The elderly woman took my hand when it was time for me to get off and squeezed my hand. We arrived safely thanks to the young and old.

We looked about the neighborhood and went into the shop. The tourist shops are only for foreigners to buy Russian souvenirs. I was interested in the wooden dolls that teach children to count and black lacquer plated candy dishes. After a few hours we headed back to the hotel, for some reason it always seemed easier to go back that it was to go forward.

On December 29, a train ride was scheduled. It was farewell to Moscow and hello to Leningrad (St. Petersburg). On the train I sat with some of my new friends. We were sharing stories and laughing when the tour guide motioned for me to come to her. She said, "Why are you sitting with the Jews? You are not Jewish." I replied, "They are my friends. She continued to comment, "Why are they are so noisy?" Once again I replied, "They are happy people." Excuse me now I would like to return to my friends." I left. This ended the encounter.

We arrived in Leningrad early in the evening and began to get comfortable in our modern student-like room. The shower situation in both Moscow and Leningrad was terrible. The water had a powerful odor, and the acids burned ones skin when attempting to bathe. It seems that the plumbing system was all torn up during the war, and the people are still without good water.

The next day the sun was brightly shining (which was not usual in our experiences) and we were off to meet some of the Russian children and young adults. We were going to the Friendship House. Our group was divided into tens, and group of ten assigned a college age student. One student was studying physics for her father was a physicist. I asked her if she wanted to study physics and she said, "No."

After a few questions and answers I asked the group if we could let her ask us a question. They agreed. Her first question was "Do high school students have cars and drive the cars to school?" "Yes, that is true." I answered. "Do students sometimes get angry and break windows at the school?" Again I replied, "Yes, they do." She stopped and thought, saying, "The students here would be sent to a labor-colony for re-education if they broke windows." It was my turn. "In the United States people are free to express their anger but they must also take responsibility for their actions."

We were having this honest dialogue when a supervisor came and spoke critically to our student. We quickly switched to asking her questions once again. When the half-hour was over, it was time to assemble for a talent show.

While moving to the next room, our young student gave me her favorite pin. She explained to me how all the children collect and exchange pins. She also asked if I would meet her tomorrow. I said, "I would be happy to meet with you, but I had been told it was against the rules for foreigners to meet with the Russian people." I continued, "Perhaps you could ask you Papa about what to do as I did not want to bring trouble to her or her family." I asked her to tell her family that many people send love and encouragement and we ask that you continue to have strong courage. We parted in sadness.

Our last day was filled with both fun and fear. We began the morning with a long distance ride to a wooded area to take a troika ride. When we arrived, the bus was surrounded with soldier dressed in white and rifles drawn. We were to told the men were here to protect us from going into forbidden areas. How quickly the images of Nazi Germany flashed into mind, and the statement, "Here to protect you" sounded all too familiar. We slowly dismounted the bus questioning everything.

We walked into a large room where a decorated table with caviar, orange juice and vodka were being served. It was a Father Frost New Year celebration. Part of the group stayed indoors and ate while others began to line up for their troika ride. The sleigh carried three to four people and took us in around the woods. As we completed our rides, Father Frost came to us with sparklers for all. Our farewell to Russia was completed. We boarded the bus to the music of Dr. Zhivago singing in our hearts and to smiles on every face. We were homeward bound.

At the airport, I had one more purchase to make. I had seen many men of distinction wearing a fur hat with ear flaps so I thought I could buy this hat and make it be a sign for the Soviet Jewry. I needed a sign to keep my conscience ever alert. I purchased a sable hat with mixed feeling for I was using a sign (fur hat) that went against Jewish teachings regarding the sacredness of life. I had to believe that the remembrance of Soviet Jewry was just as important and that my sign each winter would enable me to tell the story of their struggle. I was ready to go home.

The flight back to the United States was peaceful. We had gone and we had seen. As the plane headed in direction of the airport, the co-pilot said, "We have been instructed to land in Pittsburgh. The weather conditions are too severe. You will stay overnight and fly out in the morning." Boos and cries rang out, "Try to land…We want to sleep in our own homes." A few minutes passed and the co-pilot said, "We have decided to land…Destination…Home!" Cheers broke out and joy returned to the tired travelers. Just a few more hours and we would be landing.

The wheels were lowered and soon we felt the bumps of touchdown. It was the most delightful touchdown that I had ever experienced. How good it was to be home!

We had seen oppression, poverty and people trapped in a police state. We had experienced restricted freedom of speech, programmed activities (instead of planned) and control through constant monitoring. We had experienced the limitations of rights to assemble, of rights to privacy and of rights for freedom of movement.

We had learned about the manipulations of truth through lies, the misuse of the art of questioning by ignoring the question and giving an answer that has nothing to do with the question. We have been told about the new program to have people work where they live thus limiting their movement to go from one area of Moscow to another area without special permission.

We appreciated the arts, the talented youth, the people who had extended themselves to us and the faithful ones. In ten days we had strengthened our determination to protect the freedoms of America and thank Gd. for democracy.

In the middle of a cold winter night, we exchanged hugs and bid each other good night. We were free once again. ©

My Travels
By Bonnie Branim

I have traveled to many beautiful destinations. I have dug for diamonds in Arkansas and New York. I have ridden a whaleboat off Cape Cod, standing on the bow with my arms outstretched. I have camped in Monument Valley, Utah, where many of John Wayne's westerns were filmed. I have followed the colorful sandstone rock formations on the Oregon Trail. I stayed in tepees on scenic Route 66. I watched the yellow and orange sky blend together at sunset on the southern most tip of Florida. Each place has its' own unique style of beauty. It is difficult for me to pick the most gorgeous spot that I have ever been.

Let me begin with the Oregon Trail. The historical societies out west have preserved places along the Oregon Trail that make the history of our pioneer forefathers live. In 1993, my husband and I started our trek to follow the Oregon Trail in a thirty-three foot travel trailer pulled by an F250 Ford Super Cab Truck. We had previously taken a trip to St. Louis, Missouri, to see the pioneer museum under the arch. Therefore, we started our journey on Route 80 this time, headed west for Nebraska. We stopped in Gathernberg, Nebraska, to visit the original Pony Express Station.

So that we could get the actual pioneer feel of the land under our feet, we camped at the Oregon Trail Wagon Train in Bayard, Nebraska. The next morning we climbed aboard the covered wagon headed to the landmark of Chimney Rock. The early pioneers found their way by watching for the well-known landmarks. We took turns driving the wagon and riding horses. Most of the pioneers walked beside their wagons for hundreds and thousands of miles. There was no air conditioning. The temperature was a sweltering 100 degrees. I wore a western hat to protect me from the hot sun beating down on me. They gave us handkerchiefs to wear around our neck.

In 1842, the immigrants measured miles per day, not miles per hour. They averaged about ten to fifteen miles per day. It was dustier back then. I could smell the sweet prairie grasses and the sparse cottonwood trees and the mud on the trail. We camped at the foot of Chimney Rock and set up our tents. Our trail guide started dinner over the red coals of the campfire. He made fresh homemade bread in the Dutch oven. It

149

tasted as delicious as it smelled, with butter and jam, along with our main course, beef stew. We drank boiled sassafras root tea. It tasted tangy, like root beer. We washed the dishes in the sand and went to bed. We zipped our tent up tight, so no rattlesnakes would slither in during the night. We had a dark, peaceful, quiet, starry night. I fell asleep listening to the coyotes howling. The pioneer's greatest fear was a thunderstorm.

The next morning we awoke to the luscious smell of bacon frying and French toast wafting through our campground. Our guide was frying last night's homemade bread in a large, black, cast iron skillet. We were all given a loaf of the scrumptious bread to take home with us. As we were writing in our journals, provided to us, the Pony Express rider came over the mountain. He collected our letters, put them in the pouch slung over his horse, and then rode off.

The next day we took off again in our RV in the direction of Scottsbluff. We passed the fast-flowing, bubbling Platte River that helped the pioneers find their way. We stopped to feel the cool, fresh water. That night we pulled into a riverside campground. We were tired. It was late. We went right to sleep. We opened the windows to let the balmy breezes flow through the travel trailer. I neglected to tell Jim that we were camped on the edge of the Riverside Zoo. The next morning we were literally raised out of bed by the roar of the king of the jungle. I now understand why the lion is called the king. Our seven thousand-pound vehicle trailer shook as her growled our welcome!

The last stop on the trail was Fort Laramie in Wyoming. This was a welcome stop for the pioneers. They felt safe from the Indians here. They knew they were getting close to their destination. Near the fort, I walked through the wagon ruts made by the heavy covered wagons pulled by oxen and mules. A sign read: ***"Watch Out For Rattlesnakes!"***

I felt the six foot smoothed down sandstone that was soft enough to make a trail. This three-week trip has remained one of my favorites because of its authenticity. ©

Boyhood Summers

by Thomas Torango

Nothing conjures up fond memories of my boyhood more than the sights and sounds of summer. I still love to hear the chirping of the crickets at night, the buzzing of the cicadas in the trees, the sight of dragon flies skimming over the water and the bees flying from flower to flower. There is nothing in winter to compare.

As a young boy in the 40's, our playground was the fields, creeks and woods that were at the end of our street. Our subdivision was new and just developing in 1939. The street was not paved. Oil trucks would spread used oil on the roadway to keep the dust down in summer. There were ditches on either side of the road. We'd wade in them after a rain. Our house was one of the first to be built. There were no houses across the street from us. By 1942, we were a nice little community with plenty of open space in which to play. My closest friends were the McConnell brothers, Tom and Jim. Tom was my age, Jim a year younger. We roamed the fields in the spring, picking wild strawberries and raspberries. We would wade in the creeks and ponds collecting pollywogs and grayfish, which we erroneously called crabs, and we'd catch spiders that we'd put into cigar boxes and be amazed at the webs that they would spin inside. We would invade our fathers' garages and workshops for hammers, nails and shovels. Out to the fields and woods we'd go. Digging holes and covering them over with sod and scraps of wood from home to make hide-outs. Or we'd build platforms up in the trees and pretend we were Tarzan. We'd collect horse chestnuts and hickory nuts. Our mothers never seemed to be concerned about where we were, or what we were doing. We would have to be called home at supper time. After supper, we'd be out playing again and wouldn't come home until it was getting dark. I'd arrive home usually pretty filthy, but baths were Saturday night affairs so it was just a case of washing my face and hands.

With the end of World War II, the landscape began to change. In 1946, in came the bulldozers and steam shovels. Our street was paved. A culvert was installed in the creek at the end of the street and covered over and the street extended. No more pollywogging! The trees were cut down in the woods. No more tree climbing and tree house making! The fields were bulldozed and basements dug. No more strawberries, raspberries and wild flowers! Our men and women were home from the war and needed places to live. So they put up what mother disparagingly called "those postwar cracker boxes". Our activities turned to sandlot baseball, or playing in the new houses as they were built. We had a new kind of fun. When given a lemon, make lemonade.

Whenever I hear the crickets and cicadas, whenever I see the dragonflies, bees, horse chestnuts and hickory nuts, I'm transported back into the happy times of my boyhood where life was innocent and carefree. ©

Inheriting a Melody
by Janis Schuon

Music has always been incredibly important and powerful for me. I grew up among family with a love for music. My mother is an accomplished musician, as are her siblings. The house she grew up in was well entrenched with music lessons, participation in school music programs and music competitions. My grandfather did not read music, but played the violin quite well. All the children in the family played at least one musical instrument; most played two.

That love for music sifted down through the next generation and similar abilities were cultivated. One of my sisters has the ability as my grandfather did—unable to read music but able to play incredibly beautiful piano music. And so with that heritage came an unspoken rule in our family; if you should find yourself in a position of having to choose between a washing machine and a piano, choose the piano.

As I grew older my appreciation for music and the transforming ability it has to soothe the soul also grew. Like my mother, the first purchase after college, entering adult life was the purchase of a small spinet piano. As the years passed, the piano moved with our family from one Midwestern city to another and finally to the east coast; our seventh move in nineteen years.

I had always wished if not envisioned a piano of grander scale and sound quality but my wish remained a wish because the little spinet provided a respectable piano experience for my children and me. My daughter began her piano studies at age five and continued throughout high school providing us with many colorful memories of piano recitals and a plethora of idiosyncratic piano tutors. The little spinet was an integral part of our family and was faithfully tuned and played regularly.

Then in 1993 my Uncle Bob died. As unexpectedly as his death from cancer, came word that his entire estate had been left to my sisters and me. Uncle Bob had never married nor had children of his own and his nieces received much attention, jokes, hugs, and interested listening throughout our childhood and adult years. What happy memories we all have of the love and attention he bestowed upon us. He was generous with his attention and interest in our lives as we matured. He never lost interest in us or our children as we each married and our lives took different directions and focus. Ours was a mutual admiration society. Robert Eldon Holman, born in 1910, was also an integral part of our family.

Within the year as Uncle Bob's estate was settled and we the heirs, each received an equal cash portion. I had not anticipated any inheritance and wanted to use it as wisely, carefully, and respectfully as possible. I felt as if uncle Bob was smiling down at each of us and undoubtedly curious about what each would choose to do with our money.

I thought long and hard about what I would do with this money. Uncle Bob was a frugal man and so I considered putting the money in a savings account or investment. But there wasn't much enjoyment for me in that idea. Anything tangible I considered as a purchase seemed temporary and would depreciate over time. I wanted something I could enjoy, keep with me, and yet I wanted something that would hold its value if not appreciate.

One sister chose plastic surgery to have her eye lids lifted. One sister used her money to take a cruise and reduce her mortgage. One sister bought furniture. Another used the money for an in-ground swimming pool. All were appealing ideas, but still undecided, none of those choices seemed quite right for me.

Soon the answer became crystal clear—a piano. A piano would give me and the rest of my family enjoyment and its value would appreciate if I chose carefully. I felt uncle Bob would approve.

I consulted with my piano tuner, who in-turn introduced me to a reputable piano restorer. I visited the workshop prepared to purchase a grand piano. The feel or touch of the keys and the sound were the highest priorities. The cabinet I imagined would be either black or brown but plain. I could not have been more excited to explore the choices there in the workshop.

George Smith was a gracious old-world craftsman who loved his work, his music, and the combined outcome. Each year George and his wife, Catherine, hosted a new year's day party. Each guest brought something to share for the buffet supper. But the best part of the evening was the music. Every guest came prepared to play one selection of music. It was both an elegant and grand way to begin a new year.

There in the workshop, George directed me to three or four pianos that were near completion; ready to find homes for wanting musicians. I carefully fingered the keyboards of several fine pianos. But then my eyes locked on one piano and I was mesmerized by the beauty of a gleaming finish across the broad lid opened proudly atop the dark burl walnut cabinet. Intricate carvings graced the corners at each end of the keyboard and the legs were stately and dignified. Not convinced its sound would be equaled, I sat at the keyboard and was surprised to feel a touch that was gentle yet confidently firm. The sound resonated with pride and passion. The sound, the touch, the cabinet—a love affair had begun. My decision had been made. But was it I who had chosen the piano, or did the piano choose me?

George told me the history of the piano I had selected. It was built in New York City in 1915 and had belonged to a concert pianist. From markings on the underside, George also knew it had been in Paris before coming back to the east coast to retire. I was thrilled and eagerly anticipated the delivery date.

The small spinet back at home gave me some cause for concern however. That piano had been in our house for 20 years by now. It was the piano on which my daughter had learned to play. I had perfected "The Sting" on that piano and logged uncountable hours trying to improve my own skills. How could I just dismiss that piano because I had found one bigger and better? I felt guilty contemplating its departure. I lived in a neighborhood with many young children. Perhaps I could find a home with a good family who would care for it as I had. My conscience was soothed only slightly. Nevertheless, I wrote a small advertisement and included it in our monthly neighborhood newsletter.

Within the week a neighbor called and came to see the piano. Within minutes she had made her decision to buy it for my asking price. She concluded our deal by explaining that she wanted all three of her children to learn to read music and have the exposure of a piano in their home. But she went on to say that most of all she wanted her youngest child, who had been diagnosed with deteriorating hearing loss, to experience the sound of a piano, to feel the vibration of the sound, before his hearing was completely gone. The spinet had found the perfect home and I could be happy knowing it would have such a noble continued life.

The day my new piano arrived was a sunny crisp New England day. There was great fanfare. George was wearing a bow tie and corduroy jacket looking more like a proud father at the birth of his first child than delivering a piano. Turned on its side, legless, the piano came in carefully wrapped in swaddling clothes (or so it seemed). The legs were attached, casters put into place, and then three strong men set the piano upright. It was there, it was mine, and it was magnificent. A gift I had only dreamed of but not believed could be realized. Handing me the papers of pedigree, George broke my mesmerized gaze to say he'd made a mistake about the year of the piano. It wasn't built in 1915 after all. It was built in 1910—the year uncle Bob was born. I knew I'd made the right decision. I knew uncle Bob approved. Every time I sit at the piano and feel the stress leave my body and replaced by peaceful calm energy, I remember Uncle Bob and thank him for the gift of a lifetime. ©

The Day I Made a Movie with Julia Roberts

by Bonnie Branim

My friend, Rhonda, of Las Vegas, called me and said, "How would you like to be in a movie?"

"Of course, I answered. Assuming it was probably just some small-budget insignificant, unknown film, I asked, what movie is it?"

Rhonda replied, "Oceans 11."

Knowing this was possibly one of the most popular movies of the year, loaded with well-known, good looking and talented stars, I said, "Are you kidding?"

I called the casting number that Rhonda gave me. They asked me if I was a SAG member. I told them I wasn't. They were delighted since the SAG Union was expected to go on strike. The man said to come to the MGM Arena tomorrow, in formal wear, give the password of Barney Rubble and I would be admitted. I hurried out to a bridal salon to pick up a long black velvet dress on the sale rack. I ran around the corner to Payless shoes and found a pair of black heels.

As Rhonda and I walked through one of the worlds' largest hotels, all dressed up, people invariably would ask us what was going on in the arena. "Oh, nothing much," I said, "just a boxing match." We joined a long line, went through a metal detector and had our purses checked through. We didn't have to say "Barney Rubble," but the name was used in the movie.

We sat in the huge garden area that holds approximately eight-thousand people. There were only about one thousand of us extras. They compensated for this by moving us all around the area, shooting us in sections. (In the finished movie it looks like the entire arena is filled to capacity.) As the crew shot each short take, they would describe and explain exactly what they were going to do next. After each segment, the director, Steven Soderberg, would view it on a small monitor. If it weren't perfect it would be done again and again. We spent all day filming the fight scenes between the famous boxer, Lenix Lewis and a Russian boxer.

If we became bored, they would play YMCA inspire us to dance. They offered us free food and drink at the concession stand anytime we were hungry. The little, short stout assistant director, Dave entertained us by lifting the tall, Steven Soderberg over his head, spinning around in the boxing ring.

The second day of filming was much more eventful and interesting. As Rhonda and I were sitting in the bleachers, everyone began to clap. In walked the stars of the show, Julia Roberts and Andy Garcia, looking very serious. Julia was wearing a beautiful sleek gold dress. Behind them came Wayne Newton and his magnificent blonde wife. Wayne kept busy waving and talking to everyone. Next came Roy Horn and Sigfried Fishbacker of

Sigfried and Roy fame. A little later, in walked Elliot Gould. The assistant director walked behind him showing that we should be clapping for him too. George Clooney and Brad Pitt were unfortunately not in this particular scene. They could usually be found at the Gentleman's Club. (Julia Roberts got in trouble with the hotel for being nude in the hot tub with her friends.)

Normally people do not dress up to attend a boxing match. But in the movies Las Vegas makes likes to make people think it is a fancy place. Usually everyone in Vegas dresses very casually. However, tickets for a front-row boxing seat can run around a thousand dollars.

They began to film the fight scenes, showing all the stars sitting in the front rows. At the end of each take, Andy Garcia had a woman pat his makeup and fix his hair so it was perfect all the time. After one particular scene, Julia Roberts said to us, "I'm sorry, but we will have to shoot that scene again because the cameraman caught me with my finger up my nose. I promise we will get it right this time."

When we were all finished for the night, Julia Roberts and Andy Garcia thanked all of the extras. Andy invited us to a partying Steven Soderberg's hotel room. He was, of course, being factitious, because there were about a thousand of us.

This was truly my fifteen minutes of fame. It was very interesting to see how our favorite movies are actually made. Steven Soderberg, his crew, Julia Roberts, Andy Garcia, and all the other stars were very gracious to us. Rhonda and I enjoyed it tremendously. We had the opportunity to meet some very nice personalities and even were paid for doing it. ©

The Big Bird

by Pat Spriggel

I was standing beside my Mother who was washing dishes. Looking out the window above the sink was rather had for me because I was in the 2nd. grade and stood only as high as the bottom of the window pane. My Mother said she had always wanted a window above the kitchen sink. Because she and my Father designed the new additions of the kitchen, living room and utility room – well, my Mother got what she wanted. Looking back I can really appreciate how modern Mother's interior designs were for the time. She almost did not get the square wood panels for the kitchen ceiling because the man putting them up said this had never been done before but Mother got her way!

Although I could barely see out the kitchen window, I could make out the back woods because it was on a slight hill, covered with golden weeds. We had six acres. Today six acres seems quite small to me as my brother has a one hundred and eighty acre farm and six acres is only the proverbial drop in the bucket.

But to me, growing up, the whole six acres was a Winnie the Pooh kind of magical land where all my fantasies of cowboys and Indians living under the leaves could be played out.

So this particular morning stands out to me, in my memory. It was a sunny day, so normally I would already be outside on the tire swing, or playing with an imaginary friend, or climbing on various trees, especially on "Roger's tree." (Roger is my older brother and my other older brother, Kenneth, had trees named after them. Thinking this was unfair, at some point in my childhood, I decided all the rest were mine!

On this day, however, I had something else on my mind. I was scared! Too scared to go too far back into the woods because my brothers had told me about this large black bird with talons so strong they could pick me up and fly away with me.

"Was it a crow?"

"Oh no, something bigger!"

"Was it a vulture?"

"No, something much bigger."

It had a six-foot wingspan! My brother showed me with his arms outstretched, "It's bigger that this!"

I wasn't sure. Was this just another story that my brothers made up? Or was it true this time? I had seen black birds (probably crows) flying back there. In fact I loved seeing crows fly – their stark black against all the greens and blues of the back field.

I must have asked my Mother if such a thing as a bird that could lift me off the ground was really true. I don't remember what she said. It was probably to state the truth that there was no such big bird. Eventually I went to play outdoors, although maybe not all the way back to the woods.

But, I do remembering that big bird, just as my brothers described it. I remember the big bird today. ©

Christmas Took a Back Seat

by Joanne Savas

One Christmas we did not go to Aunt Demetria's house in Muskegon, Michigan. Instead, my father accepted an invitation to Boston and Cape Cod, Massachusetts from his friend. Our parents were friends in Athens, Greece, and the friendship continues in America.

"A gathering of friends does not come often enough." Our father said as we made the long road trip. The friend's house was on the Atlantic Ocean. A thick stone wall enclosed the house. At the gate entrance were two cement lions sitting as if guarding the house. My brother and I sat motionless in the back seat of our shiny black Oldsmobile. Our father took pride in his cars. They were always new and always spotless.

Our mother had spoken telling us to behave as we approached the house. She was the family disciplinarian. Our faces turned solemn as we aligned our legs neatly on the back seat. We were eighteen months apart in age, but almost the same height. Our knees matched. Docilely our hands lay on our laps.

Father stopped the car abruptly and we cascaded out, following our parents through the brief shock of cold air, we clumped noisily into a big square front foyer. As we stood there among the suitcases, on the Turkish carpet, we blinked into the light of an enormous chandelier that looked larger than a small car.

Our parents called out, "Well, hello, we're here!" in a general celebratory way in Greek. I waited for someone in the house to speak. I thought of how ashamed I would feel if I got lost in this house. Just then the master of the house appeared in the large doorway leading to the living room. He was tall and dignified, with a neat, thick silver gray mustache. He held himself very straight like an officer in the Turkish army. He was in charge that was certain. About him was a air of order. I could only stare.

"Hello, you Jones's' and children!" He said in a deep voice, his manner ceremonial. I could see underneath his mustache the traces of a smile. He included all of us in his smile, then, he opened his arms broad in a welcoming gesture. I knew then that he was truly our father's friend. He spoke in Greek, "Here you all are at last!" He looked pleased, yet exhausted somehow as if Christmas guests were already too much for him.

We milled around, taking off winter coats, and being kissed many times, a Greek custom sometimes practiced to extremes. Our host's authoritative voice told us to go to our rooms and unpack. We dragged our suitcases up the winding staircase. The staircase was wide and curving with heavy mahogany rails and carved banisters. I felt I was falling, but the steps were sturdy, broad and shallow under my feet. Lugging our suitcases behind us we went up step by step in slow motion. I was thinking how I was too small to undertake such a big task..

I counted six bedrooms and wondered where I would stay. Then the door to my room was opened for me. It was a picture from a movie setting. I stared into a world I had never seen. A scene bigger than our living room, times three! A fireplace was already burning and there were windows, windows everywhere. Was Santa Claus ever in this fireplace? I laughed at myself knowing it couldn't be true.

Our father said this Christmas would be different than any we had before. We children explored the house and ended up in the kitchen. Hot, sweet, buttery Greek twist cookies were waiting for us, served up by a skinny woman who looked like she could not talk. She wore a white uniform, a white apron, white stockings and lace up shoes with thick low heels. She ruled the kitchen, absolutely, but did she like children. This time she stared at us. My brother and I drew quiet.

"Come over here and let me have a look at you." Suddenly she spoke. We presented ourselves expectantly, waiting to see what she would find. To me she said, "Could there be a girl so sweet as you, here in this lonely house!" To my brother, she said, "Do boys wear short velvet pants like yours?" She liked us. I could tell. We did not speak as we gobbled up the cookies.

The skinny woman sent us through the pantry into the ten-seating dining room, into the living room where we found the grown-ups. I decided my favorite place would include trees and water. Liquid darkness filled the outside deck and the Atlantic Ocean disappeared. Our parents were engrossed deep in conversation. It was a journey to happiness for them. I believe a great joy filled their hearts as they laughed and conversed about the past.

Did anyone notice the Christmas tree? I guess the best time is always spent with best friends and surroundings don't matter. Coming into the living room I saw our parents sitting in front of a mammoth stone fireplace. The stones climbed from the floor to the ceiling. The sofas were covered with fabric that had blurry flowers scattered about. They passed the Christmas tree, tall and glittering. I stopped and stared. Imagine a ladder that could reach high enough to put the star at the top of the tree. I tilted my head sideways to look at it all. It was beautiful!

A discovery turns on the brain and lights flash just like on this tree and this make-believe house. I did not speak to our parents then. Instead I went over to the orange and yellow fire to feel the heat on my face. Outside, the snow covered the long lawn that sloped down to the ocean. The Christmas tree rose high in shimmering tiers, fragrant brilliant, intricate, much more so than the biggest tree at J.L. Hudson's Department store in our Detroit, Michigan parade.

My brother was asleep now on the large sofa. I just sat. I couldn't sleep. The reason we were there? Our father wanted to tell us about friendship, to share this friend with us. It wasn't about this grand house, the overfilled stockings, the lavish presents; but the ecstasy of a child's anticipation was still there. I smiled and put my hands carefully in my lap as my mother had instructed, and I waited for it to be Christmas morning as always.

(In honor of Father's Day) ©

Falling Leaves
by Sally Wu

Silently I walked along the streets after a day's work, listening to the crunching sound of the fallen leaves which were on the streets, the sidewalks, the lawns, the driveways, everywhere I stepped. Some of the leaves were still hanging on the trees, like colorful clouds floating in the sky. I felt that I was swimming in an ocean of greens, yellows, oranges, reds and every shade color in between. Their dazzling colors glowing as if on fire under the bright afternoon sun gave me a feeling that I was out of this world.

The houses on both sides of the streets were equally colorful. It seems to me there were no two of them alike. So delicate was the architecture, the wrap-around porches, the cathedral like houses, the church spike roofs and many more I could not find words to describe. Here an old man swept the leaves and there an old woman sat on a rocking chair on the front porch. I was completely taken by the peace and tranquility surrounded me as if I was in a fairyland.

That was in the autumn of 1961, the year I came to America, my first autumn at Worcester, Massachusetts. It was so enchanted that I shall never forget. It has been more than 45 years since I left Worcester. I am longing to go back to walk along the same streets in another autumn. ©

Retirement

By Sally Wu

I am retired. I feel so happy that I could fly. I get up in the morning whenever I like and go to bed as I please. I do the things that I have wanted to do all my life and have enjoyed every little bit of it. I don't have to take any responsibility if I choose not to. I am free like a bird. Yes, these are the golden years in my life.

Some of my friends ask me with curiosity and sincere concern, when they find out that I am retired, "Now that you are not working, isn't it boring staying home all day long?" "Did you say that you are busy, but you are retired?" Some even told me, "you know that you can do some part time consulting or teaching. Lots of people do that. It makes the day go by fast,"

Why would I want the day to go by fast? I have too many things that I want to do but don't have time for. As a matter of fact, I wish that I had forty-eight hours a day. Most people are puzzled, they cannot imagine that a retired person would be so busy.

Definitely there is life, an active and fun life, after retirement. First I signed up at a health club after I retired so I could keep my exercise routine in case the weather does not allow me to hike or do some other outdoor activity. Exercise always makes me feel good. Like taking a hot water shower, it releases the tension and stress from every cell of my body.

Hiking in Kennesaw Mountain in Marietta, Georgia (only twenty minutes driving from home) is always a great joy and treat for me: the green trees, seasonal flowers, rocks, birds and lizards, the far away mountains and city buildings, all delight me. Once there are five of us went to Kennesaw Mountain hiking. After a three hours hike, we went to our favorite eatery for lunch. Frank exclaimed: "This is the good life." We all echoed: This is a good life indeed. Who can ask for anything more?"

From the telephone directory I located the nearest senior center and joined the line dance class there. I met many young active seniors who enjoy dancing. Our instructor is an energetic woman in her eighties. She dances with such graceful movement. She is really a great inspiration to me.

I took a jewelry design class at Los Angeles Community College many years ago. When I found that Spruill Art Center in Dunwoody offering a similar class, I signed up for the class right after I retired. The class gives us hands on experience. From designing to finishing, we do it step by step: drawing the pattern, cutting the sterling silver sheet metal or bending the wire, forming the silver pieces into shapes, soldering pieces together, and finally polishing the jewelry surface. Whenever I complete one piece of jewelry, I cannot help staring at it with such admiration, fulfillment and happiness. "Whoa, this is so very beautiful, did I really make it?" The joy was so overwhelming; no words can describe it.

When I received the course catalogue from the Kennesaw University extension program, I found a creative writing class for senior. I have always been interested in writing. When I was in my junior high years I dreamed to be a writer. It has been a long time since I last wrote something. I was a little apprehensive that I might make foul of myself, since English is not my native language. But I enrolled in the class anyway.

Travel is my passion too. Through the newspaper and magazine advertisements I found many organizations which offer activities and tours specifically for mature people. There are Elderhostel, a non-profit organization, which provides learning vacations worldwide; Eldertrak, a Canadian version of Elderhostel on a small scale; Grand Circle, a travel company offers adventure travels; Gala Holiday and many others. The most popular one is Elderhostel. It issues several catalogues for learning vacations each year both domestic and overseas. Just reading through page after page of trips descriptions, I get so excited, like a small child walking into a candy store, that I just feel like taking all of them at once. Finally, I settled for a trip to Grand Teton National Park for geological study. We stayed in the Grand Targree Ski and Summer Resort near the Great Teton in Wyoming. We had classes in the morning to study the earth formation, the animals and plants in the region. Our naturist had some many samples of the plants and animals. She gave us an assignment to identify the animal from their droppings. I saw some smooth elliptical shaped thing like olive in a glass jar, very beautiful. I asked the naturist "What is this made of?" She gave me a funny face. She told me those were the drops or stool from an animal that she asked us to identify. I was embarrassed.

In the afternoon we hiked to the nearby mountain with our geology and naturist teachers as our tour guides. It was an awesome view with high mountain range standing right nest to the vast plain. How amazing that we found fossils on the top of the mountain 5000 feet above see level. In the evening we always had activities, such as slide show, line dance and even local author of ninety years old Bertha Chambers Gillette, told us stories of frontier life in Jackson Hole, Wyoming. All class and activities were very interesting and entertaining. We even had a free afternoon to take a 10 -mile floating trip on the Snake River. Best of all I got to meet many people who share my interest.

The classes, the hiking, the learning vacations and the trips to visit my relatives and friends surely have kept me busy and made my life interesting that I don't need to find anything to kill my time. ©

Grand Canyon West Skywalk

by Bonnie Branim

At 6:45 a.m., one hundred of us brave souls headed from Las Vegas to the Grand Canyon West to see the newly opened skywalk. The motor coach drove over the huge Hoover Dam and the man made Lake Mead. Two towers fell over two months before and slowed down construction on the new bridge across the Colorado River. We traveled to Arizona for about three hours. We went through a three thousand-year-old Joshua tree forest. The bus had to go for fourteen miles on a dusty, windy, dry and bumpy dirt road. It reminded me of a ATV path. Fortunately, we didn't meet another huge, wide bus coming the other way.

When we arrived early the Grand Canyon Airport and Hotel, the Hualapai Indians were just beginning their brightly colored hoop dance. Next, we went on the skywalk built by Indians. We paid $25.00 extra and gave them our purses and valuables and cameras. We proceeded through the metal detector and to walk what looked like a fairly short walk around the loop. We put on booties to walk on the clear Plexiglas walkway, so as to not scratch it. Many people took a few steps, then changed their minds, turned around and came back. I figured I had already paid my money and I was going to get my picture taken on the walkway as proof that I had been there. I walked the entire loop. I probably would not get back this way anytime soon, so I might as well do it the first time.

My friends and I were glad that we made the extra effort to walk out around the loop. When we looked down past our feet, there was the eerie four thousand-mile drop to the deep, beautiful multicolored Grand Canyon.

Our next stop was the Indian buffet at Guano Point. The Hualapai's were selling their renowned turquoise and silver jewelry. We sat at a picnic table overlooking the calm and peaceful Colorado River. The lack of guardrails made me very nervous. The rich browns, smoky gray blues, black shadows, yellow buffs, and terra cotta oranges of the canyon were spectacular. We didn't have time to take the trip to the ranch that offered a Western barbecue and horseback riding.

We all felt very happy that we had accomplished the one-day trip to see the new, controversial Grand Canyon West skywalk. It was exciting, interesting, and fun to see and be a part of modern history. ©

Fred Torango

by Thomas F. Torango

I never knew my grandpa Torango. He died six years before I was born at the relatively young age of 63. By all accounts he was a colorful man. Not in the sense that he was eccentric, but rather he was a well -rounded individual who was quite popular in his church and community, although he did have his detractors. Much of what I have learned about him was related to me by his older grandchildren, my cousins, or my aunts. Strangely, I never heard my father talk about him, good nor bad. Mother said they didn't get along too well and dad left home and boarded out elsewhere when he was about 18 years old. She characterized his childhood with the rhyme, "His father was the butcher, but his mother ground the meat. And he was the little hotdog that ran around the street." This implied that grandpa was busy with his other interests, so grandma ran the butcher shop while the kids fended for themselves. Dad being the only surviving son with three sisters seems to have taken the brunt of grandpa's expectations.

Grandpa was born on December 3, 1867 in Ecorse Township, Michigan. He was the son of a dirt farmer, Thomas Torango and his wife Matilda. He had an older brother George also known as Ballard, his middle name. Grandpa always went by the name of Fred. He apparently didn't have a middle name as did his brother. It was always assumed that grandpa's real name was Frederick. Hence my middle name. I have found in several records that his name was actually given as Alfred, but he always went by just plain Fred.

Grandpa was a devout Catholic, as was grandma. Grandpa didn't have much of an education; probably no more than the eighth grade. He worked on the small family farm until he married. He and grandma married on September 13, 1892 when he was 24 years old and grandma was 18. They probably met each other while attending social functions at their church, St. Francis Xavier in Ecorse, Michigan. That is where they were married. A photograph of the occasion shows his hair noticeably thinning. He would be nearly bald by the time he died. He was considered tall for being a Frenchman. While he was only 5'-9" or 10" tall, he was head and shoulders above all the other members of his family. This no doubt gave him an air of authority.

Not too long after he and grandma married, they built a home on Biddle Avenue or River Road as it was known at the time, in the Village of Ford, Michigan which would eventually be incorporated into the city of Wyandotte. They built a meat market next door to the house and ran a butcher shop for the next 25 years.

Grandpa had a life long passion for horses. He had many horses over the years and raced them competitively on the grand circuit. These weren't saddle horses, but rather pacers, sulky racing horses. He had a penchant for naming them after his daughters. Hazel T was one of his horses that won many races. In one race she ran the mile in 2 minutes, 15 seconds or nearly 30 miles per hour! He was a great story teller and never was he more at home than in reciting a tale of horse racing in the old days.

Outstanding among his races, was a race at Dundee on a track owned by the American Trotting Association in 1906. Grandpa drove Hazel T against some of the best horses in the class. He drove hard and skillfully, and as a result won second-prize money. During the winter that followed, after extensive investigations, it was found that the horse which had been awarded first prize money was a ringer. (A ringer is a contestant that is entered dishonestly into a competition.) In consequence this horse was disqualified, and the secretary of the American Trotting Association mailed grandpa a check covering the difference between first and second-prize money. Friends and family rejoiced at this distinction.

In another thrilling race, grandpa's Hazel T and another horse were evenly matched, and neither could seem to win an advantage. Much excitement held sway in the grandstands. Grandpa worked Hazel T hard, but the judges didn't seem to appreciate this, and they informed him that he would be fined if he didn't make a greater effort to win. After five heats, grandpa was finally victorious.

A bronze trophy was offered at one time by a Mr. Cavanaugh of River Rouge for a race between Simoline, a pacer driven by grandpa for another Wyandotte man, and a trotter owned by Dr. Belanger, of River Rouge, on the ice of the Rouge river.

On the day set for the race, grandpa informed his opponents that the day was too rough for a race and urged that it be postponed. Dr. Belanger's supporters insisted that they go ahead, and grandpa agreeing, they ran off one heat, which grandpa won. His opponents then decided that, after all, the day was too rough for a race and postponed it for a week. On the day the race was to be resumed, grandpa found that his competitors had switched horses on him, but he said nothing, and proceeded to win two more heats, and then go home. "Where are you going" he was asked. "Home," he said. "Last week, I won one heat and today two more. The terms specified three out of five heats, "That's right," said the River Rouge men, "but we changed horses; you must win three heats with this horse." and grandpa, ever obliging, won another heat and the trophy.

Over the years, grandpa was actively interested in the political life of the village. He served three terms as assessor and one term as justice of the peace. He had an addition built onto the meat market and used this space as his office as justice of the peace. The building still stands there today. As evidence of his sense of humor, the story goes of his seeming defeat in an election. At the first counting of the ballots, it became apparent that he lost. "What happened," asked his friends, "that you let that man beat you?" Grandpa told them a large number of votes for him had to be thrown out because they were improperly marked. "Not enough of my friends know how to make the sign of the cross!" he explained.

In addition to his meat business, horse racing and political activities, grandpa also belonged to the Knights of Columbus, the Arbiter Society, and the Holy Name Society.

In about 1915, grandpa had an agreement with the Michigan Alkali Company to furnish meat to the company's ships which were docked at their property a short distance from the market. My dad was delivering meat to the ships one day and was scalded on the legs by steam as he passed through the plant. His burns left lasting scars. If grandpa agreed not to sue the company they would promise a life long job to both my dad and grandpa. Thus, grandpa closed the meat market and went to work as a laborer at the Michigan Alkali Co.

Grandpa's father died on Armistice Day, November 11, 1918. When his estate was settled, grandpa and his brother George came into some money. About 1922, grandpa had three houses built just around the corner from the family home on Biddle Ave. two were side by side on Davis St. and one on Sullivan St. He rented these houses to his daughters and their husbands and to dad and mother. He charged his daughters $40 per month for their houses, but he charged dad $45 per month for his. The partiality was never explained.

Grandma's father died in 1923 leaving a considerable sum of money to his two daughters and his widow. It was about this time that grandpa decided to sell the meat market property and the family home next door to it. Grandpa and grandma had a new home built on Emmons Blvd. at the north end of Wyandotte. It was also about this time that grandpa bought his first car. Mother said that it was with grandma's money.

It seems that grandpa went on a spending spree with grandma's inheritance, for they also had a cottage built at Woodland Beach near Monroe. This cottage became a favorite family gathering place in the 1920's and 30's. He also bought a large cemetery plot at the new catholic cemetery in Southfield, Holy Sepulchre. Grandma and grandpa had the bodies of grandma's mother and their son Aloysious disinterred from Ecorse cemetery and reburied at Holy Sepulchre.

While grandpa's daughters expressed a fondness for their father, calling him papa, my mother didn't share their affection for him. While she liked grandma very much, she didn't have much use for her father-in-law. This dislike stemmed from an incident during the depression. Mother and dad were having a hard time making ends meet with two small boys. Mother took in sewing to augment dad's income at Michigan Alkali. But in view of this, grandpa thought nothing of pulling a wad of bills from his pocket and counting it in front of everyone. Mother didn't resent his money, but felt it was in extremely poor taste to flaunt his prosperity and subsequently lost all respect for him.

As the year 1930 came to a close, grandpa celebrated his 63rd birthday on December 3. He had retired from the Michigan Alkali and was living comfortably with grandma and Aunt Marguerite, their youngest daughter, on Emmons Blvd. Christmas came and went. Grandma celebrated her 57 birthday on New Years day. On Sunday, January 25, grandpa and grandma entertained friends. They played bridge. After everyone had gone home grandpa remarked on what a good time he had. He couldn't remember when he had laughed so much. They retired. The next morning grandpa awoke and complained that he wasn't feeling well. Perhaps grandma should call Dr. Engle. Dr. Engle came to the house and examined grandpa. I don't know what his diagnosis was, but he left the house and before he got back to his office, grandpa died in his bed. It was 11:15 Monday morning; the cause of death, Angina Pectoris with coronary embolism, a heart attack!

It was grandma's decision to have grandpa laid out at home. This custom was rapidly disappearing, but grandma thought that that is what grandpa would want. The coffin was set up in the living room and guests were received for the next two days. The funeral would be held on Thursday. A look at the weather forecast in the paper called for unsettled conditions with temperatures about 25 to 30 degrees and rain or snow over night. On Thursday morning with friends and family at the house preparations began for moving grandpa to St. Elizabeth's church for mass followed by a funeral procession to Holy Sepulchre Cemetery. It was soon discovered that the casket with grandpa in it wouldn't go through the front door!

What to do? With their tape measures out, the funeral director determined that the only course of action with everyone standing around would be to move the dining room furniture to the side, take the casket through the dining room, through the kitchen and out the back door! What a spectacle that must have been, (and stressful for grandma.) Following the mass at St. Elizabeth's the funeral procession began it's long route to the cemetery along wet and slippery roads in cars that had no heaters. Grandpa was the first in the family to be buried in his plot aside from the reburial of his son and mother-in-law. Mother vowed from then on that she'd never allow herself or any other member of her family to be buried in the family plot as it was too far out. ©

A Connecting Story
(Portraits of Great Grandparents)

by Joanne Savas

"When my father died, mid October, 1951, we were living in Dearborn, Michigan. I was only seventeen years old. His sudden, fatal heart attack left my mother emotionally scarred and unable to face her grief. There was personal change that happened to your grandmother so many years ago, a challenge that affected me the rest of my life. These memories come rushing back to me as it is time to visit the family grave markers with your great uncle Taky.

My mother (your Great Grandmother) cared for my physical needs beyond anyone's expectations. She was a fastidious housekeeper, a role in those days that was honored and admired. My father and I would laugh about it. He would say she was right there in every season. In the spring, I was told not to track mud into the house; in the summer, I was told not to let the screen door slam; in the fall, when she shooed away my friends and I when we came home from school (but only after she gave us her favorite Greek koulourakia butter cookies); and finally in the cold snowy Michigan winters, she always complained and screamed about dripping wet mittens on her freshly scrubbed kitchen floor.

Even now, at age sixty-eight, I can remember every detail about my mother as I stood there at her grave site; from the slippers she wore all day, (with holes cut to relieve her bunions), to her pretty wavy hair of chestnut pinned up with polished curved combs. She was short in stature, her complexion a beautiful milky flawless white, her eyes, unusual for her Greek heritage, green-gray with tiny sunset streaks of gold. She was so energetic! Like a little vole, her quick movements and stride, that of someone much younger. She moved about completely centered in her tasks.

Great grandmother, in the midst of some crazy project that could not be interrupted, such as polishing the linoleum or spraying the pantry with Lysol, was so busy that sadly she didn't have time to talk to me. "Get out of the house," she would say, "Go play, leave me in my peace." (This does not translate as well as it sounds in Greek.) Your parents heard the same phrase as they grew up. It was generational.

God knows she did her best. She minded the house and mother took this job seriously! No one would have a cleaner house than she. Many times I would hear her downstairs, cleaning until well after midnight. When I was sick she overly pampered me, but when I misbehaved, she slapped and cursed me until it seemed to never end. I don't remember her ever carrying on a sustained conversation with me. That was what your great-grandfather did.

My father would arrive home late in the afternoon when he wasn't on the road selling china and restaurant supplies. Most days he would get up at six in the morning, do his paperwork, and plan his road trips. He ate breakfast with me which my mother served without joining us. She was certain he or I would ask for something, so she remained standing at the kitchen sink waiting for any requests. Pleasing us was her role. Uncle Taky told me that when he attended Howe Military School, she would take his dirty laundry home, clean it and press it and mail it back because she felt the school laundry did not clean it properly. I had forgotten that!

Father was a delight when he came home because he talked to me. T He talked with me during my days in high school. It was a ritual. He would walk through the front door (he never used the back door) put down his briefcase, go directly to his favorite lunge chair and motion to me with a pat on the arm of the chair. This signified, "Come talk to me about your day." Mother served a strong Turkish coffee in a demitasse. After a few sips he was ready to talk, making sure his news told a story. I remember how first he would hand me a wrapped peppermint from a restaurant he serviced that day. The wrapping stuck so tight from his body heat that I would have to spit out little pieces of cellophane as I chewed it. I didn't mind.

Your great-grandfather Jack had a nice way of telling a story. His big chest cavity gave his voice some depth and he sounded his 'r s' in a wholesome mid-western way. He told stories slowly, dramatically, not neglecting details. This great storyteller told me about watching Chicago burn. "I looked over Michigan Avenue and saw black clouds rising in the sky," he would say knowing very well, that I knew he wasn't in Chicago then. "Dad, that was in 1871," I would reply. He loved it when I could be smart with my responses and show that I was listening!

Before he went to bed, comfortable in his striped pajamas, we would talk again on the steps of the dark front porch. That too was controlled by ritual. He would smoke one cigarette, drink one glass of cold fruit juice and say, "Is there anything we didn't talk about? The day is ending." Every topic I brought up was followed by an interesting story from him until I got sleepy and went to bed dragging my feet.

Jack Jones entertained and informed many friends with his stories. He was not a moralist. He looked for a laugh and some appreciation. It was a wonderful time for me with your great grandfather. I could even talk back and he would listen patiently. I could ask questions and he was right there, face to face. Growing up as I did in a post World War II era in a busy society that worked long hours, I wonder now whether in absence of my special time with a devoted loving father for seventeen years, what would have become of me?

I wish there was some way I could bring a little essence of this man and this woman to you, then again, maybe I just did." ©

World War II and On the Home Front

By Tom Torango

Although I was only four years old on December 7, 1941, my recollection of the war years between 1942 and 1945 are quite vivid. Perhaps it is because my two older brothers, two uncles and some cousins were in various branches of the military. Being very young, events on the home front did not seem unusual to me because I could not remember what life was like during peace time. Everyone knew someone who was serving time in the military.

It was a war unlike any that we have witnessed since. The whole country came together and each contributed in his or her own way to defeat our enemies. We had our Victory Gardens. We collected scrap metal. I remember mother cutting the ends out of the tin cans and stepping on them to flatten the cans, then tossing them into a bin to be collected. We saved newspapers for paper drives. We kids collected tin foil from cigarette packages and gum wrappers after peeling it from the waxed paper backing. We collected the seeds from weed pods for filling life vests. Housewives were exhorted to save bacon and other greases. "Ladies take your fat cans down to the corner butcher!" one radio announcer urged apparently oblivious to the unintended double entendre!

Gasoline was rationed as was almost everything else. Our toys were made of paper or wood. Lines formed everywhere. "What are we standing in line for?" one might ask. "Cigarettes" might be the reply, or "nylons"! Such a luxury! At a time when the country came together on short notice and switched from butter to guns. Turning out thousands of planes, ships, ammunition and other war supplies and bringing the enemy to his knees in four years time, it is incomprehensible to me that we can't find a solution to today's war on terror and capture its troublemakers. ©

A Never To Be Forgotten Beach
by Daniel Kent

In 1943, I was a seventh grade student at Blessed Sacrament School in Hollywood, California. For a few months of that year I lived with my mom and two sisters in an apartment building managed by my grandmother. We lived on Orchid Avenue hardly a block from the famed Grauman's Chinese Theatre.

In November of the year, thousands of American troops stormed the beaches of tiny Tarawa Atoll in the Gilbert Islands. That little island took the lives of over one thousand Americans and cost the Japanese defenders thousands of lives more in the space of some seventy hours of fighting.

Only days after the famous battle, the boys and girls of my class would be taken to the Hitching Post Theatre to see the first combat films from the island of Tarawa. Getting out of school was one thing, but what was this place, Tarawa?

To our horror, we saw bodies floating in the shallows, lifeless legs and arms moving with the rhythm of the incoming sea. We probably saw much more than that, but that was enough for a youngster to remember.

To this day, I fail to grasp the worth of taking us from school and exposing children to the harshest reality of warfare. There was enough time for that later on in life. I'm sure some would say their sacrifice will never be forgotten. Last week a veteran of that fierce battle revealed that one of the beach areas that claimed the lives and limbs of so many young men had now become a city dump.©

A writing project led to this short story. Members selected random words from a drawing, wrote a short paragraph including the word, then the paragraphs were woven together to make this tale! 'Elle'

Bits & Pieces

A Joint effort by Pittsfield Creative Writers – November 19, 2007

His name was Bob; a short stout man of about fifty. He worked in the shipyard as a boilermaker. He had lived in BalMain across the bay from Sydney, Australia, for years, living alone in the boarding house up on the hill overlooking the harbors. Aside from volunteering his spare time to the Salvation Army no one knew anything about his past. Most people who are immigrants to Australia have "pasts," pasts that they don't share with anyone. What did Bob leave behind? What was HE running from?

"Don't push me!" He shouted.

"I didn't push you!" He screamed back.

Both faces showed strain, ruddy and wet with sweat from the effort of holding back, hoping not to make a bad situation worse by physical violence. Bob's dark eyes flashed with anger.

"She was my wife!" He cried loudly.

"But I loved her too!" He replied just as passionately.

Each man had a different picture inside his head. Bob's memory stirred; remembering how their first offspring came into the world at the cost of seven bucks. This included the new mother's food at the Air Force Hospital in Tinkerfield, Midwest City, Oklahoma. Since he was in the Navy, and without a car, wife and her girlfriend went by taxi to the base hospital. He went to the Navy base, borrowed a car for the twenty mile trip. By the time he arrived, the blessed event was over and he was a new father. How they had arrived in such an obscure place as Oklahoma was another memory.

Jacob's memory of Mary went back to his childhood. For three summers in a row his brother and he were sent to his paternal grandparent's farm. The whole family was going through the depression and his grandparents needed all the help they could get on the farm for chores.

His Aunt Mary was about twenty-five, still single and ran the whole show! As an example, there were twenty-two families on the party line and she would run for every ring, even if it was not hers. (for Lent, she would only answer her ring.) Frequently the wolves would howl at night, Jacob's Aunt Mary would go out on the back porch and scream, "Shut up!" He was amazed at how many times they did!

This reverie was broken by the chiming of the clock on the wall. Their world had become lonely since she left this place; a place where we all come together to find comfort. An imaginary place called Freedom, brings us characters solace and a chance to relive parts of our lives forgotten. We characters decide life was difficult during formative years. Freedom place allows us a second chance to make it better if we choose.

Some choose senior life. What would they restructure to accomplish that? Living in a place like Freedom, reminds me of a town near Disneyworld, Celebration, where people decide they will be in Paradise for the rest of their lives. We don't hear much about their community, I wonder why. Bob continued to muse as he put his arm around his nephew Jacob. Both men picked up their whittling where they had left it before the argument.

Jacob's eyes wandered far away. He was again remembering Mary. They were in New York. She called it an "odd object." It became a prized possession. Mary had not expected this antique gift, but she guessed the elderly Mrs. Jacobson could afford it. She and her son were just leaving Paris, the five star restaurant, when Mary was jogging by. Mrs. Jacobson tripped, and without giving a second thought Mary caught her just before the wealthy matron fell into the moving stream of traffic. Thanking Mary profusely while still holding her arm, Mrs. Jacobson insisted that she ride with her in the waiting limo to her condo. Then the driver would return her to any spot she requested. Once there, Mrs. Jacobson told Mary to pick out anything from the collection that she liked. Mary chose the smallest object she could find. That is how Mary became the proud owner of a tiny gold hummingbird finial for her bedside lamp. Jacob pictured dear Aunt Mary polishing and shining the hummingbird until it glowed warm in the sunny old bedroom. ©

Generation to Generation

by Beverly Lee Bixler

In 1991, after my father learned of his Jewish heritage, my mother said, sheepishly "I have something to give to you." She quickly went to the basement and went straight to a box that was hidden away with my grandmother's dishes.

She came running up the stairs with a sparkling glass bowl. I knew immediately the bowl was Jewish for it had a big Star of David in the middle, with a little Star of David hidden inside-just like our Jewish heritage...hidden. Encircled around the star are twelve small circles representing the twelve tribes of Israel. The scalloped edging adds to the beauty of the bowl.

I asked how the bowl had been used. My mother replied "It was used every day for it was our fruit bowl."

My next question was "Did anyone ever talk about the bowl?"

She said "No it was never discussed." (It is thought that the bowl is from the 1800's.)

This bowl had been passed from my mother Frances M. Holbert, from the hand of her mother Effie Polhemus from the hand of her mother Nora Dragoo and from the hand of my great-great grandmother Mary Frances Frasuer (Polish spelling) Fraizer (German spelling) whose Jewish heritage she tried to preserve. She left the bowl without a note but all who saw the bowl kept the secret.

The bowl represents to me the perseverance of the Jewish people and the strong desire to have tradition and heritage passed on from generation to generation. It represents to me the power of love of my great, great grandmother for her Jewish roots. She was able to instill in her family the value of family and the history of who we are. In spite of having to hide this knowledge (because the family lived in a small town (Parker, Indiana)about twelve miles from Middletown U.S.A. She must have had the assurance that her daughter Nora Frasuer (Frazier) Dragoo would protect the bowl and pass it onto the next generation. ©

Moonlight Sonata

by Sally Wu

We met at Pittsfield Senior Center for our weekly creative writing class. After we shared our stories from our last week's homework, 'Elle', our facilitator played music and asked to write whatever came into our minds. It was very beautiful music, Beethoven's Moonlight Sonata, one of my favorite pieces, so lively, sweet, delicate and delicious. As I listened, I drifted back to an autumn evening in Taiwan.

It was 1954, Ching, and old friend from China just got a teaching job offer from the Tah-Yuang middle school. He invited me to have dinner at his place to celebrate his new job and also the Mid-Autumn Festival. Tah –Yaung was in the county next to Taipei where I lived at that time. I invited my best friend, Betty to come with me, although it was not far to Chings. I had met Betty at freshman orientation and since then we had become very close friends, seeing each other all the time in the dormitory.

We took the train to Tah-Yuang and found his place. He lived in a small house surrounded by a nice garden with trees and flowers. He set a small table in his backyard and prepared special delicious dishes for us. There was even a bottle of red wine. We sat around the table enjoying the wine and food while the moon climbed slowly into the sky. Gradually the stars, one by one appeared around the full moon. We were talking about those memories, things that had happened in school back in China. I don't recall when we stopped conversing. We just sat there, listening to the music of the night, the chirping of the autumn insects, the whispering of the leaves as they danced in the gentle breeze under that full moon, the low voice of toads and the occasional lonely bark of a dog, far away. It seemed that we were surrounded by soft, sweet music. It was such a peaceful, lovely, and tranquil night. We all enjoyed it.

Suddenly, the music stopped. Then I realized that I was sitting in the writer's group meeting. The music, conversation and friendship of that beautiful mid-autumn full moon night in Taiwan faded away. ©

Today's Culture
Carole Hendreckson

Our writing group was given nine topics to choose from for a writing project. The nine were: T-shirts, vanity plates, bumper stickers, tattoos, billboards, commercials, identity theft, web sites, the internet and rap. All seemed to speak to my lack of creativity or at least, my lack of appreciation for creative expression in today's culture. Not one spoke to my knowledge base or life experience. I am so very simple, practical and unworldly.

This TV prompted and youthful culture just leaves me, well, out of it. So I chose to write a snippet about each topic.

T-shirts make sense on some levels. They can be inexpensive and easy care. They can also be very elaborate, colorful and fun. I occasionally buy them for my husband or kids. There is only one I really want. It says in bold letters, "You don't know me," and the fine print says, "Federal

Witness Protection Program." But T-shirts are everywhere; it makes one wonder if they breed like rabbits.

As for **vanity plates** and bumper stickers they are expensive, plentiful, often offensive, and frequently tiresome. I might add; I have enough trouble reading street signs and seeing traffic lights. So please, don't distract me, it may be at your peril.

Tattoos- Why? I was plagued with acne so why would I choose more holes put in my body? Tattoos seek attention, just like pimples. Besides, being a nurse, I focus on the health risks. Also, I have not seen many tattoos that age well. For heavens sake! I haven't even had my ears pierced!

Billboards and **commercials** are often clever expressions of creativity, even art. But they are so…commercial! Let's enjoy the scenery and nature's beauty without a billboard block-out.

Commercials are seldom welcome; they are more often interruptions. There was that poster in Utah for Polygamy Beer that said, "You'll want more than one." That made me chuckle.

Today there are multiple news articles about **identity** theft. It can be devastating and certainly is on the increase. Nothing funny about that, except, if a person really had to accept my total identity it would be poetic justice.

If I were computer literate, I could write volumes on **web sites** or the **Internet**. Unfortunately that is not the case. Occasionally however, when my husband, George, says I couldn't possibly find a web site. I am overwhelmed by the challenge. I have proven him wrong. There is no doubt, that if one makes technology a friend it is a wonderful tool.

The last topic, **rap** makes me think of baggy pants, and they bring out the devil in me. Secretly when passing a young man, practically hobbled by drooping pants, I'm tempted to give a quick tug and then very innocently walk on. Back to rap – I suppose it is all right if done well and doesn't include my least favorite four letter words.

You can tell I am not in tune with the world but stuck like an old gramophone needle. I am an aged alien in this culture of youth and I am limited in the ways of creative expression. These topics seldom add to my life's enjoyment. But, would you like to hear about the great book I am reading? ©

Glen Miller's Big Band Sound
by Joanne Savas

Bodies swing and sway to the bands sound. The musicians play as if it were their last performance. The dancers find their way to the best way to show their appreciation of the bands talented efforts and personal pride in performing. There is no end to the energy and positive vibes of all who witness this phenomenal starry night. Dancers cling to each other unsure of when they will see each other again. Laughter and love mask the real feelings of fear and sadness that no one present wishes to reveal. It is an unreal experience in a very real tragic time of war, but tonight the mood is magical and tomorrow is far away.

A Childhood Dream

by Sally Wu
(condensed and edited by 'Elle')

My name is Szu-I Wu. It is so very difficult to pronounce in English that I use the nick-name 'Sally." As a child, I dreamed of becoming a writer. Sometimes I sat by the window looking out to see the bats flying in the summer evening sky or walked the footpath between the rice paddies watching the tadpoles swimming in the water. Words and sentences, like water in a downhill stream rushed into my mind then onto the paper that carried me away into another world.

Gradually, I grew up drifting away living another dream. Now I am retired, I found my old dream of writing coming true. I have lived and had experiences and adventures that need sharing with my children and their children. Although the situation is different, writing them in English, my second language, it is challenging, I welcome it. So with encouragement from the Creative Writers Group, slowly I start to tell these stories. I am fulfilling my childhood dream at last! ©

(When Sally's bio came in I could not help but extract these beautiful thoughts for a last minute addition to our works! 'Elle')

Draw a circle, not a heart,
around the one you love
because a heart can break,
but a circle goes on forever."
Unknown

Z-Z-Z-Z-Z-Z-Z

by Janis Schuon

If I could sleep for some time
I'm sure I would feel just fine.
But my brain's in a fog;
Full of fuzz balls and bog--
Oh, why can't I just go to sleep?
I tried the trick of counting sheep

Thinking that would put me to sleep.
But no matter the number
There still is no slumber,
Oh, why can't I just go to sleep?
I'm done writing rhymes about sleep.
I'm done picturing white leaping sheep.
I'll pick up a broom
Go straight to my room
And sweep and sweep and sweep!! ©

THE WIND IS CURLY

by G. OTTO FANGER

The wind is curly this time of year,
It blows with a gentle ripple, or…
With the fury of an Alberta Clipper. (tumult)
It meanders among shivering boughs,
Of arborary silhouettes,
Sometimes distributing
Albino flakes, as it passes.
Another task…for the curly wind.

It tosses rainbow leaves in whirlpool gusts,
Dancing them into irregular gatherings.
Its path is marked by quivering squirrel tails,
Busily burying their winter food.

Overhead aerial acrobats
Flutter in its wake, magically
Modifying their ethereal routes, (undulating)
Buffeted by the stuttering velocity
Of the curly wind.

Bristling wooly worms curl, and plummet
Onto the grassy terrain to "ride out"
The persistent invisible turbulence,
Doing its own thing,
On a chilly pre-winter day
A task for the curly wind.

Soon a more piercing curly wind,
Will stir the fragile leafless branches,
Scattering powdery bark chips,
Above the restless debris,
Now covered with a cold crystal carpet.
Blow with gusto curly wind,
your time to rule! ©

The River

by Pat Spriggel

I am no longer flesh and bone
but spirit,
as I step into a fast-running river.
I am one with the surface of the water,
reaching across the width,
feeling the bobbing of each ripple
circling out further and further
until I mesh with the grassy bank.
I am being massaged through the bubbling and tingling
of small waves,
rushing over logs and stones,
being one with the texture of water
and the rhythm of the fish
swimming alongside.
I hear the silence
as I pass in the shadows of birds and branches.
I smell the mosses and mud
as a river perfume.
Stepping out
I recognize that this bit of osmosis
transforms my world
into what is truly beautiful.
Thank you, River. ©

*"A river seems a magic thing. A magic moving
living part of the earth itself."*

Laura Gilpin

You Can't Have It All

by Joanne Savas

You **can** have the touch of a single finger on
your cheek waking you at 7 a m to say,
"Come to breakfast."

You **can** have the soulful look of your
parents that tells you, if we could we would
take your every sorrow away.

And when it is May you will have Love and
so abundantly that it carries you to the next
wonderful year.

You **can** have happiness though sometimes
it can be mysterious like the white foam that
bubbles up on the chili pot when your father
adds red kidney beans.

You **can** have the fig trees in Greece with
the fat green leaves like gloved clown
hands; the smell of lamb with lemon sauce
and rosemary.

You **can** have a foreign language that can
mean something like a Sunrise ready to
burst!

You **can** visit grandmother's grave marker
where your mother wept openly.

We can't bring back our loved ones but we
can have the words '*forgive*' and '*forget*'
hold hands as if they mean to spend a
lifetime together.

You **can** have GiagGia sitting in
the rocker next to your bed
At least for a little while.

You can be grateful for the rain, the way it kisses your soft doll-like face, the sweet smelling towels sucking up the drops on your beautiful skin.

The treats we give you when everyone else is fast asleep.

You can have the many notes of Mozart racing one another to the melody of Life!

And when adulthood fails you, you can summon the memory of your childhood, the ducks swimming on Quarton Pond.

Then my dear child there is the voice that will always whisper, but you can't have it all. ©

Best Advice

by Thomas Torango

The best advice I ever received was to live within your means and don't borrow money unnecessarily. If you must borrow money, pay it back promptly. This advice was given to me by my father. He led by example.

I am the namesake of my father called Thomas
Who exhorted me to make him a promise
Please pay off your debts
And don't place any bets
Then life won't push you over the precipice. ©

The Darker Side of Spriggel

Along side the road
Dead deer
Dead skunk
Dead groundhog
Dead possum
Dead sparrow
Dead turtle
Dead dog
Sprinkle sweet grass
Say a prayer
Respect life
Accept death
I only hope
Someone will do the same…For me. ©

Family Tree
by Beverly Lee Bixler

I think that I shall never see
Such beauty as a family tree
The branches of two hundred and eighty five years
Spread out across the U.S.A.

Poems are made by people like me
But only Elohaynu creates a family tree

The tree was transplanted from
Outside Munich Germany

Out of Europe they came in 1723
And before
Just to enter at Philadelphia's door

This is how the story began for Great Grandpa
He had a letter dated 1909 stating
Manchester, Maryland, is where the family settled in

Great Grandpa attended a co-educational school
Called the "Old Academy" near the Old Methodist
Church grounds in Manchester, Maryland

At the age of 22 on March 29, 1855 he took
Melvina Egoffstein for his wife and soon
They began their family

The last daughter died as an infant with
Gravestone I.K.B. (Ida) buried now with
Great Great Grandpa Fredrick Bixler in Manchester, MD

Great Grandpa John Bixler with Elvina S.A.
Her name in the West
Traveled with their eight children and settled in
Indianapolis around 1874 and established a
Rope factory on Sixth Avenue

The Industrial Revolution came along and ropes
Were replaced so it was time to move again.

Great Grandpa moved the family to the farm near
Fortville, Indiana, where ducks, geese, and cows
Kept the family fed

I think that I should never understand how we Jews
Found each other in this new land

Yet Papa's family on both sides and Mama's
Families too
Came together in one accord to find their unique place

Synagogues were not on the route
No inns to take them in
Yet Elohaynu's holy light brought them
Near to "Middletown, USA"

Living in little towns, scattered from farm to farm
These faithful ones raised their kin
Now through two hundred and eighty-five years of growth the tree is
Solidly planted with new rays of hope and
Visions for tomorrow

Give Praise and Thanksgiving to our Gd. ©

~Eulogy~
"AND ALL THAT MIGHTY HEART LIES STILL"

by Walter Palesch

In keeping with his wishes'
Papa's remains were borne aloft today.
On gentle wisps of smoke
To the high, towering cirrus.

The trade winds now carry his ashes
To the far corners of our world.
Even to the place of his birth.
He is now part of the sunrise.
Part of the sunset.

Author's note:
Dad died of heart failure, after saving Mother's life. She had gone out after the blizzard to shovel snow on the steep, icy driveway. How many times I told her not to do that! She fell and could not get up. Dad was inside, sensed something was wrong, and went out with his cane. He went to help her up, risked his life, and pulled her to safety. Back inside, he sat down and died from the enormous exertion and the fear he almost lost his best friend. His heart stopped five minutes later. He had traded his life for hers, I wrote this eulogy two days later, late at night. He was cremated. ©

On January 27, 1992, Anno Domini.

PAPA!

by Walter Palesch

Papa! You were always so stubborn!
We told you about your 82nd Birthday party.
Just two weeks to go.....and you could not wait?
As you can see, we're giving you a party anyway.
But the party favors are now useless.
So I talked to your buddy Lou.
"Eighty two years. That's all?" Then he adds:
"With your mother's cooking and his easy schedule, that's no big deal."
So you see, Dad. You can't please some people, even in death.

I am laughing because I have not yet let you go.
Soon it will hit me.
I will stop reminiscing,
And face that you are gone.
And curse the days I did not honor you.

How dare you leave me like this,
After all we've been through.
I have tried my damnest to ignore your advice.
All these years.
And now I'm supposed to be the eldest?
Head of our clan?
How am I gonna do that?

And another thing,
With you around I felt protected.
Now death breeched my first line of defense.
Which means I move to the front row.
And all that scares me something awful.

So four hours later I'm standing here to talk to you,
Our family and friends.
Tell you things befitting this occasion.
What will I say?

Hey Dad! We're refugees, Immigrants.
You and me, Dad.
And Sis and Mom.
Freedom fighters and survivors
As kids we played with tanks and trucks.
Full size trucks and armed halftracks.
The T34 and T70 Soviet tanks
Almost got blown away.
But we took care of each other, like a clan.
Anybody can have a family.
We have a clan!

What a story!
Your life I mean.
Pieces out of "Fiddler on the Roof" and "The Sound of Music."
But the hills were alive with the sound of howitzers, not music.
And Austria rejected us, gave us no safe haven.
How that changed everything.

P.S. The lotto numbers you picked on your last day lost.
With that went a story that would have made every paper in the world.
Can you see it? Dead man wins seventy nine million dollars!
Read all about it.

You were born on the eve
of World War I,
The war to end all wars.
A rifle shot from its epicenter.
Ground zero of hell!
In the idyllic village of Gaidel.
For those of you who are not familiar,
This Germanic area in Czechoslovakia was settled in the twelfth century.
So what were we? Germans? Czechs? Who?
This area was the bartered bride in geo-politics,
And a stone's throw from either Vienna or Prague,
Two of the most elegant cities in the world.
Cradled between the Danube and the Tatra Mountains.
I was too young to remember the place.
You said it was beautiful.

You and Mom had it all.
But history would not wait.
You were barely married
And the World exploded again,
Not twenty years after the War to end all wars!
World War II trampled your friends and homeland,
And you were at ground zero once again.

You could never go back until just now
And just now you can't again.

I was almost eight the first time I saw you.
That I can remember I mean.
Why?
Soviet Prison Camp Tula
Prisoner of war.
Charged with: Saboteur, Specialist in explosives and demolition
Your mission: Destroy strategic targets to slow down fast moving Soviet
Divisions at the collapsing Eastern Front. They roll with scorched earth
orders to secure the farthest possible Western Front. The Iron Curtain
is destined to go up where those troops stand at the hour marking the
Armistice.
That means your homeland is swallowed up.
In your own words:
Humanity has rendered all visions of Hell redundant and irrelevant.
Replaced them with vastly depraved versions here on earth.
Visions beyond the reach of even lunatics' nightmares,
Images to drive madmen sane.
You sealed up those memories like an oyster does,
When it takes that sliver of stone
And builds around that pain a pearl.
A glistening, shimmering, beautiful thing.
You failed to save your homeland, Dad. But note this:
That iron curtain fell before you did.
It was made of steel and stone.
But not nearly eighty two years old.

When I was a kid, maybe twelve, I tagged along with Dad.
He worked at a granite quarry to cut up a stone.
A boulder 60 feet by 20 feet tall.

It was to be cut into foot thick slabs.
He measured and examined this enormous gem.
Looked at the veins.
Had hundreds of holes drilled.
Set the explosives,
Routed fuses every which way.

As we watched from a distance, the earth erupted
Fragments of stone were raining down a kilometer away
As that mountainous boulder shattered into smaller sections of stone.
Like slices from a loaf of bread. Neat and fairly smooth.
To be cut into markers,
Grave stones to mourn that area's share of seventy million dead.
And then I understood: Specialist, Explosives. My Dad.
Head of our clan.

Wrote Shakespeare, if I remember correctly:
"Out,out brief candle, life's but a shadow.
A poor player who struts and frets his hour upon the stage,
And then is heard no more.
It is a tale told by an Idiot, full of sound and fury
Signifying nothing."

How easily you might have succumbed to these words.
So many,
Countless many,
Did.

But you did not.
You made a pearl instead.
And because I did not ask you how you did that,
I have never fully understood you.
And that finally is what makes me sad.
I did not learn to do pearls.
So gimme a nudge now and then.
We gotta work out some signals.
It ain't easy being an elder, head of a clan.
"It's not easy being green". At anything.
Even at grieving.
So Dad, for your gift of unending wonder,

About the works of man and God alike,
You will live in your children's, children's children,
"To the last syllable of recorded time.
This marker is dedicated to makers of pearls,
Be they oysters or children of God.
See that wisp of smoke, that flickering light? Where?
"Straight on 'til morning, second star to the right."

Contributors: William Shakespeare, John Milton, Kermit, the Frog, and Peter Pan ©

M' Lady

Janis Schuon

I think of her now with her thick ankled narrow feet
seemingly impossible to support the stalks of heavy limbs
above.

There's a shrillness to her voice with over-tones punctuated
with superiority.

Small grey eyes squint with displeasure and disapproval.

When was it she decided she was regal;
deserving an extra slice of white cake?

Each mouthful calms and soothes until it is finished
and her attention is diverted to the next self-declared crisis.

The exhilaration quickens her breath.

Nostrils flare and the sensual urge begins again. The familiar
sweetness
on the tongue is intoxicating, disguising its addiction with
pleasure until there is no distinction between the queen and the slave.©

Three Free Verse

by Pat Spriggel

Trees exhale
Water breathes
Air surrounds the living and the dead.

The dead are not gone,
only transformed.
Death and life is a circle
* * * * *

There are vulture shadows
on the walls
of my room
I move slightly
so the vulture knows I'm not dead.

I don't see the vultures so clearly
that are eating my inward parts.
I only know
they are having a feast.

*

Losing consciousness
seems like a good idea
when life is blank ©

Open Windows

by Elle

Windows open
Curtains billow outside
That giant living inside
Has just exhaled.
He inhales,
Sucking them back in again. ©

Affirmation

by Joanne Savas

I'm safe.
I'm intelligent.
I'm caring.
I'm strong.
I'm capable.
I'm calm.
I'm loving.
I can handle this day forward, whatever it may bring,
Because I'm ME! ©

I was, am, and will be invisible.
Worth is worthless.
Hope is stagnant.
Love is hidden.

Surely the strength of the Loving Spirit
will care
will lift
will spring the dead to life.
Or not.

All I know is
I still don't see
My ship coming in.

Pat Spriggel -Simplifies

The Secret of Life!

At a reunion,
my uncle was asked what was the secret
to a long life.
He was 90.

Breath circulates then stops.
Blood circulates then stops
It's so simple
Breathe in and out

Until dust returns to dust. ©

When You Recognize Me No More

To my grandma by Yueh Tsau (14 years old, eighth grade)
Translated by Sally Wu

Once
It was your strong and powerful hands
That guided me taking my first step into the world.

Once,
It was your assuring smile
That gave me the motivation
To stride with confidence toward success in my life.

Once,
Your kind and loving heart had forgiven
My arrogant and rebellious attitude.

Once again,
Your sweet loving face that had deeply imprinted in my mind,
Will never, never fade away.

Life is so unpredictable and hard to grasp.
That day, I looked at you and asked softly,
Who am I?
You looked at me silently.
"I just could not remember."

That moment, my heart was broken
into thousand pieces.
Tears were flowing down my cheeks.
I cried.
But what was the use?
I cried.

I knew I could not blame you.
It was the disease.
But why did it destroy the sweet,
Sweet memory that once I had?

When you remember me no more,
When you recognize the surroundings no more,
Everything is lost in a blurring dream.
No memory, no relationship
Only an immensely hollow mind, And a fragile life. ©

Butterflies and Me

by Janis Schuon

I wonder about butterflies fluttering around,
Soaring and swirling where flowers abound.
Did they dream as a small fuzzy worm
Of leaving the tight dark space where they squirmed?
Did they imagine their new life carefree?
How one day their only worry would be
How high and how far to fly for their fun
Or where to alight as they glide toward the sun?
I think I began as something less
Than I had dreamed, I must confess.
Fighting and wiggling my way to be free;
Wanting the light to shine on me.
Crawling and crying why are things so?
I don't know where but I know I must go
Where butterflies dance and spread gossamer wings
Yawning and dreaming long before spring.

I dream of a place far, far from here;
Away from the drone of sadness and fear.
I dream of a time when rain will be sweet
Like a lily's deep nectar in mid-summer's heat.
I would stay in that place for a very long time;
Watching clouds, naming which ones are mine.
I would give each blossom a caress and a kiss.
I think these are the reasons butterflies exist.

If I were a butterfly and you should pass by
I would sing to you all the reasons why.
I have the wind as my sister, the moon as a friend
And though life is short, it doesn't really end.
Michelangelo painted these wings of mine;
My thirst is quenched by jasmine wine;
I feast on flowers flawless and sweet.
My life may be short
but my life is complete. ©

A Tribute for May 4, 1970

Kent State University, Kent, Ohio
by Pat Spriggel

Do you remember May 4?
Think back.
It was the other side of the '60's
when idealism was supposed to win.
When the Peace Corps was hard work
of soft young people
following Kennedy's challenge.

Do you remember May 4?
Think college students.
Young people
who didn't know how young they were.
They walked to and from classes
with books and weekly reminders
and skirting around the soldiers.
Do you remember May 4?
Think National Guard.
Young people
who didn't know how young they were.
They were under orders, under pressure,
Under old-guard officers.

Here a stone, there a yell,
the sound of feet scrambling
to classes,
to marching in line.
With covered faces and minds trained to obey,
Lethal bullets soared into buildings
seared into young people.

Do you remember May 4?
Today those young people are not so young,
and realize how young they were then.

Four were killed
never allowed to grow old.
victims all.
Do you want to forget May 4? ©

Winter View

Carole Hendrickson

You look out on tawny, barren trees
Clothed in their patchy snowy blanket
It is so cold silence hangs in the air
All is in retreat or repose
Waiting, waiting
A cardinal alights, it's color shedding a glow
Then you see a twig shiver in the stillness
Sensing buds, blossoms and springs sunrise
Sensing, sensing the promise ©

October

Elaine 'Elle' Cousino

October is…the surprise of early frost.
October is…stolen sun-drenched afternoons.
October is …eye widening magnificent crimson and gold maples
October is …showing your grandchildren
the old man who lives in the orange full moon.
October is…leaf- raking, then the first fire in the fireplace.
October is…pumpkins, bats, witches, black cats and ghost stories.
October is…time for reflecting golden days of summer. ©

Backwash

by Gene O. Fanger

A watery ditch, edging the fast road
Paper, cloth, metal and elastic
Backwash
A windy city, edging stone towers, sky-pointed
Gray shadows huddle, in oversize garments,
Beside raggedy - sacked possessions.
Backwash
An orange – jacketed crew,
Reach to gather the debris,
In tied black plastic, waiting,
To be trucked away,
To a dusty earthen grave
Backwash
A blue- silver badged cop
Surveys the gray shadows,
Solitaire hulks cower over air ducts,
On concrete ribbons, as the city sleeps.
Sometimes he calls for a white truck,
With swirling colored lights,
Using black – bags, zippered shut,
Trucked away to an earthen grave.
Backwash
What difference?
Between the two black bags
Both discards of a disposable society
Backwash? ©

Dreaming

by Beverly Lee Bixler

(Words written to the tune of White Christmas by Irving Berlin)
I 'm dreaming of a world in peace with everyone in one accord
Where the air is pure and rivers clean and lakes with fish galore
I'm dreaming of a nuclear free world just like the one we used to know
Where the children played and adults did too and listened to each
other's dreams.

I'm dreaming of a drug free world with every adult and child
Seeing life through the vision of hope and truth and not hidden in
disguises

I'm dreaming of a world in peace where old values are restored
Where Gd is first and hospitality is second and everyone's dignity is
secured

I'm dreaming of a world of peace with everyone in one accord.

Where human rights and justice are instruments of Gd's way of
providing
no more war

I'm dreaming of a world of peace that will take both you and me
to see ourselves in our foolish deeds, the bigotry and the long time
focus of "me." ©

TIME

by Janis Schuon

Untouchable
yet we feel its weight or its ghost
Unconquerable
yet we live as if command were our boast.

TIMES TWO

by Janis Schuon

Our past never really leaves us
but reappears on a distant day.
Time presents itself in another form,
another experience, or way. ©

Untitled

Family Memory
by Pat Spriggel

Father comes to Grandma's and Grandpa's house
where we three children were staying overnight.

I run into my Father's arms, as a common greeting
for my being 4 1/2 years old.

Something cold came inside the house,
though it was June.

My Father's smile was gone in a flash
when he let me slip out of his arms.

He talked of something gone wrong,
he'd have to leave again.

Babies were thrown into corners of graveyard buildings,
Forgotten

He'd make sure that wouldn't happen,
it was the doctor's fault

A conversation between adults,
knowing that children wouldn't understand

As if children had no hearts or minds.

Grandma made Campbell's vegetable beef soup
for our supper that evening.

Years later, as an adult,
I learned that was the day my Mother
gave birth to a baby boy
who died within an hour.

I hate vegetable beef soup. ©

Sea Dream

by Elaine 'Elle' Cousino

Gossamer dreams of verdant seas
Flit in and out on delicate wings.
Astounded, I see myself mounted
on silver flying fish and scaly brown dragons.
I ride on the white foam of waves.
They break on the shore,
Pulling the caramel sand into the sea
Leaving only traces of footprints.
A simple reminder that I was once here!
Waves of green and snow
quickly wash away that detail
and I am gone.
©

~ *Book Excerpts* ~

"*If you can carry your childhood
with you, you never become older.*"
Abraham Sutzkwever

Refugee Children
by Walter Palesch

Notes from the Author – "This an excerpt from an upcoming non-fictional publication. You will note that I write in truncated sentences and fragments. I have asked my work to remain unedited because my feeling is that to use proper grammar would destroy my story. Improper events require jolting, twisted and improper grammar. It is my 'train of thought' style."

Chapter 2

February 1944: It is bitter cold, as if the elements were punishing all who have wrought this war. We are refugees from German settlements in Czechoslovakia. Our forebears settled in this beautiful, hilly area in the thirteenth century. Vienna and Prague, two of the most elegant cities in Europe were only 90 miles distant from our village Gaidel. Hitler naturally demanded that this Germanic area be rightfully reunited with the Vaterland. Britain's Chamberlain ceded this Sudetenland to him, in the hope that this would satiate Hitler's ravenous appetite for "Lebensraum", or living space. That was like giving in to a bully to shut him up, and make him go away. Problem is, bullies always come back and this was a bully of unmatched capacity for terror. His actions resulted in deadly consequences for many of our folk.

Escaping from the onslaught of motorized Russian Divisions from the East, we were herded into freight trains, mostly cattle cars. Heading north. In the confusion created by constant Stuka dive bombers strafing the train, and Russian planes shooting at us, we ended up in the wrong city. Both armies attacked what they thought to be troop and material carriers. We were Germans as far as the Russians were concerned, and to save our lives, we all had to flee. We were now in a small village near Hohenerxleben, East Germany. The terms of the armistice dictated that this place was now in Soviet occupied Germany. This land would end up behind the Iron Curtain. Millions had already escaped, but more millions would spend their lives here, never knowing or seeing the outside world. Many died trying to escape. They tended to be young people and children.

These are my memories, and those of people I interviewed. Mostly they are about children, and a few about adults. This is a tale of unimaginable terror and pain, but also about courage, survival, hope, triumph, and escape to freedom. These stories were encapsulated in the hearts and minds of young children. I have tried to recover some of them. So after a half century, I will awaken some of those memories. Bring them up from that long locked up, cobwebbed sub-basement of our souls. That is very painful, because we have to relive those memories in complete detail.

Ancient tree branches creaked and moaned in the courtyard below our window, under a heavy new blanket of snow. Nighttime temperatures dipped to 30 F below zero. Daytime temperatures barely reached 10 above. The season was as grim and punishing as the aftermath of the war. Mother had to constantly yell at sister and me to stay inside, which is hard to accept when you're young kids. I mean our whole refugee apartment was 5 by 12 meters small. How do you play hide and go seek or cowboys and Indians in that space? You could hurt yourself!

Among the 121 refugees from our home village of Gaidel, there were two fathers who had suffered war injuries, and no "men" over 14 years old. Those were being taught to kill and maim for the Wehrmacht or the Russians in this lunatic war. In fact they were only cannon fodder! The rumor was that both Germans and Soviets were forcing 13 year olds into battle, so heavy were the losses in the ranks. Those in our group were the two Fathers, mothers, children, the sickly, and grand parents. All the fathers and brothers 14 years old on up were already dead, dying, missing or prisoners of war. Our father was one of them. At this time we don't know which.

The war destroyed most sanitation and infrastructure. That brought typhoid, cholera, tuberculosis, yellow jaundice, unmanageable dysentery, and worse things that were not identified. There was only a modest little hospital with almost no equipment or medicines, dealing with its share of seventy million dead. This war produced maybe 12 Holocausts. A Holocaust is not only an atrocity where Germans kill Jews. Horrible and as unforgivable that is, there is a far more unfathomable, threatening, recurring characteristic built into the fabric of humanity. Look at the Russian Pogroms, Kosovo, Iraq, Sudan, and Somalia, and many more. Sex Slavery, illegal drug trafficking, and immigrant trafficking-the horrors of man's inhumanity to man appears to be a basic human condition. Holocausts are a genetic aberration in man's DNA, a regressive gene that rears up with some regularity. Only way to explain it. Maybe research will conquer it some day. Please convince yourself of this mutant gene by reading back a few hundred years. There is in fact a Super Holocaust gene that nobody ever identifies. Historically, humanity has violently taken the lives of hundreds of millions. Now we have some perspective! How would you fix that problem? With a monument? How many war monuments have prevented the next war? With a museum? By endlessly showing refugee and war movies? Come again! Could we generalize a little here?

Several of our young friends died. Helmut of Cholera, Christian eventually of Tuberculosis, Seppl and Bernd of unidentified causes. Mom forbade us to visit anyone of our friends if they were even mildly feverish. There was no daytime supervision, as the mothers were all working in the fields for food. That command was impossible for 7-15 year olds to obey. The 2 grandmothers that were to watch over us were a joke. They couldn't possibly keep up with us kids. We easily fooled them into believing we were only up to good.

Even more pressing, as I said-there was very little food. The farm animals either died or were shot either by retreating or invading armies. They were left to rot in place, because high-powered shells, mines or bombs killed them. What was left was neither recognizable nor useable. Looking back I can say that much of the countryside, especially the Dresden perimeter, looked like Hiroshima without radioactivity. Devastation was total. The Allied air attacks were purely and purposely against civilians, here and in several other cities. The combined armed forces of Russia, Great Britain, America, Canada, Australia, and others fought 5 years against a nation the size of Montana! With that unholy Allied might, we either had too little skill, technology, effectiveness, will or military strategic where with all, that bombing civilians was necessary! Recall our national outrage when it was trumpeted that Sadam had killed 5000 civilians.

Alternatively the Allies are binned by some as bestial creatures. You decide The only thing that saved major controversy over the bombing was that everybody wanted to end the war, go home, buy a new car and refrigerator and make babies. Hence the baby boom.

Thousands of British and U.S. bombers dropped tens of thousands tons of bombs. The asphalt streets caught on fire. People fled their burning buildings and ran of course, into the streets. The pavement melted 10 inches deep and ignited at hundreds of degrees. Their charred skeletons were imbedded in the road like gnats stuck to burning flypaper. The firestorm fed on itself and superheated the air. The city burned for several days. Anyone needing to breathe will die of charred lungs, and then be cremated. Sometime later came Tokyo and Nagasaki. Probably 200 thousand civilians died in these bombings. How did those civilian deaths diminish the military capability of Germany or Japan? It was crystal clear that Hitler would fight to the end, independent of any civilian death counts. It took no advanced level intelligence to see that. My friend Mark sums up the atomic bombings. "We developed the atomic bomb at the expense of billions. Truman was gonna use it, by God. After all, we paid for the damn thing. It will save many American lives, was the mantra. How many? Politically, it made a statement to Russia of just who was top dog now. Irony is, Japan was at the verge of capitulating, and Russia got its own nukes a short time later." I can't argue that one with Mark, but it is interesting. All of this is not a bright beacon from the alabaster cities on the hill. Human tears surely should dim them. And certainly God did not shed his grace on any of that. In Japan, mutations in newborn children and future damage to adults were part of many years of tragedy.

Hunger was ever present. It was a monotonous drone that permeated all thoughts. It robbed us of energy and joy. You would vividly dream about food. I would wake up and look in the little dresser next to my bed, where I remember placing that jelly sandwich-in my dream. Picture a six year old girl, undernourished, hollow eyed, unable to speak at all because of the terrors she has seen, in deep depression. I believe none of us have enough tears to deal with that.

Mom worked in the fields all day for two eggs, half a loaf of bread, and a half-liter of milk. This for four people-Gram, Lili my baby sister, me and Mom. After the harvests, and only then, we were allowed to glean what we could by digging out onions, beets, radishes, and potatoes. There wasn't much left. We used a short stubby knife to dig in the soil that was beginning to freeze in the early onset of winter. Bernd nearly cut his thumb off by hurrying too much. His glasses were lost some time ago, and he got hurt a lot because he tripped and fell. The only people who ate well were farmers whose property was spared damage. To them we were DP's, or displaced persons. We were seen as a drain on Germany's economy, as third class citizens. All that after leaving every last possession behind to a damn war caused by these same damn Germans. We still carry a noticeable amount of hatred for these "Holier than thou Krauts." First they annex our homeland, making us targets for the Soviets, then they treat us like crap.

Because of the lack of protein and other foods, some of us grew up to be smaller than our parents, and suffered diet deficiency problems. This whole diet issue left us open to diseases, which a healthier child might have resisted. So our food pyramid had one tier-scraps! These were our formative years, the crucible within which our personalities and character were molded. Where our little bodies developed. Where 10 whole years of our childhood were stolen, never to be returned. And where nightmares were born to last a lifetime.

A thin dusting of snow falls on Hohenerxleben. Each flake reflects the full moon, shimmering like a sea of diamonds. It happens only when snow falls in perfect calm, so as not to break the crystal structure of each flake. An occasional sliver of high cirrus clouds hurry across the moon, momentarily slicing the disk into pieces. It is eerily silent, as it always is after new snow has fallen. Across the road, large fields stretch in every direction, frozen solid. No more digging out scraps. Occasionally the ghostly shadow of a tree attests to the brightness of a full moon. In another place and time, this would have been beautiful, but here it is not. Here there is only unrelenting and unimaginable tragedy. Our nights will forever be filled with unexplained noises, visions of horror and fitful sleep. Some children will wet their beds, some will be afraid of everything. Others will have learning and concentration issues or become painfully shy. Various neuroses will spring up, along with rashes and sleeplessness. One boy named Mirko began to cut and hurt himself. How many Psychiatrists do you think were available to refugees then? Saddest were the horrible nightmares, the mechanism by which the mind somehow tries to sort things out. To hear a seven-year-old scream in his dream, jump out of bed and race mindlessly around in the dark, beating himself is really hell.

The walls are paper thin, so everything that happens is community property. Children cannot possibly deal with this world. In this story about child refugees there is not a single solitary shred of normal life, a life that should be filled with joys and discoveries. With comforts and nurturing. With a father and mother and happy children's stories; with toys, outings, and presents. Here there is no Christmas, no Easter, no birthday cake or laughter. We are trapped in a strange and dangerous land. We are not welcome here. We are poor in ways you cannot imagine. We came from a middle class home. We had a farm, a store, animals, and a good life. Today we own a small wagon, a featherbed, two blankets, two sets of clothes, and two pillows. What we ate, when or how, what we did and saw, how we played, all that was abnormal. How we managed to sleep while children and mothers wept well into the night is beyond me. Add to that the ugly habit of lamentation, practiced by the oldest Grandmothers. They would lament and wail their troubles in a continuous cadence, while rocking back and forth in the chair, for maybe two hours. We were tempted to poison these cantors, or is it cantresses? They now reached a point in their lives where they had control over absolutely nothing, had absolutely nothing, hence the lament. It is a spin off of those Eastern European funerals, where the older women wailed endlessly. Depressing. We kids thought they were possessed, and stayed clear of them. As I said nothing, but nothing was normal.

We will repress much of what we've experienced. That is a survival mechanism to retain sanity. In some derivative form we will carry the echoes of these events to our deathbed. So some of us will live a lifetime without discussing the events that forged us into adults. But in the winter of my years I discover that, much like the Oyster, I had encapsulated that pain with a sort of pearl. We have benefited from our experiences. We have triumphed over huge odds. We have become survivors, in a baptism by fire.

I have been a refugee all my life—always seeking the next refuge, the next sheltered port. Perhaps that fate befalls many of us, in different ways. As an adult you cannot possibly comprehend what happens to children in war. That is conceptually impossible, and even if somehow you could feel their hurts, the pain would damage you irreversibly and you would never see war or violence the same way again. So let us now tell the story of some of those children. My sister, Anton and I are the only survivors of a group of 15 children who came from that village, who shared some of that journey. The rest are dead by age 12, in one case 30. They never made it to freedom.

A thick layer of frost covers the window. The pot bellied stove is unable to raise the temperature much above 50. We have no real logs, just branches that have fallen from trees. They are mostly rotted and provide little heat. Gleaning has become an important supplement to our diet in years to come. Refugees don't own land, so they have to glean.

Temporary housing for refugees like us was cheap and poorly built. Mostly cinderblock walls with wooden plank floors. There were only a wood stove, two beds, no electricity, no water, and a communal bathroom down the hall. There was a cistern in the courtyard for water.

At the end of WWII, the flame of civilization in Europe had flickered and all but gone out. The massive damage to infrastructure was so total that without outside help that flame could not have rekindled itself. America, the victor, did something that no conquering nation had done since the Roman Legions marched across this continent. America rebuilt or helped to rebuild the European nations shattered by war. There were many compelling reasons for this beyond the humanitarian. I will cover this later in the book. We were praying for the Amis to win, explained the adults, because all other alternatives were unimaginably abhorrent. We were outside that American protectorate. That place was West Germany. We were now in East Germany at the end of WWII, cut off from the rest of the world by an Iron Curtain. It was actually barbed wire fencing, secured by minefields, machine gun towers and patrolled by guards with dogs. All that to keep people from escaping! Imagine a country where you could never escape or travel. The only good news is, the "Bear" sometimes forgot where the mines are, especially when tanked on vodka and taking a shortcut across a minefield. Contrary to belief, Yuri Gagarin was not the first Russian in orbit.

I sat up in my bed, next to my four year old little sister. She would grow up to be a really beautiful person, in every way. She is truly too young to react, except for sympathetically responding to the adults' body languages and cues. She saved my life twice as I did hers. On the next room, Mother and Grandmother were sleeping in the other bed. Pressing my thumb against the glass, I could, for an instant, melt the thin icy layer and look down the street for maybe 5 seconds, until my breath froze the thumbprint over in those iridescent fans of crystals. It might have been midnight. I could actually read by full moon. I have always liked to stay up late, and got a lot of lectures on that habit.

Magnificent Linden Trees once stood along the Boulevard. They were planted a century or two ago in a more civilized time, a time unrecognizably different from now. Measuring 3 feet in diameter, they lined the broad street with elegant grace. Their foliage was so dense that you could sit under them for 15 minutes in the rain before you started to get wet. A giant umbrella! They came in handy to wait out a rain without having to go home. These trees had witnessed enormous slices of European history, looked on as the nation states defined themselves, as the Enlightenment produced many of the intellectual and scientific achievements of western civilization. They were timeless reminders of nature's beauty, with a permanence not granted to humans. Now they looked like exploded and shredded stumps. Soviet tanks used them for cannon target practice. The armor piercing rounds would explode in the tree with unbelievable force The instant steam pressure from the vaporized sap would shatter that magnificent centurion into mere shards.

There it was again-Fritz barked that cross between a yelp and whine that meant trouble. It also meant he was tied up and couldn't protect us. He was a mixture of Shepherd and some more elegant breed, the product of a one night stand. We thought that maybe mama was a Greyhound. He was not at all pretty. His fur managed to always look like shag carpet from a 1969 Hippy Volkswagen Microbus. His legs however were really long. That made him one fast pup. Nothing outran this one. The Russkies twice shot at him, but our Fritzl lost them. We did cure him of chasing Soviet trucks, which I won't tell you about. Fritz barked only if he sensed real danger. He was really smart, not like those yappy dogs that bark at everything and are afraid of everything. But best of all, he was our buddy. He was one of us. He was always with us, keeping an eye out for us. Then the slam of a distant truck door. I turned in time to see mother rushing towards us in the dark. She had painted her front teeth and tongue black. Put gray soot on her face. Rapes by drunken Soviets were not uncommon, because these boys were a long way from home, and she was a pretty lady. Her face scared us to near incontinence! She hissed" Quick hide under the bed"- the only place out of view. She tells us to not make a peep, no matter what. We stopped breathing until almost passed out. Grandmother came trundling behind. She was out of it most of the time. Had reached her elastic limit. At this point, she had lost her son, nephew, dozens of friends, her homeland and all possessions. She was about to lose the only valuable possession left, her mind. By age 60! She was in a permanent state of deep depression. We cowered by moonlight in our second floor Room. We had heard these sounds before.

Closer and closer came the truck sounds. We knew it was a Soviet Army truck, the kind we saw every day driving up and down the street, sometimes with a mission but mostly to impress the civilian population of their place in this brave new world. The Russians had a lot of army gear left all of it in bad repair. The driver ripped up the gears and cooked the clutch. He and his companion were running on pure 100 proof vodka. The truck ran on Diesel. The truck stopped and we stopped breathing. Grandmother whispers "Heilige Maria und Josef". The truck tires break through the icy snow. The ice over the frozen puddles splinters as if made of glass, sounding just like that. They stop directly below our second story window. We stop breathing.

Soviet soldiers wore size 14 boots, not because they had feet that big, but to allow a foot wrap of rabbit fur against the terrible cold. Some of these idiots used machine gun fire to get a rabbit. Then they were looking for the pieces in the next town. Frostbite was the typical winter signature of the Soviet soldiers. Even the 100 proof Vodka antifreeze could not protect their toes and fingers. As you know, alcohol actually restricts circulation. The Soviets now controlled an empire of 11 time zones, bridging from the Arctic Circle to Mongolia, from Central Europe to the Bering Strait. This massive landmass contained more than 100 separate lands and languages, several races, including Eskimo, Mongolian and European. To secure this empire of loose configurations, only insurmountable and even unassailable military force would do. They recruited the most threatening and fearsome soldiers to keep the civilian population in control. They were threatening because these fellows were not related to us, did not have any sympathies for the likes of us, and did not speak our language.

Almost falling out of the truck, the two well-tanked soldiers marched towards the door below our window. One looked to be sort of European, not all that scary. The other, a six foot 8 inch Mongolian whose face was totally covered with hair, except for eyes and mouth-- lifted his boot and sent the door into 3 chards, skittering across the floor, actually hitting the family huddled in the corner. There was momentary silence, the impact of the incomprehensible unfolding, and then the screams of mother, the twin 6 year olds. For any other child to hear this may result in a sympathetic response. Mother knew this and cupped her hands over our mouths, nearly asphyxiating us. She knew they would come up the stairs after us if we made any noise. We knew what was next- the soldiers pistol whipped the father, finally subdued him with their carbines and dragged him out to the truck. Mother and the twins hopelessly clung to father who was now unconscious. They kicked the mother and children off their father, leaving them lying in the snow, unable to comprehend what happened, and sobbing only silently now. Later we saw that several of their fingernails were ripped out, trying to save their father. This scene was repeated somewhere every week or so. Such were the tactics to keep the civilians from rebelling against authority

And such was the glue that held the mighty Soviet Empire together for decades. In the years leading to the end of WWII, millions of refugees left the Baltic, Russian, Balkan and Nordic states because they saw the Russian front coming across Europe. Many just did not make it out in time. That includes our little community. So we are now here, some 60 miles east of Berlin, part of that empire. Eventually there were revolts in Hungary, Poland, Czechoslovakia, and finally in the German Democratic Republic. By then we had escaped to the West. Our village was totally destroyed, and 1300 of 2000 had been killed.

Mother and Grandma flew down the stairs the instant the truck left, to help bring our neighbors inside. We tried to comfort them, but we all knew their father will never be seen again. Just like our Dad. He is gone too. Mom holds Mrs. Hausman. Oma (Grandma) dutifully stokes the oven until it put out some comforting warmth. Little Lili, now 5 held the twins' hands, as if she understood their need. They were shaking uncontrollably now, and Mom was worried about them going into shock. I recall the beds being moved together in front of the stove and everybody piled in under the featherbed, blankets and such.

Herr Hausman will be shipped to a forced labor camp in Siberia, to that Empire's far terminus of the Trans Siberian Railroad. This prison camp has no fences, no machine gun nests, only some armed guards. You were free to escape, the guards would even encourage it. They placed bets on how far a given escapee would get. If you tried, you faced 5000 miles of Siberian winter between here and civilization. You have no food, weapons, shelter or suitable clothing. The low temperatures reached to minus 70. Hence escape proof. Those that tried to escape were recovered by the guards a day later, frozen stiff. They took satanic delight in pounding the corpses into the ground and hanging a sign on them telling how many kilometers they were able to cover before collapsing, and keeping track of the number of attempts. Hausman's only escape is: Early Death.

One man I know, of the few who managed to escape from a different Concentration camp is our father. His story comes later. Somehow in his journey home he managed to mail a letter to the American Red Cross. We miraculously received it 14 months later. No one could figure out how that happened. The best guest is that he befriended another prisoner who managed to escape and got the letter to the Red Cross. Mother had placed it in a family bible. I found it while sorting through old books. An excerpt from that letter, written when he was convinced he would not see us ever again. It was part of his diary:

Tula Labor Camp, Russia.

I am now prisoner of the Soviets.
Because I am a specialist in explosives.
My mission: Destroy strategic targets.
To slow down fast moving Soviet Divisions,
At the collapsing Eastern Front.
They march with scorched earth orders
To secure the farthest western front.
Because a wall will be erected, you will see
Where those troops stand on the day of the Armistice.
That means our homeland is now swallowed up
Where I am, we have rendered all visions of hell irrelevant.
Replaced them with vastly depraved versions here on earth.
Visions beyond the reach of even lunatics nightmares,
Images that will surely drive madmen sane.

The rest of the letter was his good- bye to us. I cannot bring myself to deal with that just now. The tears are blurring my vision, so I am stopping here. ©

The Loss of Only Friends
by Dan Kent

Chapter 49
The Seventh of Her Kind
139 Manzanita Road
Tulare
Residence and Offices of M.F. Foxwell, M.D.

She wondered how her old friend from college simply found the time. If Penny's two children were not enough, the family cared for an assortment of animal life in addition to her practice. This time it was an injured pelican. As usual her letters were amusing although she had tried to pen a return letter this evening, the words were not at her command. With a sigh, she set the unfinished letter aside, pushed her glasses to her forehand and switched off the bedside light. It was time for the late news.

Near the end of the telecast, the announcer said that staff reporter, Allison Boyd, had been on special assignment in Redding to cover the U.S. Forestry Service, forest fires, and the men who undertake to quell them. When the filmed report began rolling, the newswoman Boyd was shown walking to a parked aircraft where its pilot appeared to be waiting.

Boyd paused to address the viewing audience, "On our first segment, we spoke to a number of individuals responsible for organizing men, materials and equipment needed to wage war on our annual forest fires. Most viewers have been exposed to footage depicting aerial tankers or fire bombers dropping retardant chemicals. Today we will met one of the pilots of those planes. He is Steven Hand, owner and operator of Aeroflame Aviation, a tanker firm headquartered in Mesa, Arizona."

Hand was shown standing next to his machine with vivid yellow helmet and oxygen mask. In his had he held a small black clipboard with maps and notes fluttering in the light breeze. As Hand's name appeared on the bottom of the TV screen, the woman in the darkened bedroom sat bold up-right and murmured a startled, Oh my God!" exclamation.

In an instant she was kneeling on the bed in rapt attention, the fingertips of both hands pressed to her lips in amazement at what was unfolding before her.

He looked fit and trim in his flying outfit. His thick dark hair shone with some graying just at the temples. How old was he now? Thirty-seven or so- about her age of course. He still maintained the mustache she remembered, and the ever-present sunglasses completed the image.

The camera began panning the overall length of the aircraft with its chrome yellow glossy paint, black engine cowling and black number 14 lettered on the tail. The camera moved to the front of the machine and paused at a name painted in flowing silver script on the cowling. The lens zoomed in to focus on the name Marilou. The Roman numeral seven would seem to indicate that seven successive aircraft had been so named.

"We are standing next to a near-legend. Many viewers will recognize the airplane as one of the Yellowbirds or Canaries that we have heard of or seen. With us is Steven Hand, founder of the firm that operates the Yellowbirds. This particular airplane is one of Mr. Hand's favorites and as you have seen is christened Marilou. The crew ahs been told that a fascinating story may lay with the name on the plane. Is it true that your employees and friends say that you have never revealed to anyone who the mysterious lady was? We wonder if just this once you might be persuaded to tell something - maybe a little clue about her?"

There was chuckling and muffled laughter in the background as Hand glowered at the culprits who had arranged to have him put on the spot in such fashion.

When hesitated to reply, Allison Boyd introduced still another question. "We understand that the company's business plane has never had a name applied to it, but instead it features a pair of exotic feminine green eyes where the name is normally found. Is this true Mr. Hand?"

More laughter followed and an embarrassed pilot stared the pavement and nodded in discomfort and admission.

"Another source that shall remain anonymous says that this matter over the name has even appeared in magazine and newspaper articles, and yet you have remained steadfast and admitted little, if anything. It seems that over the years, no one has ever made you budge from your position of silence and avoidance. I am willing to bet it's an old girl friend. Is that it?"

With an agitated frown on his face, Hand declined again.

"Well can you at least tell us why the name is always present?"

Growing irritated over the pointed questioning he looked away from the camera as if pondering the answer and coolly replied, "Simply for luck, you might say."

"Won't you tell us who she was?"

With patience growing thin, he shifted the helmet under his arm and paused to consider. "Well Miss Boyd, if you will forgive the terrible pun considering the business I am in, I will now admit- if you can let this line of questioning drop - that she was an old flame."

Boyd took the hint, and continued the interview in the manner of the professional that she was. Her questions were forthright and intelligent dealing with the airplane, its military origins and current methods of retardant application. When the interview ended, the camera followed the movements of the pilot as he inspected his machine and its readiness for flight. As he walked about the plane, background music was added to the soundtrack. It was a group singing a lyric that went, "Oh I don't want to set the world on fire." He was shown entering the cockpit and fitting his helmet with the oxygen mask. When his cockpit check was complete, he nodded to a mechanic standing by with a fire extinguisher and the black propeller began slowly turning. Suddenly the huge, round engine belched a cloud of blue smoke and the propeller blades merged into an indistinct blur. After a check of instruments, the pilot gave a nod and a quick had movement. Yellow chocks were pulled from the wheels and with a burst of power the veteran Avenger began to move. The machine was filmed as it taxied away in snake-like movements seeking the active runway. Minutes later it was shown rushing at the camera and as the machine swept by, the pilot could be clearly seen in the open cockpit, oxygen mask on, and then he turned his head to the camera for an instant and was gone. The ex-Navy torpedo boomer lifted from the runway, gear retracting, and lights flashing as it faded into the deepening twilight. "Smoke Gets In Your Eyes" was now on the soundtrack As the aircraft grew smaller and smaller in the distance, the voice of the reported could then be heard.

"Well if there is a real Marilou out there somewhere, we think you know a fire still smolders. This has been Allison Boyd reporting for Channel Six."

Yes, a real Marilou did see the telecast, and by ten the next morning she was on the phone. The first call went to a Phoenix detective agency. A gentleman there would gladly examine the current affairs of one Steven Hand with utmost discretion for a reasonable fee. All particulars regarding the subject would be made available within a 30-day period.

The second call went to a television station that aired the Steven Hand interview the previous day. They agreed to furnish a copy of the interview for a nominal sum and forward the film recording to one, M.F. Foxwell, in the care of a Los Angeles law firm. She had no idea how she would view the film, but she would find a way. Perhaps the local library could help. Clearly Marilou was again captivated by the likes of Mr. Hand.

PHOENIX (AP)

Late Thursday afternoon, Steven Hand, noted aviation figure and owner of Aeroflame Aviation, A mesa based aerial tanker firm, was injured in a spectacular crash of his converted ex-Navy torpedo bomber.

Those on the scene say that Hand, while attempting to land at Falcon Field, threw a propeller blade leading to severe engine vibrations. Moments later he lost control of his machine, swerved off the runway and collided with parked construction equipment. Upon impact, Hand's aircraft overturned pining him in the cockpit. He was feed shortly thereafter by rescue crews and rushed to the hospital by ambulance.

A hospital spokesman said his injuries were not life threatening and he should be released from the hospital within a week or so.

Hand said in the past, that all his airplanes are named Marilou for luck, out of consideration for his line of work. Associates say that Hand may retire from firefighting upon release from the hospital. With the total loss of Hand's recently built Marilou IX, some are now wondering if the legendary line of aircraft so named has come to an abrupt end. ✈
©

Meet the Authors

Dan Kent –retired book printer from Edwards Brothers in 1992, married to Helen for 57 years, 4 children, 3 grandchildren and 1 great grandchild.

Youthful years were spent in Boys Town, Nebraska, where his writing career budded early, writing a comic script in the 4th. grade. Dan was the Blue Streak! A Navy veteran and military expert authored, printed and published two technical books that have been exported world-wide. Currently, he has completed a novel, and twelve short stories to be published.

Beverly Lee Bixler – graduate of Western Michigan University, receiving her B.S. in 1967 and her M.A. in 1970 and another M.A. in 1971, in 1978 she earned her Ph.D. in Education from Michigan State University. Bev, a retired high school teacher and community college English teacher and is a budding author with an interest in family history.

Bonnie L. Branim – A retired native of Ann Arbor, Michigan also lives part time in Las Vegas, Nevada. She has written several magazine articles for Vette Vues, Bird Talk, Left-hander and Michigan Snowmobile Magazine. Bonnie mother of two and grandmother of three, Cody, Alexander, Alexis and Katie. She is one we always count on to give the group a highly interesting presentation each Monday.

Joanne Savas –A retired social worker that enjoys creative writing, enjoys writing true happenings about her three children, only brother and six grandchildren. Joanne was born in Athens, Greece and now lives in Michigan. She never knew her grandparents due to WWII. Now she wants to use her animated stories to tell her family history as she knows it.

Janis Shuon – has been a free lance artist and writer for over thirty years. Having an equal passion for art and writing, she earned a degree in Communication and Fine Art from Eastern Michigan University in 1991. Janis finds it impossible to separate her passion for writing, art, and music and uses all three art forms to express, communicate and entertain. Janis and her husband John lived in Pittsfield Township at the time this book was being composed, and very recently has relocated to a new home in North Carolina.

Thomas (Tom) Torango – Retired Mechanical Design Engineer in the power and chemical industries, does genealogical research, enjoys outdoor recreation and traveling. Tom is the father of four children, grandfather of seven and great grandfather of three. He lives in Ann Arbor with his wife Gerry. They have been married for a little more than fifty years.

G. Otto Fanger – Artist, wood carver, author. Gene recently joined Creative Writers, charming us with his wit, imagination, short fictional stories, and honing his writing skills. Experience in writing technical articles as well as editing fit his forte. Numerous awards he has received have noted artistic abilities in the fields of wood/metal sculpture, watercolor.

Michael Anderoni- Published free lance author and small business owner, lives near Ann Arbor. Michael, a newcomer to the group keeps tickling our funny bone and stimulating our brains and just generally amazes us with his broad range of interesting, thoughtful articles.

Walter Palesch-Walt lived in four countries as a refugee before arriving in America. Against all odds, he is the solitary survivor of eleven boys who attempted to escape to freedom from behind the Iron Curtain. You will find an excerpt is from his upcoming non-fictional work, which tells these stories through the voices and eyes of the refugee children. Walter is regularly published locally in both newspapers and journals on a wide variety of subjects.

Marge Anderson -author of a weekly human interest column for the Saginaw Township Times before retiring to Ann Arbor in 2000, where she became involved in several senior writing groups. Although her essays are filled with anecdotes of her life experiences it's those about her family, especially her five grandchildren and two great grandsons that are closest to her heart. The story offered here, "The Mystery of the Small White Sea Shell," is one of her rare ventures into the land of make believe.

Carole Hendrickson -Wife, mother, retired nurse, writer and our own version of Laura Ingalls Wilder, growing up on a farm on the prairies of Canada, her adventures and life experiences make good reading for all, her children and grandchildren and the public. These glimpses of prairie life and characters of that era lead us back to a more labor intensive yet less complicated time.

Edna Massey -A woman with a sense of humor only outdone by her lovely, lively spirit. Edna is new to the group however, we feel as if we have always known her. She is both innocent and wise by noted her comments and writing.

Szu-I 'Sally' Wu –born in Changsha City, Mainland China, but due to the wars moved many times and eventually settled in Taiwan. Emigrated to the U.S. as a graduate student 1961.

As a child I dreamed of being a writer. Now I am fulfilling that dream, writing them in English, my second language and in my children's mother tongue.

Pat Spriggel -Born in Akron, Ohio, Pat is a graduate from Kent State, and from Louisville Seminary. Her work has ranged form social work, art teacher, Director of Christian Education and Pastor in the United Methodist Church. She has always been active in the arts and music.

Elaine 'Elle' Cousino –Facilitator of the Creative Writing Group is a lifelong writer. Before relocating to the Ann Arbor area authored two bi-lines appearing in 3 different newspapers. Her passions are writing, reading, and travel.